TRIATHLON

A Personal History

SCOTT TINLEY

Selena —
I hope this carries you
through all the tough spots —
and helps you float across the
miles. Kick some tail!!
♡ Liz

VELO
press

BOULDER, COLORADO USA

Triathlon: A Personal History

Copyright © 1998 by Scott Tinley

ISBN: 1-884737-49-8

Printed in Hong Kong

A tremendous thank you to the many photographers who provided their invaluable work for this book, including Mike Plant, David Epperson, Richard Graham, Harald Johnson, Robert Oliver, C.J. Olivares, Carol Hogan, Betty Jenewin, Bob Babbitt, Ron Haase, Reggie David, Anheuser Busch US Triathlon Series, Sharri Hogan, David Petkiewicz, Lois Schwartz, Peter Read Miller, Russell Moore and Rich Cruse.

Library of Congress Cataloging-in-Publication data applied for.
Distributed in the U.S. and Canada by Publishers Group West.

10 9 8 7 6 5 4 3 2 1

VeloPress
1830 N 55th Street
Boulder, Colorado 80301-2700
303/440-0601, ext. 172 • fax 303/444-6788 • e-mail: velopress@7dogs.com

To purchase additional copies of this book or other VeloPress products,
call 800/234-8356 or visit us on the Web at www.velogear.com.

Cover photographs by Mike Plant (left) and David Epperson (right).
Design by Erin Johnson

To the Sneaker,
for all of it

CONTENTS

INTRODUCTION

We athletes are great bleeders. We bleed pain from our bodies during intense periods of training and competition. We bleed sweat from our pores when it's hot, steam from our lungs when it's cold. We bleed disgust and disappointment upon failure and other-worldly elation when victory is ours. Indeed, it is not uncommon for an athlete to look upon his or her own blood, spilled upon the playing field in a collision with earth, or another competitor, and wonder if the red contents contain some personal proprietary element that *belongs* inside; but maybe it's okay if a little, just a little, flows back from whence it came. Sort of a "remember thou art dust" kind of thing.

Any athlete who allows themselves to bleed pain, sweat and tears of emotion joins a unique subculture with thousands, maybe millions of individuals who realize the intrinsic beauty and benefits of this purging process. Maybe it's only two-on-two down at the old schoolyard, but for those four, it's a chance to release pent-up tension, blocked frustrations, a chance to burn up last night's cheeseburger, this morning's argument, last week's traffic ticket. The process of physical movement ignites a fire within us that bleeds out many of life's impurities that constantly find their way inside. For some, a more cerebral purge is adequate. They can find solace in the arts, in open space, in the mental joust that is constant in the commerce arena. But for the athlete, movement is paramount. Without it we will implode with the unreleased energy of volcanic proportions.

There was a story many years ago about an athlete convicted of a crime and sent to solitary confinement for an extended period. As the story goes, he was allowed 20 minutes each day to stretch his legs within a 50 x 200 foot dirt strip. The prisoner would begin his mental preparation hours before his allocated time in the yard. He would see himself moving effortlessly over miles of virgin grass hills, the wind on his face, the smell of oak and sage in the air. When the door to his cell was opened, out he went to the yard and for 20 minutes straight, up and back he would run, as fast as his caged legs would carry him. But inside his head, his athlete's soul would soar over the fence, straight into vastness that would never be his again.

When interviewed years later, the prisoner would say he sometimes he wished he was born without the burning desire to move ... but then again, even in prison, he couldn't imagine a sedentary life. He, like most of us, bleeds movement.

INTRO

. . . . .

Every once in a while, we look back on our career decisions and wonder if we did the right thing, if the path we chose will lead us toward whatever it is that we seek. And it is a natural tendency to let doubt and regret enter our thoughts. I am not immune from this malice of hindsight. Not long ago I met a man on an airplane, a nondescript but interesting individual who was much like any other business traveler except that he seemed to have more than a cursory and polite interest in the fellow sitting next to him. Maybe it was the fact that you don't often see someone in shorts, black numbers drawn on their calves, sitting in first class (a result of a partially scammed "accidental" upgrade). In any case, this fellow told me his story, quite successful as it was, and I told him mine.

Well, he didn't say anything for awhile and I thought I must have bored him. Quite possibly he thought I was a prick when I told him about the time I convinced a couple of German triathletes out for a ride in San Diego that I was John Denver and proceeded to show them where Mark Allen and Julie Moss lived, assuring them that people go up to their door all the time to get autographs and swap training stories. After his prolonged silence though, he took a long sip of his third cocktail, looked out the window and said with no small amount of whimsy, "Man, if I had it to do all over again…." And that was it.

It wasn't the time to launch into some rhetoric on 100-mile rides in the rain or lost paychecks due to flat tires, for he was weaving a dream that I was liv-

ing. Who was I to downplay a dream that every Little League baseball player goes to sleep with? What I wanted to say was that God gave me a good pair of legs and I was *not* going to lock them under a desk all day. But all I could come up with was, "Well, the job security is low and you have to work weekends, but I wouldn't trade the view from my bike seat for one of downtown Manhattan for anything."

. . . . .

This book is, more than anything, a disjointed, but eclectic collection of thoughts, ideas and memories sandwiched between a whole bunch of really cool photographs. The pictures, like any strong graphic image, rekindled memories and sparked ideas. And as you will see, there is a healthy dose of introspection. Not being overly emotional, you may find quite a few of my beliefs and opinions hidden inside lighter comments. While I doubt many people will be offended by my wisecracks, I make no apologies if they are. There's a high degree of jest in here, but it is up to you, the reader, to find it. This sport has enjoyed an interesting past, checkered with intrigue, mystery, dishonesty and nobility in the highest degree. I tried hard to offend no one. Too many whitewashed interpretations of history detract from the soulful truisms that reign supreme. Still, if you wanted a fluffy, white bread book — sorry. This is my book. If you don't like it, write your own.

I've tried not to ramble on about things. Heaven knows, there are enough worn-out armchair jocks who have nothing better to do than relive their glory days. Please, if I ever get to that point, take me out to the barn and push my head into the spokes of a spinning wheel. I've tried to keep things succinct, even though parts of the book were written many years ago. It was tough deciding which events warranted inclusion, which people had some historical significance. I know that I've left out a few, sometimes for no reason other than I couldn't find a photo of them. For that, I do apologize. Off the top of my head, I know that a few competitors and friends slipped through the cracks: Ruben Chappins, Garrett McCarthy, Dan Rock, Dan Maher, Stoney Mayock, Keri Puhl, Paul Copesky, Roch Frey … oh, the list goes on.

Some of the references found here might seem too "inside" for the casual reader. That's a tough one. The sport is headed for the big time and someone had to document a portion of triathlon history that pertains primarily to the early players. Though everything in the book other than quotes came from my own pen, in many ways it is a collection of the efforts of many. Indeed, the success of this project, in feeling or finance, is reliant on all the incredible photographs contributed by the many photographers. Their creative artistry often outshines the written word. The images found here will be different things to different people. I have tried to expand their meaning to affect others, but in the end, you can either take them or leave them. Each generation of triathletes, as well as most genres of photographic style, are represented. From Mike Plant's stark depiction of mid-1970s competitive style, to Rich Graham's mid-'80s tightly focused profiles, to Dave

Epperson's unmatched catalog of artful mood expressions, to Robert Oliver and Lois Schwartz' early-90s high action drama — and the many other contributing photographers (see photo credit recap for a complete listing) — I believe this to be an unparalleled visual depiction of every aspect I could think of, while maintaining a "G" rating.

This is not the time nor place for me to launch into a lengthy Academy Award-esque thank-you speech directed at all those who made this project happen. But you know how people love to see their names in print, so I will say this:

"Thanks everybody, I know who you are. You know who you are. Hopefully, that is enough." Take away the family, friends, sponsors, race directors, media, and the complete package of this sport is hardly that. We are left with ourselves, which in some ways is okay, for triathlon has no equal when it comes to teaching self-reliance. Without the support, the sharing, the esprit de corps and the opportunity to take our place in this growing faction and concern, well … you know how hard it is to finish that last mile repeat all by yourself.

I've enjoyed the whole trip. And I hope and pray that I have the opportunity to ride the journey out. Like I said once before, there is little I would change. When you roll through these pages, I ask only this:

Find your own place, your own memories, your own glimpse into the next 20 years of triathlon. Hear the words of Jackson Browne's "The Road and the Sky":

"When we come to the place where the road and the sky collide,

throw me over the edge and let my spirit fly. They told me I was gonna' have to work for a living, but all I want to do is ride. I don't care where we're going from here, honey, you decide."

Thanks, ST

ACKNOWLEDGMENTS

The only thing worth more than a long, protract-ed good-bye is false praise and shallow patroniz-ing. There have so many people who have contributed not only to this book, but to the 25 years of triathlon history, that I would seem gushing and, excuse the word, plastic if I even attempted to thank them all here. But in an attempt to put credit where it's due, I will only embarrass a handful.

Thanks to the crew at VeloPress for believ-ing in the project, especially Amy Sorrells for sharing my vision (and selling it to the boss, Felix Magowan, who signs the checks); Lori Hobkirk for coordination; Erin Johnson for design; Lisa DeYoung for a bunch of little things; and a big mahalo to Anne Stein for editing. You folks are great.

One man I am hopelessly indebted to is Mike Plant. Not only did he graciously supply his entire catalogue of priceless photos, but he got me started on the right track in writing well. His support over the years is incalculable.

To all the race directors who have put up with us athletes since day one: Thank you. Now that I have dabbled in this field a bit I am even more grateful. Racing is easy compared to race production.

To all my sponsors without which I would never have had the chance to do what I do, espe-cially Reebok, Timex, PowerBar, Oakley, Litespeed, Giro, Hed and Champion Nutrition. You are all awesome.

To all the folks at the Ironman Corporation: Dr. Gills, Dave, Lew, Ken, Sharron — the list goes on and on. I really appreciate your belief in me over the years. I'm with you for the long run, as long as there's a slot.

My training partners, Skid, Welchy, Brown-stone, Fritz and Tex — don't be quittin' on me now. I still need you. And there's a whole list of other people who have been integral in some way over the years: Ron Smith; my hero, Bob Babbitt; Jeffrey Essakow; Jim Riley; Harald Johnson; Bill Katovsky; John Duke; Steve Hed; John Mueller; Patrice Shimrack; Mike Reilly; Mike Greer; Terry Davis; Kenny Souza; Hopper; Iron; Sparky Dan; Roach; RDM; Sickie; Norm Paul; and my biggest fan, Keri Puhl; well, you guys know who you are. Thanks, really.

And to the original crew who agreed to help in any way they could: Dave Pain, Don Shana-han, Jack Johnstone, Bill Phillips, and of course, Tug Warren. I owe you dudes. Hey, we all do.

And finally, thanks to my wife, Virginia, and our kids, Torrie and Dane. I hope I've made you proud.

Thanks everybody. Now, let's keep the party going!

— ST

FOREWORD

Every sport needs an historian — someone to remind us how an athletic event evolved. Tennis has Bud Collins. Baseball has Thomas Boswell. The relatively new sport of triathlon now has Scott Tinley.

Scott, however, is more than a chronicler of the past. He lived it; he witnessed its groundbreaking; he won the honors; and he still competes. When you talk about triathlon, you automatically think of the name Tinley. When you read this book, you are seeing an insider's perspective of the sport from its inception. This isn't some third-hand account passed down through generations. This is the real deal from the dude who saw the sport emerge and got involved in it.

And maybe this book will get you involved, too. You may not ever be an Ironman like Scott. You may wind up like me; by comparison to Scott, I'm an aluminumfoilman. But if this book gets your adrenaline flowing, like it does mine, then, by all means, put down the book right now, get your gear and get going. Then, after you swim a few kilometers, bike 100 miles, and run until your muscles cry "Uncle!" sit down and finish the book. It's worth it.

— *Robin Williams*
actor/comedian

"If you haven't the strength to impose your own terms upon life, you must accept the terms it offers you." — T. S. Eliot, 1888-1965

ORIGINS

MIKE PLANT

I don't care who started the sport of triathlon. You shouldn't either. Great controversies have surrounded bragging rights to various beginnings. People get quite possessive when it comes to the claim of origination, of the right to say, "Hey, that was my idea!" Wars have been fought, people killed, feelings hurt over such petty things as, say, who invented the telephone or who discovered gold in California. Once it's done and the guy or gal gets a few pats on the back, maybe a patent or at least a gold watch, any discovery of note becomes the property of Society. Hey, just pay the dude a royalty for his generosity and enjoy the fruits of our good fortune to have such great minds living in our time.

I can't tell you the exact moment in time and space that the sport of triathlon was conceived. Oh, for sure we'll discuss the common theory of its creation, but the very raw and simple act of play, of athletics and sport go as far back as you'd care to imagine. Just because a handful of men and women, somewhere, at some time, decided to combine three different endurance sports into one loosely organized event, does not necessarily give them claim to Ground Zero. It makes them a part of triathlon's rich and varied past, but putting a label on something as evolutionary as that requires un-political substantiation.

Take the case of the 1904 Olympic Games in St. Louis, Missouri. If you look at the results, you may notice that a gentleman named Emerich from the U.S. won an event consisting of the long jump (he went 21-feet 7-inches), the shot put (32-feet 2-inches), and the 100-yard dash (10.6 seconds). In many Olympic Almanacs and resource guides the event in question is referred to as the "triathlon." Was this a predecessor to what we have come to know as triathlon? Of course not.

And then there is the very interesting story of one Charles Secter, who at 19 years old claimed to have competed in a bike/run/swim event in Marseilles on the southern coast of France on September 4, 1921. John McBride, Secter's grandson, recounts the story: "Our family owned a hotel in Marseilles called De Paris. It was just across the street from the train station, which was still damaged from the war. We started the race at palace Castellane, south of the old Port. I recall maybe 10 or 12 racers — the bicycle was the first event. Mine was an everyday model with no gearshift. We raced down Avenue du Prado, a beautiful tree-lined route, for 5 to 7 kilos to a sign-in table.

"There we started our run along the Corniche Road. We then ran to the pool at Petit Pavillon, a distance of about 5 kilometers. From

DAVID EPPERSON

ABOVE Triathlon was heavily influenced by beach lifeguard competitions in the early 1970s. In Australia, an Ironman is a beach competition with swimming, paddling, and rowing.

there we ran down a flight of steps to the beach and into the Mediterranean. We swam out to a buoy 100 yards or so and then back to the shore for the finish."

McBride remembers asking his grandfather, "Were you the top man?"

"Oh no, not me," he answered. For the record, the race was won by a woman named Lulu Helmet.

. . . . .

F ast forward to 1972, when a lawyer from San Diego decides to celebrate his 50th birthday by inviting a few of his friends (and anybody else who wants to show up) to a run/swim event he conceives and organizes.

Dave Pain recalls: "My birthday biathlon was an entity unto itself. Triathlon evolved. It really wasn't just one person's idea, but a logical progression from the biathlons already in existence. My birthday race was just another one of those. We rode around Fiesta Island, 4.2 miles, then swam across the estuary there just south of the Hilton Hotel. Tony Sucec won that. I just wanted to celebrate my 50th birthday and create an excuse to drink beer. The real star of the whole thing was Bill Gookin (creator of Gookinade E.R.G., the first electrolyte replacement drink), who was the best runner and the worst swimmer. He would hit the water first after leading the run and then end up near last place overall in a 300- to 400-yard swim.

"The date was July 31, 1972, my birthday. It proved to be very popular. We had 50 to 75 people the first year and there was either no entry fee

DAVID EPPERSON

TOP From left to right, Tom Warren, Jack Johnstone, Dave Pain and Don Shanahan. Take these guys away and you're holding a book on the history of long-distance running in your hands. In the far background, just above Pain's head, is a faint but noticeable spit of land on the edge of Mission Bay in San Diego. That is Fiesta Island, Ground Zero for triathlon. The shot was taken from the roof of Warren's house in the fall of 1997. Bill Phillips had just left to go to a

or a very low one. My law firm always funded the minimal expenses and it was sort of like by invitation. From time to time I would get calls from running magazines wanting to make it into a much bigger event, but I wasn't interested."

In late 1997, I asked Dave Pain, now retired from his law firm and quite successful as an age-group cyclist (national record for the 20km time trial in the 75-79 age bracket): Why running and swimming? Why not fishing and croquet, or lawn darts and high jump? "Simple," he said. "I was always a decent swimmer and back then, everybody ran. You just did. "

Agreeing wholeheartedly with Pain was Sucec, who won the first race. A 37-year-old professor of exercise physiology at San Diego State University, Sucec ran for fun and fitness. Never very competitive, he was a decent swimmer and overall, much fitter than many of the younger, faster runners.

He laughs when I tell him that his seemingly inconsequential victory at a tiny, oddball race held 25 years ago makes him "a figure" in the history books. "Well," he said, "the thing sounded interesting. I knew I could finish it without much effort, and besides, it just sounded like fun, something a bit different."

He remembers entering the water alongside Bill Stock, another runner in his late 30s, and another guy he couldn't remember. "We were all just a bit behind Bill Gookin, but it became obvious that not only might Bill lose the race, he might even drown. He was just awful in the water. We were only swimming 400 or so yards, but quite a few people diverted their course to a small island of sand off to the side of the course just to take a rest."

Dave wasn't they only member of the San Diego Track Club to have thoughts about staging a multisport event. Jack Johnston, a 38-year-old

swim workout. If you are a triathlete, these four are at the bottom of the family tree. LEFT For a long time, the one piece tri-suit was a popular option for race wear. This was before people thought it was acceptable to not only run in a small, racing swim suit, but to wear one around town as well. Good for fast transitions, bad for tan lines. LEFT CENTER Transition area, mid-to-late-70s style. Bike rack? What for, when you could get your girlfriend to hold your bike? By the way, this bike cost me $119, complete. I thought it was so bitchin'. ABOVE Ron Smith. A former member of the Underwater Demolition teams, predecessor to the SEAL Teams, a hell of a nice guy and one of the fastest 60-year-olds on the planet. He surfs, too.

school teacher from San Diego and a regular at many track club events, had an idea to put on what he was going to call an "advanced biathlon." Sort of a run/swim event with multiple segments. Twenty-five years later Jack recalls how it all came about.

Really it was Don Shanahan who had the original idea. I was going to put on an advanced biathlon with a whole bunch of running and swimming legs…. I actually got the idea from Dave Pain's Birthday Biathlon. There's no question about that. So I submitted the idea to Bill Stock who was the Calendar Chairman for the track club at the time. I had never put an event on before. Bill said, "Tell me when you want to do it and if the calendar is free I'll list it." As an afterthought he said, "Why don't you call Shanahan? He's got some sort of weird race in mind too … just so we don't have too many of these strange things going on."

Don Shanahan was a 31-year-old lawyer and running enthusiast in 1973. He was also on the board of directors of the San Diego track club at the time. To stop for a moment, if your analness necessitates that you have only one father of triathlon, Don Shanahan is it. Independently, without knowledge of Pain's bash or any other swim/bike/run event, Shanahan conceived of the idea to stage a triathlon. Don recalls the sequence of events: "At that point in 1972 and '73, there were a number of biathlons going on in Southern California, most of which were lifeguard competitions. I was on the board of the San Diego Track Club at the time and as usual, I would peridically

get hurt. That's when I started taking up the bike. One day, I thought, 'Geez, that wouldn't be a bad idea to throw the bike on the back end of a biathlon.' Well, I tossed the idea out at a board meeting, and most of the others looked at me kind of weird. But another member, a guy named Dave Pain, told me to get ahold of Jack Johnston. We ended up talking soon after that and Jack, wanting to put a race on, had already thought up a course. So one day we went out to Fiesta Island and he basically had the whole course mapped."

Jack adds a footnote or two. "When Don Shanahan and I spoke, I discovered that he wanted to add a bike portion. I wasn't too thrilled, never having ridden competitively. In fact, I didn't even own a bike at the time. 'What the hell,' I thought. 'Let's go for it.' We decided to call it the Mission Bay Triathlon."

THE ISLAND

I asked Jack, and Don and Dave Pain, "Why Fiesta Island?," expecting some deep, philosophical rationale. What I got was a short, almost curt answer from another guy sitting off to the side, half-distracted, half-intense. "Because it was close to where we all lived," Tom piped in. The Tom I speak of is Tom Warren, former bar owner and defacto king of prehistoric triathlon. Tom didn't race that first event in 1974, but he did go on to compete in nearly every triathlon in San Diego in the mid to late '70s, winning more than anybody, including the 1979 Hawaii Ironman. He was an enigma and, more than anybody, represented the

ABOVE I think this couple is Rich and Leslie Landreth. She still looks this good 15 years and four kids later. Rich could stand to lose some weight, but is faster than me on a dirt bike so I can't tell him anything.

ABOVE Old helmet, tank top jersey, cotton gloves, aviator sunglasses, leather shoes, toe clips, high pressure gumball tires and a handlebar-mounted computer as big as your current laptop. Just think — 15 years ago, this was state-of-the-art.

raw, grainy personalities that would typify the early participants. Even as the sport has evolved into its current state of high tech, structured speedfest, Warren has refused to allow the changes to gloss over his shaggy soul.

Tom lived in a 4000 square foot, one bedroom, bachelor villa with an entire floor built out like a cocktail lounge, overlooking Mission Bay and Fiesta Island in the background. From his hilltop bungalow, he could nearly coast all the way to the start of most multisport events in and around Mission Bay.

Jack Johnstone also had a very pragmatic reason for chosing this venue. "It had pretty good parking," Jack said. "And the traffic was light, especially late in the afternoon on a Wednesday." But Dave Pain takes a longer look at the whole thing. "I doubt our thinking went beyond that. Besides, it was just, what, a Wednesday night get-together to try something different. We weren't thinking of a marathon. We weren't thinking of a 100-mile bike ride. We ran around Fiesta Island once and thought it was a big deal, nothing in comparison to what those guys do now. Holy Cow!" Which is, of course, why it is so amazing that the current crop of world beaters can go as fast as they can in such a short evolutionary period of the sport.

EARLY PHILOSOPHY

The so-called 'founders' of the sport didn't expect it to blossom overnight. They may have known, after the enthusiasm generated from the

TOP I think this was the Mission Bay Triathlon somewhere around 1977. The blond guy running second is Daniel Einar Odun. For many years he worked as a beach lifeguard during the summer and a ski instructor at Mammoth in the winters — just a really bitchin' setup. In the early 1990s he developed cancer that ultimately spread, and two years later he was gone. Dano was so full of life that when you got within 20 feet of him, everything seemed cool. We miss him.

first few races, that people would sign up to do their "weird event," but the general thinking was that it was still uncharted waters and probably too challenging for more than the hardiest few. Don recalls, "Jack and I both thought that in terms of endurance, we were putting on a monster event; I mean, total running was probably a little over five miles, you had to ride five miles and then a total of 800 yards swimming! Oh boy, that seemed like a really tough event." Jack concurs: "The winners were just under an hour and being runners, we equated it to the half-marathon distance … that was hard. People were scared of what their bodies would do after all that racing."

"You see, people didn't train for it," adds Bill Phillips. "The triathlon as I had envisioned it was something different from the normal training regime of running or swimming. It was an 'unevent' that you just paid your 50 cents and did it. It alleviated the boredom of running and gave the injured folks a place to compete."

Now that's a concept, I thought. Triathlon becomes popular because runners who can't race their beloved 10km and marathons due to injuries now had a chance to compete in a race that was less traumatic on the runners' legs. But still, no one trained specifically for the triathlon … except maybe the cofounder himself, Jack Johnstone.

Jack reminisces: "I was 35 in 1971 and had just joined millions of other Americans in the jogging craze, all to lose a few pounds, you know. One thing led to another and before I knew it, I was competing in road races, which at the time were relatively small, inexpensive affairs. Like many of the subsequent triathlon afficionados, my athletic background consisted of several mediocre years as a high school runner and part-time swimmer. As I approached middle age, I longed for at least that same level of 'averageness.'

In '73 I heard of the Dave Pain Birthday Biathlon and thought, 'Geez, how many of these guys could swim and run equally as well as I, however bad I was? This is my race ! Well, I don't remember the exact place, but I think I finished around 14th place in the '73 Dave Pain race. Nothing to write home about, but much better than anything I had done as a runner."

"In much better shape the next year, I broke into the top 10. That rather modest success got me thinking. There should be more of these races and the swim should be longer. The Dave Pain Race advertised a swim of one-quarter mile but some of the racers contend it was only 200 yards," said Jack.

At the time though, there was much thought in the minds of those early pioneers on what sports should make up this new competition. The distances of each were still to be wrestled with. Tom Warren couldn't care less what they were, so long as they were far and uncomplicated, unique and challenging, just like his personality. Bill Phillips got a chuckle out of the non-swimmers struggling with even the shortest of distances. "The guys put the swim last because it just seemed natural, you know, to cool yourself off after a hot run. But there were problems with cramping from the very beginning. Some of the better runners would enter the water in the top five and come out in the last five. There were some really bad swimmers back then."

"Actually we were pretty lucky those first few years because as I said, it was for runners and except for Phillips and Warren and the Buckingham twins, nobody could swim," Don Shanahan added. "In fact, I don't recall having any lifeguards for a number of years."

Actually, they did. Jack Johnstone had asked his young son and his friends to keep an eye out for anybody not looking too good. The first race to

FAR LEFT As a group, the sport has never courted the kids the way they should be courted. LEFT CENTER I love the way some competitors psyche themselves up for the start of a race. It's like they are preparing to go off to war, and in some ways they are fighting battles of their making, with consequences of lesser reproach. ABOVE Why did we think that those stupid little leather hairnets did anything in a crash? Blame it on European cycling traditions if you must.

ORIGINS

actually start with a swim was the first Ironman, on Oahu in February 1978. The reason? Very few people thought that the distances of 2.4 miles of swimming, 112 miles of cycling and 26 miles of running were achievable to begin with, let alone having to swim almost two-and-a-half miles in the ocean after 10 to 12 hours of land-based exercise. It was a safety call and to this day, is still the safest order of events.

COMPETITION #0000000001

In the September 1974 issue of the San Diego Track Club Newsletter (Vol.14, No.9), there was a short paragraph announcing a run/cycle/swim event. It was headlined "Triathlon set for 25th." For all means and purposes, pretenders to the throne notwithstanding, this was the first regularly scheduled swim, bike, run triathlon. Of course, any number of people may come forth at this juncture and say things like, "Hey, wait a minute. I did a race back in '67 where we snowshoed, nordic skied and ice skated," or "Let me set you straight bud. My buddies and I did a triathlon in '52, which included horseback riding, skeet shooting and fencing." And I'm sure all these people are telling the truth. But if you trace all the different events and periods back through the years, including the USTS, the Ironman and other major regional events, you end up on September 25, 1974 at 5:45 p.m. in the afternoon.

I think it was a Wednesday because everything of note always happens on a Wednesday. Don Shanahan continues his look back to that first race: "It started in the parking lot of

MIKE PLANT

ABOVE Sally Edwards at the finish of an Ironman. No woman has contributed more to the sport of triathlon — period.

Fiesta Island near the main entrance from Sea World Drive. There were 46 people and we ran first along the dirt path that is next to Sea World Channel on Mission Bay. It was approximately a 3-mile loop that brought us back along Sea World Drive to the parking lot, where we changed clothes and started the bike ride. Remember now, very few amateur athletes had ever competed in an event that included more than one discipline at a time. This was new to all of us.

"The bike ride was two times around the short loop of the island, just about 2.5 miles each lap. The rest of the race was run/swim, run/swim, run/swim, where we ran for a half mile or so, swam across this little body of water for a quarter mile or so, and did that on up to the Information Center, then retraced our steps."

Don remembers the thinking at the time about the distances and order of events. "The emphasis at that time, until the USTS people got hold of it years later, was that it was an event put on by runners for runners. There wasn't this equality of distance thing at all. The run was emphasized and the other sports were filler. We certainly didn't want to see the event won by a swimmer."

That is exactly what happened. The inaugural Mission Bay Triathlon was won by Bill Phillips, a 44-year-old professor of exercise physiology from San Diego State University, in a time of 55:44. Dr. Phillips had been a nationally ranked swimmer at University of California at Berkeley in the individual medley. He had also achieved success as a runner, having finished in the top 20 four times at the Master's National AAU Cross-country Championship. This combination of athletic skill and background had enabled Bill to not only dominate the master's division at every local biathlon, but placed him in the top-five overall in many swim/run events.

ABOVE My all-time favorite triathlon photo. That's my brother-in-law, J.R., holding the bike for my brother, Jeff, who is right behind me. Virginia, my wife, is cheerleading on the right. If someone asked what it was like racing back then, I would just show them this photo taken by Mike Plant.

ORIGINS

Bill recalls that first race. "At the end of that first triathlon, I remember running down the muddy slough of the bay. I didn't know where the hell I was at the time because it was dark and they had automobile headlights pointing the way."

Don Shanahan chimes in: "If you can visualize what these guys were doing, the last part of the race was along the short causeway that leads over to the island, you know, where you wouldn't put your toe in the water now, and you ran into the last 100-yard swim section that leads to the finish across the little cove. It was getting dark by the time most of the racers were coming in. Remember, we started this thing at 5:45 in the afternoon in the fall. So we had to pull the cars up to the shore and turn the headlights on so the athletes could scramble up the bank." The first woman was Eileen Waters, in 23rd place overall in a time of 1:11:43. The last-place finisher was Barbara Staler in 1:34:51.

Needless to say, the equipment used in that first race was not quite up to current standards. In fact, if you look at the race notice in the track club newsletter you will see that it specifically says that you must bring your own bicycle, just to avoid the confusion that they would be provided. Don discusses this: "Most people had beach cruisers. There were very few 10 speeds at the time and nobody had anything as sophisticated as toe straps."

Bill Phillips recalls, "I borrowed my daughter's Raleigh and that was one of the best bikes there."

And what about drafting, gentlemen? "The rule was you could not draft. Period. All of the early triathlons forbade drafting."

Anything gets a little fuzzy after 25 years, selective memory or not. In some ways it's good that we have the ability to filter out the memories that are most disturbing. Without that function, the nightmares of childhood might never go away. But items of significance, good ones mostly, can get swept along in the tide of cleansing, forever flushed out of our collective memory banks. Don Shanahan doesn't recall every detail of that first race, nor should he. Who had any idea? One thing for sure is that 46 competitors, all of whom finished, far exceeded their expectations for a first-time event, mid-week no less.

EARLY WINNERS

One name in particular was gaining notice as the man to beat, if you cared at all about how you placed. But Wally didn't. A very mediocre swimmer in high school, Wally Buckingham was, like other decent triathletes at the time, a very good runner who just happened to have a bit of talent in swimming and cycling. When Wally and his twin brother Wayne competed in their first race in the early summer of 1975, they had just turned 25 and were running on the cross-country team at Grossmont Community College in San Diego. Both Wally and Wayne started running late in life, but excelled right away. In local road races, they would compete for the Jamul Toads, an eclectic group of talented runners from the area who would go on to win the AAU National Cross-country Championship in 1978.

MIKE PLANT

TOP LEFT Wally and Wayne Buckingham, two of the best triathletes in the world in 1975. They ran with goggles around their neck because many of the courses we did had two or three different short swims between small

Wally laughs when he remembers those early races. "We never thought they would amount to anything. Triathlons were just something to do during the week instead of speed work. I never trained specifically for them. And it was no big deal when I won. In fact, the other members of the Toads used to give me a hard time because I joined the San Diego Track Club to get discounts off the already cheap entry fee."

One advantage that Wally did have was a racing 10-speed. Because both Wally and Wayne were beach lifeguards at the time, they swam and ran with their teams and rode bikes around the beach area for fun and transportation. One day, Wally decided to upgrade his beach cruiser by getting a new bike.

"I came home with a Volkscycle that cost me $150. I thought it was so bitchin', but my Dad flipped 'cuz I had spent so much on just a bike. In retrospect, it was piece of junk, probably 28 pounds, but compared to the one-speed clunkers the rest of the guys had it was hot shit."

Wally and Wayne both raced well throughout the 1970s, when they stayed in school (to keep their two deferments). When the sport began to offer prize money in the early '80s, they opted to remain amateur and focus on the simple, enjoyable aspects of cross training.

SUBSEQUENT YEARS

The success of that first race in September 1974 would carry over into the next year. Don Shanahan and Jack Johnstone planned three more races in the summer of 1975. A new race that was added to the "Multisport Calendar" of the San Diego Track Club Newsletter was a popular, two-person relay. The legs were divided up, in which each competitor would run and swim, or run and

running segments. How much fun would that be to do again? BOTTOM LEFT Leslie Landreth at the 1981 Tug's Swim/Run/Swim. RIGHT Photographer Lois Schwartz took this photo of 1982 Ironman winner Kathleen McCartney. She was a great competitor and a really good lady. She left the sport too soon, but has a wonderful family with three kids and a husband who races bicycles for days at a time.

ORIGINS

bike. That race was directed by a gentleman named Tim Cohalen.

The second triathlon was staged on May 28, 1975. It drew a field of 73 and was won by Russell Jones in a time of 47:45. The course was just a bit longer than the previous race. Also participating in his first triathlon, finishing in 34th place, was a commander with the Navy named John Collins. Sound familiar? John would go on to conceive the Ironman Triathlon in January 1977 at the awards ceremony for the Oahu Perimeter relay running race. When Collins threw down the gauntlet at The Primo Gardens (next to the Primo Beer Factory) that afternoon, he unknowingly poured fuel on what was only a slow burning ember at the time. To this day, the Ironman is the single biggest influence that the sport of triathlon has on the mainstream public.

Even as the legend of Ironman took root on the shores of Hawaii, other triathlons began to sprout. Influenced by friends, word of mouth, creativity, and a personal desire to stage "one of these new multisport things," local race directors began to create new events. At first it was the biathlon — a swim/run or vice versa. It seems quite simple relative to today's adventure challenge-type races that incorporate six, eight or even 10 different sports, but you have to remember that in the mid-1970s any event that combined more than one sport was usually held over two days. Few, if any, multisport events were staged against a continuously running clock.

Dave Scott recalls his first biathlon in 1976. "I entered this swim/run deal in Foster City, Cali-

ABOVE No bike racks. The transition area was wherever you parked your car. The intensity was always there, though.

MIKE PLANT

fornia (near San Francisco) called the Redwood Shores Biathlon. I was thinking I was a good swimmer and I knew I could run 10km. It started with an 800-yard swim followed by a flat, four-mile run. I was 21 at the time and pretty confident with my fitness. Anyway, I came out of the water with the two lead swimmers, my heart nearly exploding with enthusiasm. Within several hundred yards I was suddenly back in third place and then, being passed by some 15-year-old speed demon and relegated to fourth.

I thought, "Well, not too bad, but if I could run well I could have won." I was a swimmer though, a swimmer, with an unsightly running gait. What was truly humbling was the kid that ran like a gazelle, the kid I never saw until the awards, finished two minutes ahead of second place. I wandered over to the results table and casually glanced at his name: Scott Molina, Pittsburg, California.

Few people recall that the two giants of triathlon squared off at such an early date. It's like Arnold Palmer coming up to Jack Niklaus at the Masters and saying, "Hey didn't we hit balls at the same playground 20 years ago?" Molina's mother Shirley, who would raise three national-caliber triathletes, remembers that race.

"Scott was 16 at the time. He came up to me one day and said, 'I want to do this thing where you swim a half mile and run 4 miles.' He won that race in 28 minutes, beating 60 or 70 people. He also received his first cash prize, a $25 gift certificate to a sporting goods store. He was ecstatic."

How ironic that two of the world's greatest

endurance athletes could begin their careers in such close proximity. Molina would go on to become the most prolific, competitively successful athlete in the history of the sport. His 100-plus victories remain unmatched to this day. But I am fast forwarding and I hate that.

. . . . .

On the way back to San Diego from the 1975 Oceanside Rough Water Swim, Tom Warren and Bill Phillips discussed the current format of combining a competitor's time from the Rough Water Swim with that of other running events held around the same weekend. Tom had complained to the race director about something and the guy had said, "Go put on your own race and you can do whatever you want." So Tom said to Bill, "I think I'll put on a biathlon at the beach in front of my bar (Tug's Tavern). We can swim around Crystal Pier (Mission Beach), run to the South Mission Jetty and back, about 5 miles round trip, and then swim back around the pier to the finish." Bill, of course, was ecstatic. This was just what he was waiting for because even though the combined time format existed at Oceanside and later on was instigated in Coronado, California, the fact that the rest between events, whether four hours or a full day, took away the basic endurance skill that it took to do well at these long-distance events.

Thus the legendary Tug's Tavern Swim-Run-Swim was born. To understand the aura of multi-sport events in the mid 1970s, you had to

understand the Tug's event. And to understand Tug's, you had to understand Tom Warren — which no one did. Warren was a rough-looking creature at the time, with a shaggy mustache, thick tinted glasses and unkempt hair. He was rarely seen in anything but shorts and a T-shirt. His closest friends were either endurance freaks like himself or beach rogues who rode Harleys and hung out at his bar on Felspar Avenue, one block from the ocean. But Warren was a graduate of University of Southern California Business school, and hid his quirky knack for making money from his less astute clientele. Tug's Tavern had a Thursday Night Mexican Food Special. For $1.39, you got two rolled tacos, lettuce, a dollop of beans and a bit of Tom's Secret Salsa. Being the consummate competitor that he was, each week Tom would try to set a new record for number of dinners served. The hangup, he discovered, was in producing his homemade salsa fast enough. He refused to submit to store-bought, even though most of his customers were too drunk to taste any food at all, let alone the difference between canned and fresh salsa.

So Tom pondered this challenge during one of his daily runs along the Mission Beach Boardwalk and flashed on the idea that if he put all of the ingredients, all the tomatoes, the peppers, the onions, the garlic, the works, into a large sink, pushed them down a clean, new garbage disposal with the bottom emptying into a salsa bucket instead of a drain pipe, he could keep up with the demand for fresh salsa to go with the dinners. The next week he set his all-time record of 1519 Thursday night dinners served.

The Tug's Swim-Run-Swim started right on the beach at the foot of Felspar Street in Pacific Beach. It was roughly a one-half to three-quarter mile swim around the Crystal Pier, a 5-mile beach run and a return trip swim around the pier. When

ABOVE Long-time triathlon journalist, competitor and friend Bob Babbitt is 'coached' by little known cyclist, but well-known runner Frank Shorter.

DAVID PETKIEWICZ

someone asked Tom if swim fins were allowed, he said, "Sure, but you have to wear them the whole race." Tom always shot the starting gun off himself before joining the race. Of all my victories in the sport of triathlon, I think I am most proud of having won the last Tug's race in 1985.

. . . . .

Interest in these multisport events continued to grow on three basic geographical fronts. San Diego had a bulging multisport calendar filled with five or six biathlons and triathlons. Oahu had the Ironman. And now Northern California, spurred on by the odd biathlon and triathlon, was on the verge of hosting several more races, essentially expanding the world triathlon calendar by 25 percent. Race directors still wrestled with just what exactly a triathlon was. Eppie was a kayak guy so his race was a triathlon with kayaking. The Olympic folks from St. Louis in 1904 liked the long jump, the shot put and the 100-yard dash. Even among those who favored a swim/bike/run format, there was still discussion about order, distance and equality of events. People still were leaning toward the swim as the final event, regardless of water temperature. One of the earliest recorded bike/run/swim events in Northern California was The Turkey Triathlon held in San Francisco. The race director was an ex-Marine named Buck Swannick, who kept using the word "survival" in his pre-race instructions. According to Dave Scott, who didn't know it, but was launching his illustrious new career at the time,

Tom Warren: triathlete #0000001. Twenty-five years after his first triathlon, he is still a unique character, full of stories that only people with his sense of quirkiness can appreciate.

the race had "no aid, no course officials, no wet-suits, 55 degree water, potholes the size of VWs, and was a lot of fun."

The race started with a 9-mile bike ride through Fisherman's Wharf, and shifted to a 4-mile run, finishing with a refreshing dip of a 0.75-mile swim in San Francisco Bay. Dave laughs when he recounts his triathlon baptism. "My plan was to sit out the run portion due to a knee problem that hampered my less than fluid form. I was doing the race at the urging of my sister Patty, who is 15 months older than I am and was a nursing student at the time. Assuming I would be leading my sister off the bike to pace her during the run (while I rode alongside of her), we would then swim in the Bay together. But after completing the harrowing bike ride, jumping over railroad tracks and speeding through blind intersections, I decided to hobble along through the run. Not anticipating this sudden urge of competitiveness, I dropped my bike on the grass, ran to the car, found my hidden keys in the bumper and put on my oil-changing, river-rafting, lawn-mowing tennis shoes and headed out for the 4-mile run. After the bone-chilling swim, I ended up second overall and was awarded a frozen turkey for my efforts."

As an interesting side note, the late Walt Stack of Dolphin Club fame was a participant. You may recall Walt as the old guy who would run 17 miles early every day across the Golden Gate Bridge and end up at the Dolphin Club, where he would swim in San Francisco's Aquatic Cove. He later completed the Ironman in the early 1980s, taking almost 24 hours. My favorite Walt Stack line was from a TV commercial, where he is asked how he keeps his teeth from chattering on those cold San Fran-

HARALD JOHNSON

cisco mornings when he ran, as always, bare-chested. Walt's reply, "I just take them out." For some of us, his cynical wit became an anthem for our misunderstood subculture.

. . . . .

If one were forced to list the top five seminal moments in the growth of triathlon, Tom Warren's chance meeting with former Navy Seal and second-place finisher at the 1978 Ironman, a guy by the name of John Dunbar, at the Coronado Rough Water Swim in July of 1978 would definitely be included. As you may recall, the Coronado Swim and the Coronado Half-Marathon were both held on July 4. The best combined scores were awarded a medal or something. Tom had just won when Dunbar, who was a Navy SEAL stationed in Coronado, approached him about competing in the next "Ironman" to be held in February of 1979. It was more of a challenge, really. Warren claims to vaguely remember the meeting, but when prompted, he will find minute details of where and when Dunbar issued the invitation. "I had won the little Coronado Optimist Triathlon five years in a row, 1975 through '79, and it was a bit of an embarrassment for Dunbar because he was a SEAL right where the bike turnaround on the Naval base was," remembers Warren. "I think he really wanted to beat me in Hawaii."

. . . . .

The Warren/Dunbar meeting seems innocuous enough until one realizes that ultimately, Warren's participation in and victory at the 1979

TOP Hey, don't laugh. In 1977, we all looked like this when we raced. BOTTOM Many of the early triathletes came from the beach swim/run biathlons. The guy in second place here is Bill Leach. He's 1982 Ironman winner Julie Leach's husband and one of the most formidable master's triathletes ever.

ORIGINS

Ironman led to a major publicity coup. *Sports Illustrated* writer Barry McDermott felt that the Ironman, and Warren in particular, presented a unique story opportunity, one that would chronicle an obscure but soulful side to athletic competition. McDermott, then an associate editor at SI, flew to Oahu to cover a small, obscure endurance challenge with only 15 participants. What he left with was inspiration to pen a long, lyrical piece for the May 14, 1979 issue.

I will tell you this and many other long-time triathletes will concur: That article had a big effect on many of us. I knew Warren at the time and he had mentioned the Ironman in passing before. It didn't sink in though. But as I sat on the couch and read that article, I just knew that I would be a part of it someday. McDermott did in approximately 10 pages and 4000 words what we all had been trying to do for five years: He told the world that the sport of triathlon was tough but doable and here to stay.

What "grabbed" readers wasn't so much the incredible distance, nor was it the outrageous weather conditions that were present on that particular February 13. It wasn't even the fact that "all this" would take place in one day, back-to-back. No, it was the style in which Warren approached it all. Self-effacing to a fault, people could relate to Warren because he had a bit of all of us wrapped up in him. He owned a bar and liked to drink beer, but he was a trained accountant. He hated any bureaucracy, but was so organized that he alphabetized his 'to do' notes on the dashboard of his old Buick. He had gotten mad at

MIKE PLANT

ABOVE This is Rick Delante, original star of the early Tug's Swim/Run/Swims and winner of the Chuck's Steak House Triathlon on Fiesta Island. He taught high school art for a time and then went on to become a famous and talented painter. Rick designed the original artwork for the U.S. Triathlon Association, a USA Triathlon predecessor. Many of the

a girlfriend and left the next day on a spur-of-the-moment 1600-mile bike ride. He once traded a car for 12 massages and did 400 sit-ups in a sauna only because someone said he couldn't. He owned rental property 'free and clear' because he hated banks and owing anybody anything — unless it was all in fun. Warren was the oddball individualist who had made it in the real world on his own terms. Despite his quirks and rough edges, he was a walking dichotomy that reflected the new sport like no other. In 1979, Warren *was* triathlon and Barry McDermott did an excellent job of telling us that fact.

. . . . .

When people read that article, they either shook their heads in disbelief and moved on to the cover story about the Kentucky Derby, or they did something about it. Master's swim coach Dave Scott would do a lot of things after he read that article. But first he gave it to his father, Verne Scott, a professor at University of California at Davis, to read. Verne and his wife, Dorothy, were huge fans of the Scott children's athletic endeavors. They had especially followed their only son David's swimming and water polo career.

Dave was a decent college swimmer at UC Davis, a better water polo player, and interestingly enough, an above average runner —for a swimmer. He had found this out when the water polo coach had them jogging for their "land training." This was confirmed when the 22-year-old Scott competed in a short bike/run Biathlon in Davis in 1975. The *Sports Illustrated* piece and his son's evident multisport skills prompted Verne to create the Davis Triathlon.

Starting in the summer of 1980, the Davis Triathlon had significance for several reasons. First of all, it was one of the only, if not the only swim/bike/run triathlon in existence in Northern California, maybe anywhere outside of San Diego. Second, Verne and his son Dave would go on to be two of the most influential people in the sport over the next 10 years. Verne would become the executive director of Tri-Fed, the national governing body for the sport in America, and Dave would win the Ironman Triathlon an unprecedented six times.

As with most triathlons at the time, the order of skills was not as it is now. Davis started with a 5-mile run, followed by a 20-mile bike, and ended with a one-mile swim in a small, cold manmade lake. The oddity of this was that, unlike San Diego and its 70ish degree water temperature, the water in Davis could be 60 degrees or lower. Many a triathlete entered the water with a high body temperature and suffered the cramping consequences, including yours truly.

In 1981, I was hungry for any triathlon that I could find and I was able to scam a trip up to Davis on the pretense of a business trip. I ended up borrowing a bike from a friend, led the run, maintained my lead on the bike, and suffered the humiliation of having to get out of the water for a brief period to warm up and massage out my

swimmer/biker/runner stick-figured logos that you see all over the world today are take-offs on his design. He was supposed to get $50 from the federation for his work, but I don't think he ever did. **LEFT** Race director Jack Johnstone gives Bill Phillips the award for winning a race circa 1975. I doubt there was a check in that envelope — more likely a coupon for a free meal at Tug's Tavern. **RIGHT** Annie Dandoy, on a "work-release" program from the L.A. Zoo.

cramping legs. I may have snuck into the top 10, but the damage had been done and the reputation of all San Diego triathletes was given a black eye.

Another athlete who would suffer the exact fate as myself in the Davis Triathlon was a 33-year-old businesswoman and ultra-distance runner, of Sally Edwards. At the urging of a friend, Edwards entered the 1980 Davis triathlon with the confidence that only competitive victories could give. She led the run and bike portions by large margins, and like me, entered the final swim leg with a decent lead. Five hundred yards later, she had climbed out of the 60-degree water onto the small, ice-plant covered bank that surrounded the tiny lake. Her body was rigid with cramps, her core temperature dangerously low, but her spirits soared with the high of adrenaline-fueled stoke. She had found her sport, her calling and her future.

Sally Edwards' experience mirrors that of many who dove into this brave, new sport, blindly challenging the elements, the unknown and themselves. Unprepared as they were, there was never any doubt as to the untapped potential that lay ahead.

DAVID EPPERSON

For every competitor there is a separate and distinct reason for competing, for seeking answers, and for toeing the line.

CHAPTER TWO

"Far better it is to dare mighty things, to win glorious triumphs, even though checkered by failure, than to take rank with those poor spirits who neither enjoy much nor suffer much, because they live in the gray twilight that knows not victory nor defeat" — *Theodore Roosevelt, 1858-1919*

CONTESTS

used to wonder why 15,000 people would want to run 26 miles through the streets of New York on a Sunday morning in November — until I ran my own marathon. Granted, it's probably the safest way to see New York's five boroughs, but like someone once said, "If you have to ask why, I can't explain it to you."

There are varying opinions as to what competition is or what it should be. For some, it is the struggle to climb the perennial corporate ladder, to beat out the guy in the next office. Sociologists call this a career-long race to achieve upward mobility. Often in this arena, the carrot is more money and more power. It really doesn't matter — they have become interchangeable. For others, competition is reduced to a daily struggle to feed and house a family, put a little away for tomorrow, and strive for a bit of happiness through it all.

But for a small cross-section of others, competition takes on a different meaning. Their concept of battle can be considered loftier than say, "the struggle for legal tender." It can also be considered petty and self-focusing

CONTESTS

when compared to the wars of survival that go on daily in the back streets of cities around the world.

Whatever the opinion, those who seek to compete in sports do so because they have a specific need to be met. Somewhere there is a hole that needs to be filled; their involvement in a race, game or match gives them an arena in which to seek their goal.

. . . . .

For those of us who come to accept competition in endurance sports as a way of life, we may find it difficult to explain our motivations to the layman who can't fathom why someone would possibly 'volunteer' to run that far. But their question and disbelief are completely valid. Change places for a moment with someone who partakes in an activity that you simply can't relate to. Maybe they work at a desk all day. Maybe they fight in wars. Maybe they like to cook as a hobby. To each his or her own, don't you think?

The act of competing, though, the rawest form of pitting oneself against another element, whether man, nature or time, is a trait that we all share. It is obviously more pronounced in some, but we all have an innate need to succeed. I ran my first marathon at Pasadena's Rose Bowl in 1976. It was a rather pedestrian 3:22, but I was filled with a sense of pride and accomplishment that I had not experienced in a long time. That night I lay on the floor of the living room, unable to even get up to feed myself. It wasn't so much painful as it was the total lack of function that

DAVID EPPERSON

DAVID EPPERSON

PREVIOUS PAGE June 1982, Torrey Pines Beach of Del Mar. Start of the first USTS. No wetsuits, 62 degrees air, 62 degrees water, a 2000-meter swim and $500 for the winner.   TOP Sometimes when I saw the Puntous twins go by in a race I thought to myself, "I've got to slow down. I'm hurting so bad I'm seeing double."   BOTTOM Chris Hinshaw at Ironman, racing his heart out. I sure hope this shot was taken with a telephoto lens.

ABOVE Kenny Souza climbing the infamous 'Beast' hill at America's Paradise Triathlon on St. Croix, U.S. Virgin Islands. This is still a wonderful event and Souza still can climb with the beast, I mean, best of them. **TOP RIGHT** George Yates at the 1985 Ironman. Shortly thereafter he developed a strange disease that left him with severe arthritis. He struggled for years before making a comeback. Sometimes our most difficult contests have nothing to do with athletic competition. **LOWER RIGHT** This is Mark and me at the Nice Triathlon in '85, leading the race with three miles to go, having a pie-eating contest just for the fun of it. We had just dropped Molina and Rob Barel. Five minutes later, Mark would surge, and a 15 bicycle cocoon would form fit him until the finish line.

CONTESTS

comes with the substantial destruction of muscle fibers. My roommate, a great guy named Toby Taki who had also done the race (I beat him — see, we are all competitors) was equally as immobile as I. At one point he said, "Hey, let's call out for pizza." I said, "Great, but I can't crawl to the phone. By the way, Toby, tell me again why we did this to ourselves."

Later that night I vowed to never run farther than 10 miles again. Deep inside though, very deep maybe, I knew it was only the beginning. Three days and three bottles of aspirin later, I was planning my next marathon.

You see, if there are 1000 people on the starting line of a race, there is the potential for 1000 different reasons they are there. For some, athletic success is a measure of self worth. For others it is a vehicle of self expression. And for many, a race is simply fun. My first marathon was a watershed event for me not because I had run further than ever before, but because I had competed in an organized event with 1000 other people and there was absolutely no pressure to win. Consider that for a moment. Our entire childhood we are programmed to win; get the best math score, score the most touchdowns, wear the prettiest dress to the prom. And then along comes an opportunity to compete simply for the sake of competition, for the community and *esprit de corps* of it all. In grade school there is peer pressure. In high school there are coaches and fellow teammates. Now, as an adult racing as an individual, there is only me. Egocentric? Of course. But in certain ways that is what endurance sports are all about: deeply

DAVID EPPERSON

ABOVE We all get nervous before the gun goes off, but this gal just freaked after the start of the Ironman in Kona. She eventually calmed down and started the swim. I get edgy just looking at her face.

TOP All the times I raced Dave, we were very rarely in close proximity. This shot was taken in Dallas in 1985. As soon as we got off the bike, he was gone. The guy could run in the heat! **LOWER LEFT** Contests come in all shapes and sizes. This is one of Bob Babbitt's famous Ride-and-Ties. He got a permit for this race too, honest! **LOWER RIGHT** During the course of competition, people tend to forget their manners from time to time.

CONTESTS

personal experiences, shared at the same time.

Over the years competition has come to mean many things to me, from a pat on the back to a paycheck. At times I have absolutely loved the contest, chasing down the leaders, bringing home all the marbles. Other times I have abhorred the whole process, wishing that my self worth and ability to pay the rent weren't so closely linked to my swim split. Whatever the case, I believe that every time I put on my goggles and tried to cross the finish line before the next guy, I walked away with a little more self knowledge than when I started. I honestly believe that is true for most people in this sport.

Competition can be a wonderful thing. In its purest form, it is not only a powerful teaching tool, but also a means of justifying our physical presence. It can be influenced by all sorts of external elements — from prize money, to greed, to self-promotion, to unfair officiating. With the pressure society puts on us to win, it becomes difficult to keep competition in perspective. We are taught that sports build character, but when we look at some professional athletes, we see millionaire crybabies who sell their autographs to kids for five bucks. Is this what we strive for? And just what is the ultimate reward for victory in competition? Fame and fortune? Or is victory found not in the triumph, but in the struggle?

The arena of competition in triathlon has changed dramatically over the past 20 years. People say change is necessary for survival; without growth, one will be passed by. True in some regards, not so in others. Wally Buckingham, Tom

PHOTO COURTESY USTS

PHOTO COURTESY USTS

MIKE PLANT

TOP In 1984, we raced in the Crystal Light Tri. It included a swim from the Statue of Liberty into lower Manhattan's Battery Park. Nice scenery. LOWER LEFT Molina and I in a sprint for the finish at USTS Atlanta in '84. We actually had planned to just tie and each collect first-place bonuses, but when we got going ... it sure seemed real to me. Hey Scott, where is your race number anyway? LOWER RIGHT Molina and Allen doing a team time trial at Nice in '83. Forget your Skid Lid, Grip?

ABOVE "Hey, are you guys extras for *Chariots of Fire?*

CONTESTS

Warren and Bill Philips were the first 'stars' of triathlon. None of them ever made a dime off of the sport. But each of them continue to compete in their own arena, on their own terms. Athletes have become victims of a disposable society. They emerge, they achieve, and suddenly they are gone. But the contest endures and someone else is always waiting in the wings to step up and take his or her shot at 'the show.'

Each of us will look back on our athletic career and hopefully remember all aspects, good and bad. But what will stand out will be the contests, the battles we had with other competitors, with the elements and with ourselves. I will remember taking second place to Scott Molina at the Bakersfield Triathlon eight years in a row. I will remember one of the few times I beat Mark Allen, in Avignon, France. I will remember some epic duels with Dave Scott at Ironman in the early 1980s. And I will also remember being out-sprinted by the lead female at the Pole, Pedal, Paddle Race in Bend, Oregon.

Yes, the look and feel of triathlon is different now. But you can still seek and find a race with all the flavor of days gone by. When it comes down to it, racing is still racing and a game is still a game, whether you play for a million bucks or for bragging rights on the block. The secret is to have the same attitude for both.

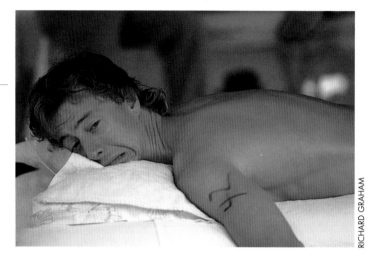

RICHARD GRAHAM

DAVID EPPERSON

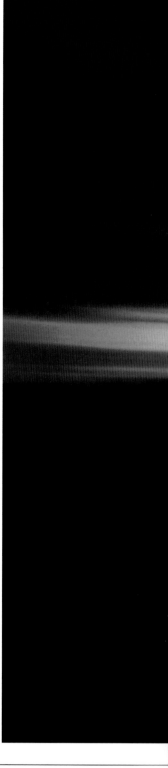

TOP LEFT Brad Kearns enjoying his post-contest massage? **MIDDLE LEFT** Mike Pigg and I watch the grass grow in a pre-race moment at the Hilton Head USTS Championship. **BOTTOM LEFT** In the early 1980s, Scott Molina moved to Boulder, Colorado, and began living and training at altitudes from 6000 to 12,000 feet. Already an excellent trail runner, he spent

countless hours roaming the Rocky Mountains. During the 1983-85 period he was unbeatable at the World's Toughest Triathlon in Lake Tahoe, on a course quite similar to his backyard of Sugarloaf Canyon outside Boulder. ABOVE … And in the end, the race is long and only with yourself.

CHAPTER THREE

"Fatigue makes a coward of us all." — *Vince Lombardi, 1913-1970*

DECADE

SHARRI HOGAN

In 1980, the sport of triathlon would enter its first full decade. If you were to use the San Diego Track Club/Dave Pain/Don Shanahan/Jack Johnston theory, you would essentially have less than 10 years of history. Narrow in scope, but 10 years nonetheless. And in that first decade, several significant trends would repeat themselves. First of all, the events were often won by older athletes; individuals who ranged in age from 30 to 45 often filled the top slots. Bill Phillips was 44 when he won the first Mission Bay Triathlon in 1974. Tom Warren was 31 that same year. Bill Stock was close to 40. Dr. Mac Larsen, a consistent top-10 finisher during the mid-1970s, was thirtyish. Tony Sucec, winner of the first Dave Pain Biathlon (who was 50 in '72), was 37 back in 1972. Conrad Will, an excellent, well-rounded competitor, was in his early thirties. Besides the Buckingham twins, Wally and Wayne, who were 22 when they did their first race in 1975, and myself, who was the baby at 21 when I began my triathlon career in 1977, almost all of the top finishers in the men's field were over 30.

The common theory on this is that only

the individuals who had a background in multiple sports or who enjoyed a career that allowed time off to train could be competitive. Warren owned a bar. Phillips was a professor. The Buckinghams were students and lifeguards.

Another lifeguard whose name would often end up near the top of the results was a 30-year-old 'kid' from San Diego named Andy O'Leary. At the time, O'Leary typified the triathlete. He worked on the beaches during the day, trained on his break, his lunch hour, whenever, and competed in these new events primarily to test his fitness level and have a bit of fun. There was no pressure, no prize money, just a handful of individuals getting together to race for a trophy, at best.

O'Leary's biggest victory came at an event aptly called 'The Balls Out Triathlon.' It consisted of a 10-mile bike, a four-mile run and a one-mile swim, all held in and around the Fiesta Island area of Mission Bay in San Diego. The significance of this event is that only eight people signed up for it because of the 'forbidding' distances, and it was held in November, proving again that air and water temperature were a key factor in the birth process of this sport. San Diego was quite agreeable seven or eight months each year. Northern California was good in the summer if you swam in an inland body of water and Hawaii was always perfect. Triathlon would have had a tough time getting started in Toronto, Canada or Berlin, Germany.

Also interesting was the fact that the San Diego Track Club, the entity to which many of these early competitors belonged, refused to print the name of the race in their newsletter. Tradition and conservatism permeated the club, and more than a few staunch runners had their feathers ruffled when these new 'weird events' started to creep into the bastion of order and tradition. Several letters were seen in the newsletter warning of potential injury and/or liability problems if the club were to continue supporting triathlon. The irony of that is thick when you consider that the very reason for the sport's existence is traced directly to a handful of men and women looking for something new, a raw athletic expression to divert them from the status quo.

February 1980 brought the third running of the Ironman and when the race was over, the sport was never the same again. Hell, the name wasn't even the same. Not wanting to be sexist in any form, Valerie Silk Grundman and her husband Hank, owner of the Nautilus Fitness Centers of Honolulu (the event's main sponsor), decided to call it the Nautilus International Triathlon. Ironman was just not politically correct.

But the cameras from big-time television were there regardless. Robert Iger's 'hunch' about this new event was going to cost the network at least $100,000, with no guarantee that it would ever air. Iger had put ABC's money on the line. Without anybody knowing a darn thing about the sport, the network's New York office phoned one of their unit managers, a guy named Phil Anast, who was filming some of the big surf on the north shore of Oahu at the time.

"I went down with the producer to talk to the race director and find out what an Ironman

DAVID EPPERSON

PREVIOUS PAGE I was happy to see this plate on an old VW bus rather than on a shiny new BMW. **TOP** East Coast triathlon style (Mighty Hamptons Triathlon on Long Island, I think): intense, determined, a bit sophisticated,

triathlon was," Anast recalls. "After hearing about it, I looked at the producer and said, 'This is crazy. Are we really going through with this?' And they almost didn't."

Friday afternoon, the day before the race, Hawaii was experiencing one of its worst storms in years. Wind, rain and high surf contributed to the already frayed nerves of the 108 competitors who huddled inside a seaside restaurant for the pre-race meeting. Hank Grundman got up and said to the crowd that ABC was here to film the event and were on a tight schedule. The film crew was set to go off and cover cliff diving or something on Sunday, so he couldn't afford to postpone the race. If the weather didn't improve in a few hours, the swim would be held in the protective waters off Ala Moana Park. Groans went out from the crowd. "This is the Ironman," they said. "Screw the 10-foot surf."

One individual who couldn't have been happier was a 28-year-old physical education teacher from San Diego, who, like countless others, had become enamored by the event after reading McDermott's *SI* piece in May 1979.

Bob Babbitt had moved from Chicago two years earlier to take a job, any job he could get that had to do with physical fitness. A certified 'sports nut,' Babbitt had grown up wrestling, playing baseball and following the Cubs. Never excelling at any one sport, he gravitated to every sport. If it was in the Olympics, Bob would give it a try.

What he wanted to try now, though, was the Ironman. By accident, he had met Tom Warren, the focus of McDermott's piece, and Warren took a liking to him and his roommate, a quiet motorcycle mechanic with a bit of a running background named Ned Overend. Warren sat them both down in the dark shadows of a Tug's Tavern booth and regaled them with stories of the

lots of people checking the time. Dinner at The Club, 6 p.m. sharp. **BOTTOM LEFT** Dave Horning, triathlete, race promoter, showman, personality. **BOTTOM CENTER** Carl Thomas, ever the diplomat, always the visionary; works in the real world now. **BOTTOM RIGHT** Sometimes the kids at the aid stations get so excited when they get a cup into your hands. Makes you want to stop and talk to them instead of running.

1979 Ironman. Warren had told me some of the same stories that year, but for whatever reason, the draw had not been enough to get me to Oahu in February 1980.

Babbitt and Overend both made the trip, along with several other San Diego athletes. Rick Kozlowski, a lifeguard and USC swimmer, was there. Ron Smith, a former Navy UDT (Underwater Demolition Team — the Navy's predecessor to the SEALS) diver and successful businessman, held high hopes. And world-class cyclist John Howard also made it to the starting line.

Only Babbitt could enjoy it in the vein of which it was conceived, though. Showing up on a bike that had solid rubber tires for which he had paid $60 at a police auction and had attached a radio to the handlebars, Babbitt had no illusions of victory. His goal was to finish. Knowing little about cycling, he listened carefully as John Howard, one of the greatest American cyclists of the 1970s, schooled a dozen competitors on bike strategy for the race.

"I didn't know much about bikes then," Babbitt recalls, "but I knew a sandbagger when I saw one. John was telling this group about one particular two-mile section of the course that was quite hilly. He suggested that if they wanted to finish they should consider walking their bikes up the hill. When I rode that hill during the race, I must have passed 20 people walking their bikes on the side of the road."

Babbitt would also witness a horrible accident later on in the bike portion. "There was this one guy who was preaching to everybody

ABOVE Someday maybe, somebody will pay $50,000 for Scott Molina's first running T-shirt at a Christy's auction.
RIGHT Sometimes it's just easier with a friend. Conrad Will and company.

night and day about the coming of the Lord. We called him 'Born Again Smitty.' Well this truck goes by and the rear view mirror clips Smitty on the back of the head. He goes down hard and is bleeding pretty bad. I come up to him and tell him we need to go to the hospital. He just looks up and says, 'The Lord will take care of me,' and gets on his bike and rides away." Babbitt laughs. "The dude ended up running like a 3:22 marathon."

Bob finishes his story about the race. "So they had the swim in Ala Moana Park and it's right next to the shore, 1.2 miles out, 1.2 miles back. Most of us are okay swimming in the calm, protected sea water, but this one guy, John Huckaby, figures out he can walk the swim course and use his arms just a little to look like he is swimming. I think he is the only person to ever walk the swim at Ironman."

In the women's division, two competitors entered and finished. At the time, there seemed to be some thought that the distance was just too tough for the females. Little did they know, though. The year before, Lynn Lemaire had been the only female competitor. Lemaire, a 27-year-old Bostonian, would show a toughness during the race that gathered the respect of everybody. Emerging from the swim in 76 minutes, Lemaire, who once held the American record for the 25-mile cycling time trial, passed everybody but Warren on the bike and came within 10 minutes of leading the entire race. She faded in the marathon, but still finished fifth overall.

· · · · ·

By 1981, the number of triathlons worldwide had doubled — from about 10 to about 20. The number of races on Fiesta Island had grown from one or two to four or five. The Northern

California connection had added a half-Ironman distance event called the Sierra Nevada Triathlon, as well as a shorter swim/bike/run version near Lodi, California. And the Ironman, which Valerie Silk had moved to Kona on the Big Island, tripled in size to include 328 competitors.

It was still being held in February each year, beholden to the somewhat limited tradition established by Collins (who was out of the picture now that he had Naval orders on the mainland). When I paid my $25 entry fee then, it seemed like a lot. Just having started a new job as a coordinator for a sailing and aquatic center, I was intent on going to the race that had eluded me in 1980. The previous summer had been my best yet in competition, primarily because, as a paramedic and firefighter, I had large chunks of time off in which to train. I can distinctively remember accepting the position, but asking for a week off the following month to go over to Kona and "get this triathlon bug out of my system."

Two other guys also had the bug: John Howard, the Olympic cyclist and third-place finisher in 1980, and Scott Molina, the wonderkid from Pittsburg, California. And they could not be more opposite in their approach to this race.

Howard had discovered that the Ironman (which was still called the Nautilus International Triathlon in 1981), was so heavily favored toward the cyclist that he only required average skills in swimming and running to be a major factor. And Howard was a superb cyclist.

During the 1970s he was one of America's pre-eminent cyclists, four times U.S. national road race champion between 1968 and '75, a gold medal winner at the 1971 Pan-American Games, and three-time Olympic team member. Howard was not only years ahead of the rest of us in cycling skills, he was *light* years ahead. He had been humbled in 1980, realizing that he needed at least rudimentary skills in the water to even have a shot at putting his cycling prowess to work for him. The marathon, John thought, would simply be a death march, a pain tolerance test in which he could keep pace with anybody.

Emerging from the swim in a very respectable 1:11, Howard could now put his head down and go, not having to worry about traffic, road conditions or getting lost. The new course over the Queen Kaahumanu Highway was perfectly suited for him. Fifty-six miles straight out over rolling terrain, wind in your face at least half the time, and back the same way. Nothing to look at, nothing to distract him; just long, lonely lava fields and hot, humid highways.

Howard rode through the field like a man possessed. To this day, I don't recall him passing me on the bike, which he most certainly did. At the time, I was on a 28-pound SR Gran Course with a tool kit containing screwdrivers, pliers, duct tape and the mother of all tools — vice grips. Sporting wool shorts, a baggy tank top and soft touring shoes, I must have resembled an accidental tourist as the sleek, skin-suited Howard roared passed me on his Campy-equipped, red and black Raleigh.

One person he didn't pass was Scott Molina. As a successful age-group swimmer and high school track and cross-country runner, Molina possessed that rare combination of skill that only the sport's best would enjoy in the years to come. What he really wanted to be, though, was a basketball player. Trouble was, he stopped growing at six feet when he was 16 years old. Sports were Molina's ticket out of

the mostly blue collar town of Pittsburg, on the Sacramento Delta. In the early months of 1981, Molina was 21 years old, newly married and father of a little girl named Jennifer. They lived in a 10 x 25 foot trailer, parked in an area that could be considered 'working class industrial' at best. Splitting his time between Dave's Liquor (stocking shelves) and Kmart (short order cook), Molina did have the luxury of a supportive family . His parents would

gladly drive him from race to race. Whether it was swimming, running, basketball or whatever, the Molinas would cover their five boys and one girl with the necessary tools.

Scott had good success at the limited number of triathlons he had participated in, but needed to hit a home run to justify the time he was spending on the training. At the 1981 Ironman he almost did that. Leading the race through both the swim and bike portions and 10 miles of the run, Molina almost accomplished his goal.

I didn't meet Molina that year and only realized he was in the race when the ABC television show featured a shot of him being taken away on a stretcher at mile 10 of the run. There is this photographic imprint in my mind of Scott, suffering from heatstroke, lying on a cot, wearing his father's lucky black work socks and a Zephyr Running Club T-shirt. The look on his face was a combination of frustration, pain, resolve and determination — but mostly disgust. How could he have blown the big lead he had on the cyclist who ran like a hip replacement patient?

My first confirmed view of Howard, the cyclist, was as he made his way back to town on the run, victory assured by his 20-minute lead on Warren and me. He looked surprisingly in control, running like … well, running like a cyclist. At the finish line I was ecstatic with my surprising third-place finish and paid no attention to Warren, who was questioning the ABC crew about the position of their van directly in front of Howard for a large portion of the bike ride. "It didn't give him any advantage," the driver told Warren. "There was no draft because we had the front windows and the back doors open. The wind would just roll right through."

In his enthusiasm, Howard made a statement at the awards ceremony that ruffled a few feathers. Addressing the ongoing debate of 'who was the fittest athlete,' he claimed, "I guess this proves that cyclists are the best." Now, Howard is a good man, and he has grown older and wiser when many have not. Thinking back, he realizes his naiveté.

"It was all in fun, but I just didn't *know* that

HARALD JOHNSON

DAVID EPPERSON

DAVID EPPERSON

OPPOSITE PAGE I have no idea who this dude is, but he owes me a sixer for putting his mug in the book. ABOVE LEFT Jim Curl, cofounder of USTS and the Jamaica James Bond Festival. TOP RIGHT Marc Surprenant and Dale Basescu model two of the ugliest tri-suits ever sewn. Hey, somebody told them they would be famous…. BOTTOM RIGHT All through the 1980s, photographer David Epperson took unique and creative pictures, always looking for a different expression. His work has withstood the test of time.

people would be offended by it." One of my favorite John Howard comments came from a Los Angeles County lifeguard and winner of the 1979 Coronado triathlon, Mark Montgomery. "I admire John because he's made a good living doing just what he wanted. He's an icon and he's never worked a day in his life."

For his own part, Montgomery had a short run at the 1981 Ironman. As a strong ocean swimmer and competent club-level bike racer, he and his buddy Kim Bushong showed up in Kona that year with high hopes. Montgomery, 27 at the time, had one Achilles heel and trouble in the heat. He and Bushong had thought about that and would carry extra Gookinaide E.R.G. (the first electrolyte replacement drink, developed by San Diegan Bill Gookin) in large, glass peanut butter jars in handlebar packs. Since the pack had a plastic pouch on the top, Mark also included a map of the Ironman bike course. He and Bushong exited the swim near the lead and rode strong enough to stay out front until Howard and Warren caught them.

Montgomery maintained a high stature in the sport for many years and is still a competitive Master's athlete today. Most people remember Bushong fondly as the guy who wore a leopard-patterned skin suit during that race. The suit, made by early clothing manufacturer Nick Forte, embodied the avante garde, devil-may-care attitude that triathlon was taking on. The mainstream media were beginning to sit up and take notice. Articles in *Outside*, *Time*, *People*, *Esquire* and the *Wall Street Journal* were proclaiming triathlon the new 'in' sport.

It is interesting to note that while some of the men were discovering aerodynamic clothing and its advantages, the women, who swam in one-piece Lycra swimsuits, were changing into cycling clothes. The women's winner in 1981 was a strong swimmer from Coronado, California, who had the unique disadvantage of challenging a new Ironman course (it was moved to Kona from Oahu in '81) that *no* woman had ever finished. In the previous three Ironman events, only three women had even completed the event. Linda Sweeney was facing new territory. Her swim was a swift 1:02, faster than all but a few men. Her bike ride, considering the equipment, was a respectable 6:53 — slow by today's standards, but you try doing it on a 30-pound bike with tennis shoes. And her run of 4:04 was gutsy enough to give her a 37-minute margin over Sally Edwards.

Though the image was shifting further to the left, triathlon's roots were still partially attached to its conservative military origins.

In 1978, when it became apparent to John Dunbar that the original Ironman would indeed be held, he began calling some of his ex-SEAL buddies back in San Diego to 'invite' them to the event. Whether this was a courtesy or a challenge, nobody but Dunbar will ever know. His buddy Dan Hendriksen took the challenge, but it became apparent that this race was *hard*. One of Dunbar's SEAL acquaintances in San Diego named Oki Moki came up with the idea of staging a half-Iron-man distance triathlon from the North Island Naval Training Center near Coronado, California. He enlisted a buddy of his to do a trial run in Sep-

RON HAASE/ANHEUSER BUSCH, USTS

tember 1978 and found it tough, but achievable.

"To be honest with you," Moki recalls, "I think we split the distance up over a couple of days." In the fall of '79, the first Super Frog Triathlon was staged in and around the base and was open to all military personnel and a few invited guests of the local triathlon community. It was won by a SEAL named Laddie Shaw. There were quite a few other SEALs on tap that first year. Martin expands on that.

"Running and swimming are the backbone of the SEAL training. Dunbar was a SEAL and some of us had been to the races on Fiesta Island. The Super Frog was a hit right away."

Without a full-time race director and a budget or a sponsor, it remained military and invitational only. Dunbar went on to win the event in 1986 and Warren finally won in 1987, though not without typical Warrenesque style. He had finished second on several occasions, but really wanted to win this race. Leading the bike portion in 1985 with a minute lead on second place, Warren was forced to stop for a train that was crossing the road. He knew it was going to be a long one and that the guy behind would catch up. After looking both ways, he slipped his bike under the barriers and took off to the sound of air-horn blasts from the conductor. Kurt Madden, who thought he might be able to catch Warren, waited almost three full, stressing minutes for the train to pass. In 1998, the Super Frog will celebrate its 20th anniversary.

THE GREAT ESCAPE

Up north in the cold waters of San Francisco Bay, the humble beginnings of the Escape From Alcatraz Triathlon came together at the Dolphin Rowing Club in 1981. A year earlier, the clubhouse had suffered near destruction in a fire.

For 110 years it had stood at the end of Fisherman's Wharf near the Golden Gate Bridge. When Joe Oakes, a long-time member, suggested a triathlon be staged as a fund-raiser, they were all for it. Though the rowing and swim club was private, the first race was open to the public and raised $4000 for reconstruction. The following year, the field was tripled, but dissension among the ranks about liability and privacy caused problems. Many club members wanted to return the race to members only, while Oakes and friends wanted to expand even further. Ultimately, Oakes and the race committee resigned from the club to run what's now called the "Alcatraz Challenge."

The swim is approximately 1.5 miles, from Alcatraz Island into Aquatic Park. Depending on wind, water temperature and tidal flows, it can range anywhere from easy to near deadly. The bike ride has changed many times in recent years, but the original route took competitors over the Golden Gate Bridge, up through the hamlet of Mill Valley and onto the famous Dipsea Trail.

The Dipsea winds 7.3 miles up and down to the turnaround at Stinson Beach. The Alcatraz event would go out and back for a leg-jarring total of 14.6 challenging miles. Interestingly enough, there is no set route for the race. Knowing the "short cuts" of the Dipsea can mean a difference of several minutes, if not more.

Throughout the early 1980s, the man to beat at Alcatraz was a 33-year-old marketing consultant and former Dolphin Club member named Dave Horning. Horning is an affable creature, large by triathlon standard, but still holder

ABOVE Start of the Nautilus International Triathlon, not yet called the Ironman, in 1981. In the middle, one of the only women you see, is women's winner Linda Sweeney.

of a 2:54 marathon personal record He is gregarious, interesting and a true self-promoter. Horning was one of the first triathletes to compete in a one-piece, Spandex suit called a skinsuit. His was royal blue and bore the logo of his sponsor, American Express.

Having run the trails of Marin County for years, he knew *all* the Dipsea secrets and guarded them with his life. But what Horning did best was add a degree of flamboyance to the sport. He once had an elaborate sitdown dinner display at the turnaround of the Ironman, with a solitary banana served by his buddies dressed up in tuxedos. The media loved him; other competitors thought he could be too full of himself at times.

He won the Alcatraz event in 1982, placed second in '83 and never really did that much again as an elite competitor. Horning now organizes one of the two, and sometimes three, Alcatraz-centered triathlons held in San Francisco each year. While he could be a bit outrageous at times, his P.T. Barnum-type stunts were good for the sport.

CONCEIVING

The sport of triathlon has been embroiled in controversy since the twin devils, money and power, emerged in the early 1980s. I don't recall much bickering in the '70s because not only was there little at stake, but people more or less policed themselves. Drafting marshals weren't needed because if a competitor "sat in" for more than a few seconds, he or she was warned first, mentally abused at the finish line for a second violation and potentially banned from further races if it became a pattern.

You can get away with this when the event is small and the *esprit de corps* is high. Not so in the

ABOVE Why did everybody want to look like Thomas Magnum back then? Rick Kozlowski coming out of the warm Caribbean Sea at the Bahamas Diamond Triathlon of the Stars. Actually, the biggest "star" there was Linda Blair from "The Exorcist." A group of us sat down with her for lunch after the race, and the first thing Rick asked her was what the stuff she vomited in the movie was made of. "Pea soup and corn flakes," she replied.

"real world."

The first major point of contention would emerge in fall 1981, when the equality of distances between the sports was questioned. In the 1970s, all the San Diego Track Club events favored the runner. Rightly so, since that was the only way they would be involved. It was not worth it if a swimmer or, heaven forbid, a cyclist would win. But a truly seminal thing occurred in the spring of 1981. Triathlon went mainstream when two gentlemen, Carl Thomas and James Curl, joined forces to build a foundation for what would become the United States Triathlon Series. The story behind the series is long, complicated and tangled. It would probably not be of interest to anybody other than a true devotee of the sport. But it is noteworthy, much like the Ironman's humble beginnings or McDermott's *SI* article. Without the USTS and its army of associates, triathlon would not be what it is today. Among the many key elements of its success, the standardization of distances remains at the top of the list.

During the summer of 1981, I was competing in a short triathlon in what's now my hometown, Del Mar, California. Having placed third at Ironman that past February, I had suddenly risen in stature in the microscopic subculture of multi-sport competition. And even though the Ironman received only cursory coverage on the back pages of our local paper (no triathlon-specific magazines existed at the time), I at least had the confidence to know that I could be very competitive in the sport.

The Del Mar Days Triathlon was a swim/bike/run event of approximately the

ABOVE Midwest triathlon style: Conservative swimsuit attire, cornbread at the aid stations.

1mi/15mi/5mi variety. Standing near the finish line, chatting with my brother Jeff, who had also competed, I was approached by a tall, familiar-looking gentleman. Carl Thomas and I had met several months before when, as a marketing associate for Speedo America, he borrowed a couple of water ski boats from the aquatic center where I worked to use in a photo shoot for Speedo's catalog. Thomas was on vacation at the time and had wandered down to the little village of Del Mar to get a cup of coffee.

When he witnessed the triathlon going on around him, it must have made an impression. Nobody but Thomas will ever know when and how the vision of his National Triathlon Series came into his head. Truth be known, it matters little. What we know is that for the next eight or nine years, Carl Thomas was a key player in almost every aspect of the sport. History may or may not treat Thomas fairly in that regard. When he suddenly left in January 1993, his company C.A.T. Sports was left owing a group of professional athletes nearly $100,000.

That was a long time ago, and people will always have selective memories. There is no doubt though, that Thomas's contribution to the sport was monumental.

U.S.T.S. IS BORN

As an All America water polo player and swimmer from UCLA, Thomas was conditioned to be a player in the sporting event business from an early age. When he left college, frustrated by having missed the 1976 Olympics by a fingernail, Thomas spent time as captain of the U.S. National Waterpolo Team and working at a small sports travel business he had started. At

DAVID EPPERSON

ABOVE Cycling legend John Howard in his trademark praying mantis pose, turning the 112-mile Ironman bike course into his own 40km time trial.

some point, Speedo asked him if he would test a new suit. Thomas wrote a comprehensive report of the item, complete with drawings and marketing suggestions. When the travel agency failed to go big, Thomas was presented with an opportunity to head up the East Coast marketing office of Speedo, located in Philadelphia. At the same time there were three individuals from the Santa Monica area who were putting out a small, fitness swimmer-targeted magazine/race calendar called *Swim Swim*. Among the owners was a former University of Southern California swimmer who knew Thomas from their college swimming days. His name was Mike Gilmore. The other two were Harald Johnson and Penny Little, a pair of freelance designers of sorts and masters swimmers. Gilmore, who also swam for fitness after college, would try to sell Thomas on the idea of having Speedo advertise in their magazine.

Stick with me now, I'm trying to piece all this together. Thomas had read about the Ironman in May 1979 in *SI*, in the piece by Barry McDermott. It apparently hit him like a ton of bricks. Not only did Carl identify with the prognosticator Warren (Warren had been a swimmer at USC, just across town from Carl's UCLA) because of his own athletic background, but as a vice president of marketing for Speedo (now based out of the San Francisco area), Thomas felt that the potential for sales of goggles, swimsuits and the like to thousands of new triathletes was a huge opportunity that Speedo couldn't miss. "My vision of this new sport took on a number of elements," Carl remembers. "I was emotionally

TOP Friend Jody Durst and myself cruising the Pacific Coast Highway a long, long time ago. I still love that hill above Torrey Pines Park (site of the original USTS). Jody is now a real estate magnate in Manhattan. ABOVE Two of the original crew: journalist Mike Plant and triathlon survivor extraordinaire Mark Montgomery.

ABOVE Dale Basescu, personal trainer, chiropractor, singer/songwriter, former pro triathlete, fond of Darth Vader-ish helmets.

involved as an athlete and as a sports enthusiast and I was strategically involved from a long-range planning point with Speedo. We needed to broaden our market, to sell suits to more than just competitive swimmers."

What Thomas didn't know was just how to put a triathlon together. "Carl was a dreamer," said his eventual partner, Jim Curl. "He had this incredible vision, never sweat the details, but could always grasp the big picture." At the same time, I started getting nice care packages of Speedo clothing delivered to my office. Nice, I thought; my first real sponsor. Carl's phone calls would follow some of those boxes and we would discuss all the ifs, ands and buts for this new sport. I didn't know much, but I knew a little, which was more than most.

At the same time, in Sacramento, California, a 29-year-old lawyer from Berkeley was looking for a new profession. Jim Curl was becoming increasingly disillusioned with his direction in law and was ready to take a flyer into something new and different. What he enjoyed was ultra-distance running. One day, one of his lawyer buddies mentioned that the race director from the Western States 100-mile ultra-marathon knew a woman at *Swim Swim* magazine who knew a guy from Speedo who wanted to hook up with someone who knew how to put a triathlon on. Follow me?

That's how Carl Thomas and Jim Curl came together. Curl explains: "I went to the National Sporting Goods show in Anaheim in the spring of 1981 and spent an entire day pitching guys at various companies to back me in putting on a series of 50-mile running races. That's where I thought the future was. Finally, late in the afternoon, having spent the entire day trying to get *anybody* to support me in my quest to become a race organizer, and disillusioned with the ultra-marathon thing, I fell back on an idea to stage triathlons, so I pitched Arena and a few other swim companies. Just before I went home, I stopped by the Speedo booth and met this guy, Carl Thomas, who I had heard about. He asked what I knew about triathlons, which wasn't much. But I had actually done a triathlon, and that gave me a lot of credibility.

"So after that we met at his San Francisco office and he hired me to put on the five races in 1982. Speedo only put in $10,000. That's it. Oh yeah, Nautilus Fitness centers put up another $10,000. So Carl said to go down to San Diego and meet with my friend Scott Tinley. He's done Ironman and knows a bunch about the sport."

With Speedo as an owner and backer of the USTS, Carl determined that the series should have five races on the West Coast that first year. "He had no interest in the details of the races," Curl continues, "so he let me determine the things like distances and course layout. Carl was always a man of big vision."

It's at this point where Curl and I disagree on how the distances of that first year were arrived at — 2km for the swim, 35km for the bike and 15km for the run; it obviously favored the runner. Curl thinks I influenced him to go with those distances because I was a better runner than most and that I had bought him a nice bottle of red wine when we went to dinner to discuss the distances in the fall of 1981. I think that we were drinking chardonnay.

DIANE JOHNSON

ABOVE The first USTS Triathlon in San Diego, June 1982. Me, Molina, Dale Basescu and Allen chase Dave Scott in the 15km run. The logo on Molina's singlet is from the Zephyr Athletic Club in Northern California, his first sponsor. Do you think they got their money's worth when they helped out with gas money to get Molina to the race?

CHAPTER FOUR

"When we see men of worth, we should think of equaling them; when we see men of a contrary character, we should turn inward and examine ourselves." — *Confucius, 551-479 B.C.*

PLAYERS

DAVID EPPERSON

Every sport, at any point in time, has its dominant figures — women and men who have reached the top and whose performances and contributions outshine all others. They are kings and queens for a day, a month or a year, or however long they maintain their position against the perpetual onslaught of competition from those intent on supplanting them. Life at the top is sweet. Excuses in any form are not necessary. But make no mistake, a price is paid for that sweetness.

Each athlete, however humble or charmed their beginnings, must steadily climb the ladder that leads upward. Athletes must walk the line that puts them on the proper road and ultimately deliver them at the station that is their own Holy Grail. As with many things, choosing the right road is half the battle. It's like going to college. If you know exactly what you want to major in from the very first semester and you get excellent counseling, you can get out in four years. On the other hand, if you are like some of us, where it takes a year or two of "experimenting" before you discover your calling and maybe you don't want to go to summer school or you live in California — well, four years can become six without much trouble.

But getting to the top of one's game doesn't always mean that you have arrived. Some people just don't have the 'tools,' which is to say that they lack a particular ingredient — physical, mental or otherwise — that prevents their best performances from bettering those of other competitors.

Have they lost out in some way? Of course not, unless their preparation has cost them some other pain in the process. But now you're talking about whether one's search and struggle in the name of a personal goal is justified. And only the individual can answer that question.

Why is it that some athletes make it to greatness and others, maybe with more talent, don't succeed beyond the club or amateur level? Why do some men and women idle along, finishing reasonably well in their age group or class and suddenly, without warning, take not one but three steps upward in their abilities to compete? Who knows? I guess when it comes down to it, you either have what it takes to be a champion, a hero, a legend, a player — or you don't.

I've known athletes who have the physical talent, the tenacity, the mental toughness and the brains to be a top triathlete, but they aren't because they don't have that extra ingredient. To have the right stuff means that you have to combine all of the above and add that extra something not found in textbooks or training camps. I can't name it and I can't tell if the people in these pictures have it. And I don't recognize it

DAVID EPPERSON

DAVID EPPERSON

RICHARD GRAHAM

HARALD JOHNSON

PREVIOUS PAGE Part of the San Diego Mafia in 1984: Sylviane and Patricia Puntous, Julie Moss, Mark Allen, Kurt Madden, Ardis Bow, Molina and me. TOP LEFT Sylviane Puntous had a sea turtle climb on top of her head in the swim and she didn't even notice. Way too focused. TOP RIGHT The Man showing his more human side. BOTTOM LEFT Mike Pigg,

always great with kids, has twins of his own now. Good things come to those who wait. BOTTOM RIGHT I love this photo of Kathleen McCartney; she looks so … lit up. She has sweat bands on just in case there's a tennis court at the run turnaround. ABOVE 'Skid' Molina wanted to be a pro basketball player until he stopped growing in tenth grade.

in my own sporting antics. But I do know that it has nothing to do with trophies and prize money. You don't always find it on the awards stand and I suspect that if you really had it, you'd just smile to yourself, confident in the fact that God gave you two strong legs, a big heart, the brains — and most importantly, the will — to do whatever it is you set out to do.

When and if you reach a pinnacle that is current with society's interpretation of success, your perspective often changes. You can begin to feel that there is everything to lose and nothing to gain; that every man and his dog wants to see you fall. It cannot be denied that much of the world cheers loudly for the underdog.

Although I have little experience at the job of top dog, I can say that the fall off the back is precipitous. You work so hard to get something, and when it appears that your goal is accomplished — well, let's just say the ride up is better than the ride down.

It also seems that our champions exist in shades of gray. Politics, business tactics and greed can and will influence the public's knowledge and perception of who's the "best." I suppose this could have been predicted years ago. Our world is big, complicated and confusing. If boxing has six different world champions and a city will pay the International Olympic Committee hundreds of millions of dollars for the rights to put on a sporting event, it's because we have let them. We approve by tolerating such outrageous things.

Maybe we just can't have one true champion in anything. We are just too far removed from a

DAVID EPPERSON

ABOVE Newby-Fraser at Ironman win number three in 1989. How do you put together eight Ironman wins, four at Nice and a Coke Grand Prix title in a 10-year period? I bet she does a lot of exercise. Probably eats her vegetables, too.

TOP LEFT "I need two tires quick, oh yeah, some size 11 bike shoes, too. I'll trade you for my 'Flashdance' headband." **TOP RIGHT** Pauli Kiuru of Finland, one of the most consistent performers to come out of Europe. **BOTTOM** "Come on, let's get this thing started. My babysitter will be here soon. " **FAR RIGHT** John Dunbar finished second in the first Ironman in 1978. The following year, he showed up ultra-fit, wearing a Superman outfit, helping to psyche-out his competitors, maybe. John never won the event, but he is an historical figure in the sport nonetheless.

PLAYERS

society that created, revered and kept their heroes.

. . . . .

F ew people have reached the top in the sport of triathlon. Fewer still have been able to maintain that position. In the early days of the sport, it was either the older guys like Warren and Bill Phillips — who had the depth of experience that came with age and won races, or it was the very fast runner who, quite by accident, was slightly less of a rock in the water, like the Buckinghams, Andy O'Leary and Mac Larsen.

For the women, it was Kathleen McCartney, Julie Moss, Sally Edwards, and a variety of women who on any given day could win. Julie Leach, Linda Sweeney, Jenny LaMont, Diane Smith, Patti Hurl, Ardis Bow, Lynn Brooks and JoAnn Dahlkoetter all come to mind.

During the salad days, from 1982 to 1990, it appeared that the same six or seven names would appear atop the men's results. But over on the women's side, a potpourri of potential champions came and went. In any case, these were the men and women champions of days past whose consistent performance, contribution to the sport and staying power have left an indelible mark on this sport for generations to follow.

For these people, reaching legendary status (truly an overused term) was a combination of several things: first, they won the big ones — Ironman, Nice, the USTS Championship or a small handful of major events where *everybody* showed up. Second, they stuck around a long

HARALD JOHNSON

RICHARD GRAHAM

C.J. OLIVARES

DAVID EPPERSON

LEFT Kenny Glah, the "beast from the east" is arguably the most durable and consistent male triathlete over the past 15 years. Kenny is always there. Doesn't get much fanfare because he is so low key and mellow. Deserves more than what he gets. Solid, likable guy. **TOP RIGHT** "Red dog to Blue leader, come in Blue leader you're breaking up." Lynn Brooks,

DAVID EPPERSON

race director. **MIDDLE RIGHT** Linda Buchanan was quite a formidable competitor in her day. One day, she just woke up and quit the sport. That must've been hard. **BOTTOM RIGHT** Big John Howard and that goofy little Campy hat. Triathletes didn't know what to think of him. Howard went on to get second in the 1982 Race Across America and seventh at Kona in '84 at age 36. The dude is still flying at 50! **ABOVE** Mark in Hawaii in 1984, when Kahunas were still pissed off at him.

time. The Big Four and Mike Pigg have more than 75 combined years as successful pros. Third, they made people feel good about themselves.

Through the action of a Molina, a Larry Bird, a Roberto Clemente, a Sally Edwards — a bunch of people took a good look at themselves and said, "Hey if he or she can do that, well, I can at least try." Or maybe what that athlete said or did restored their faith in today's youth.

A winner at any sport and at any level who receives any compensation, monetary or otherwise, has a duty to act in accordance with what we all want our young ones to aspire to. It is innate in the job description of a player who gets his or her turn at the big time. If you let it, success will teach a player that being truly successful over the long haul starts before you make your first million or get a chance to give something back. It starts when you pick up an application of some crazy new sport that sparks your interest. And you say to yourself, 'Wow, if he or she can do that Ironman thing in under eight hours, well, I certainly can jog those easy three miles. It may take me a month or two, but I'll be ready for that thing soon enough.'

TOP LEFT The importance of being Ernst. Joanne, March 1986, Northern California afternoon cool down. **TOP RIGHT** Wally and Wayne Buckingham, 'two mints in one.' **BOTTOM** Kirsten Hanssen, almost unbeatable at the short and middle distances in 1987, '88 and '89.

HARALD JOHNSON

DAVID EPPERSON

RICHARD GRAHAM

RICHARD GRAHAM

TOP LEFT Can you tell that Erin Baker saw the movie "Flashdance" the night before this race? **MIDDLE LEFT** Sally Edwards. And that ain't Kansas in the background. **BOTTOM LEFT** This is Gary Clark. He was the first triathlete with a heart transplant. Funny guy, reminded me of Kenny Rogers. Big-hearted dude, even if it used to belong to someone else. **RIGHT** Seventeen-year-old Lance Armstrong, pre-cyclist, pre-world cycling champion, just a cocky, talented high school kid looking for his way in life.

RICHARD GRAHAM

TOP LEFT Ray Browning, one of the true and solid journeyman tri'-guys of the 1980s and '90s. Won a bunch of international Ironman events when most everyone else was stuck in a USTS time warp. BOTTOM LEFT A familiar face from the Bud Light Team at Anheuser Busch Brewery. Did a lot for the sport. BOTTOM RIGHT Tom Warren: a different breed altogether. RIGHT Greg Welch, Ironman 1991, low, aero', strong, and for a brief period — serious.

CHAPTER FIVE

"The most beautiful thing we can experience is the mysterious. It is the source of all true art and all science. He to whom this emotion is a stranger, who can no longer pause to wonder and stand rapt in awe, is as good as dead: his eyes are closed. — Albert Einstein, 1879-1955

MOMENTS

DAVID EPPERSON

Life's continuum is made up of a finite number of personal experiences. Each moment is lived, then logged in our minds: creating a vast, imperfect data bank of memories that can either be recalled with an associated feeling or forgotten to time, never to be replayed, remembered or shared. A selective memory is a wonderful tool for erasing life's pain and suffering. But equally as wasteful is a mind that fails to 'bookmark' the collective moments that make up our personal history.

Make no mistake about it: It's easy to get into a rut of day-to-day existence, moving from routine to routine, comfortable in our predictable patterns. Things happen to us, both good and bad. The rhythm of life beats whether or not we like it, and we are a part of that beat. To make a lasting impression or freeze one moment in time usually takes stepping outside the flow of daily events; it takes going against the flow of everyday currents. But to seek a new experience is work, plain and simple. Ever since we were yanked from our mother's womb we have been doing things

MOMENTS

we weren't excited about, yet were thankful to have gone through.

. . . . .

That is one of the truly great advantages of being an athlete — we often enter a game or type of competition with a feeling of trepidation and cautious uncertainty and end up experiencing a whole bunch of interesting things of all sizes and shapes. Butterflies they call it. We all get them. A feeling that's equal parts anxiety, excitement, fear and joy, fueled by the knowledge that when the race begins, anything can and will happen. We are anxious and fearful that we may fail to meet ours and others' expectations, and we are excited and joyful at the prospect of success, however we define it. An athlete has this opportunity to experience and footnote a moment each and every time we climb on a bike, tie a running shoe lace or jump in a pool. It doesn't matter if it's a three-mile run that you've done 300 times before or the starting line of your first Ironman triathlon. Each has the potential to provide a notable memory to add to our list. Sport may only be a subculture in our society and I am, of course, quite biased, but no matter if it's a ball we catch and throw or a hill we race over, athletic movement and the infrastructure of competition provides an intense, compressed period in which to experience all the feelings that constitute living. Why do you think so many people want to compete in the Ironman triathlon? They know it can be incredibly painful, but they realize the

RICHARD GRAHAM

PREVIOUS PAGE Wow, that feels good. Jim Beneign, 1984 Ironman. ABOVE The moment Greg Welch won the world championship at Disney World in 1990 he was catapulted into stardom.

reward of experience is extremely difficult to reproduce in other parts of their lives.

I have many unique moments etched on my human hard drive. Some have significance, others none at all. For the simple reason that sport has always been my means of artistic expression, most of my memories have been born on a playing field. It's not to say that one can't live a full and rich existence without athletic endeavor, but like I said, I am biased. An athlete has opportunities specific to sport. I can't think of any other activity — excepting procreation — whereby the physical and sensual are melded with the mental and spiritual to form an opportunity for total involvement in the moment. Maybe it's like a sculptor who loses him or herself in the formation of light and shadow, of color and texture, in the creation of art.

Great moments in sport and in life are found not only at the height of passion and excitement, but also in the most mundane of occurrences. If you can't drag yourself out of the daily drudgery of routine, then look for the color and texture in the little things — a guy struggling to fix a flat tire in a bike race, then taking a deep breath and smiling as his new tire holds air as he rides off to chase the leaders. Or a middle-age woman laughing out loud with pleasure as she completes a long, arduous, open-water swim. Or a five-year-old boy bragging to his pal that his dad is the best triathlete in the world. The mind takes hold of anything that really touches us, so long as we let it. From an Ironman victory to a broken chain, it becomes an indelible and lasting memory, a moment to be treasured. They are something that no one can ever take away, regardless of where we go or what we do in life. A moment of significance is like a course you have passed in school, a bit of wisdom to be stored for another time and place.

TOP Dave Scott headed back to town, me chasing, and a mutual high five. BOTTOM The moments before that gun goes signaling the start can be some of the longest in one's life.

MOMENTS

Paula Newby-Fraser

"At the 1988 Ironman, I was running near the 15-mile mark of the marathon. I had no idea what place I was overall, only that I was in the lead for the women. It was just one of those rare moments when everything seemed effortless, but it had been that way all day. Then suddenly I looked up and saw my boyfriend, Paul Huddle, and fellow pro Chris Hinshaw. I went by them and Chris says to Paul, 'Let's go with her, she could be top 10!' Paul replies, 'Screw it, you go with her.' That whole race where I ended up 11th overall seemed like a protracted dream moment."

Mark Allen

"I have several consequential moments that come to mind. First one was when I sat down to watch the 1982 Ironman on TV and witnessed Julie Moss crawl across the finish line. That turned out to be a big one in hindsight because I married her. Second was in the fall of '82 when we went to Nice, France, to do that race for the first time. I couldn't sleep so I got up in the middle of the night and took a run down the Promenade des Anglaise. There I was in the south of France for the first time, a poor lifeguard with all of it in front of him. It was the first time I realized that there may be the slightest possibility of a future in this sport.

"Finally, I recall the moment in the medical tent after the '95 Ironman when it hit me that I was through with this race and would never have to come back again. That was heavy."

TOP Mike Gilmore about to give me a trophy of some sort. I didn't deserve anything with a jacket like that. BOTTOM The moment your feet feel the bottom and you know that you're not going to drown is one of the happiest of your life.

TOP LEFT East Coast triathlete and Ironman winner Karen Smyers in a quiet, pre-race moment. **BOTTOM LEFT** A young Allen and Dean Harper discuss Third World politics and sub-atomic energy theories. **RIGHT** Hey Mark, are you sure those are your shoes?

MOMENTS

Heather Fuhr

"During my running days in high school, I had a great coach that would try to push me to the limit. On one run in particular he was trying to make me feel like Mary Slaney, running behind me shouting to go faster and faster. I kept increasing the pace as he requested, despite the fact that my stomach was a bit queasy. At the end, I had my revenge. Bent over recovering, he came over to see how I was and I threw up all over his new running shoes. That was when I realized that I could push myself a little bit further than before."

Scott Molina

"It was after a very long day on my bike riding the Coast Highway that I had a revelation. I was coming out of Torrey Pines State Park in San Diego, not far from my home at the time, onto Blacks Beach at a low-tide sunset. I might have been a little delirious from the fatigue, but to me it was a perfect moment. The sun had just sunk over the bend in the ocean; the breeze was warm and the lights from La Jolla to Dana Point were the only reminder that there was a real world out there somewhere, but no one was around for miles. Truly inspirational stuff, eh? And I decided then that I would be a triathlete for a very long time; that I couldn't think of anything else I'd rather be doing."

Ray Browning

"It was the day after one of the early New Zealand Ironman races. Tinley and I were first and second, but I can't remember which was which, I really

RICHARD GRAHAM

ABOVE "Right over there, don't you see it? It was a big black fin, I swear."

DAVID EPPERSON

DAVID EPPERSON

TOP It gets awfully crowded sometimes. BOTTOM LEFT Sometimes, it's more nerve-wracking for the family of the athlete than the competitor. I'd find it hard to sit back, watch and worry, too. At least we get to sweat our fears out. BOTTOM RIGHT Sometimes, you can just go hide in the water.

can't. A group of us drove up the coast out of Auckland and stopped at this little beach for a swim on the way back. There was a small, deserted island about a kilometer off shore so we just started swimming toward it. Pretty soon we *had* to make it to the island, even though we all were pretty sore. When we got there it was filled with bird shit. Tinley and I walked around the thing doing our best Jacques Costeau commentary, you know, explaining all the different kinds of bird shit in a thick, French accent. Swimming back against the tide sucked."

Erin Baker

"My friend Colleen Cannon told me of this race on La Reunion Island off the southern coast of South Africa. She raved about how beautiful it was and what a lovely resort they would put us up at. The race was kind of long, I think an 80-mile ride up and back on the side of a very large mountain with a marathon run to top it off. The trip was hell getting there. We had to overnight in London and Johannesburg. When I finally got there, the place looked like the moon: no vegetation, all volcanic and a shitty hotel. The race was super hot, humid and hard. I won, collected my check and said *au revoir* to La Reunion. I still like Colleen, though."

Paul Huddle

"We were up in Penticton, B.C. for the Canadian Ironman when I decided to go for a short ride the day before the race. I had heard that there was a John Deere tractor store right up the street. I had

TOP Dave Scott, his wife, Anna, and his friend, Pat Finney, enjoy a moment of triumph. **BOTTOM LEFT** My daughter Torrie and I in the Ironman parade. She has the wave down. **BOTTOM RIGHT** "Okay. Who put the Kools out on my carpet?" Todd Jacobs and Lisa Lahti.

ABOVE Paula Newby-Fraser celebrates another Ironman win with boyfriend Paul Huddle.

LEFT "Yeah, some of these young punks won't even live to be as old as us. Screw 'em."   **TOP RIGHT** I asked former pro Tony Richardson what he remembers most about his 10 years as a triathlete. "When I went to China and skated on the Great Wall," he said.   **BOTTOM RIGHT** Les McDonald, president of the ITU. A penny for your thoughts Les?

to have anything with that John Deere logo on it. So, I rode out of town and couldn't find the place. Every time I asked somebody they said the same thing, 'Oh yeah, it's right on up the road there a piece.' So, I kept riding. Finally, I saw it. When I went in and the salesman told me he was out of John Deere hats, I was devastated and raced terribly the next day."

Ron Smith

"This sport is partially responsible for the fact that I have four ex-wives living in my three former residences. But I did what I did and I can't change it now."

Shirley Molina (Scott's mom)

"In the summer of 1982, Scott was 21, married, with a one-year-old daughter. He and his family lived in a 10 x 20 foot trailer and he was working two jobs, one at Dave's Liquor as a stock boy and the other at Kmart as a short order cook. After he went to the USTS in San Diego and L.A. and came home with five or six hundred dollars, we were ecstatic. And then when he was disqualified for not wearing a helmet at San Francisco, I was a wreck. You have no idea how much he could have used the $1000 he would've won. Instead, it went to Dean Harper, his training partner. His father just said, 'Hey, go ask Dean if he would give you half.'"

TOP LEFT Ron and Caroline Smith, a moment before he goes off to do his thing. TOP RIGHT Linda Buchanan, a happy winner, and Cathy Hoy Plant — a happy public relations person — sharing a moment. BOTTOM LEFT Breathing life back in. BOTTOM RIGHT "Give me a glow stick. I'm gonna' finish this thing."

CHAPTER SIX

"There is no security in life, only opportunity." — *Mark Twain, 1835-1910*

LAUNCHING

I f any one year saw more changes, new events, competitors, sponsors and media coverage than 1982, I don't know what year it would be. But the seminal occurrences of 1982 actually began a year earlier, in the spring of 1981.

IRONMAN GETS REAL

A fter the 1981 Ironman and the ABC Wide World of Sports coverage, the sport of triathlon would begin to expand. In Northern California, there was Verne Scott's Davis Triathlon, the Sierra Nevada and Lodi events (plus a new, unique race called Escape From Alcatraz Triathlon). In San Diego, with the Fiesta Island Triathlon, Del Mar Day Triathlon, Thunderboat Biathlon and Tug's Swim/Run/ Swim, the seeds would also be sewn for expansion into the rest of the world. The horsepower behind this was media, television in particular.

In 1979, a young, aggressive owner of a film production company out of Aspen, Colorado, called Freewheelin Films, read Barry McDermott's *Sports Illustrated* article and was

PREVIOUS PAGE Swim start, San Diego, USTS 1982. What a wave start meant was that the guy firing the gun waited for the biggest wave of the morning to roll in before he started the race. ABOVE Up until 1982, many of the races allowed personal aid. You could get your buddies to drive alongside of you and more or less fill your every need. Can you imagine if that was okay in Chicago with 4000 athletes?

LAUNCHING

so intrigued by the individual portrayed in the piece that he picked up the phone and called him. Rodney Jacobs was originally from Southern California and could relate to the beach lifestyle of the article's central figure, Tom Warren. After the piece came out, Warren had been besieged with requests for interviews and more information on the race. He brushed off the majority of them, choosing instead to go on dividing his time between his tavern and an idyllic Southern California lifestyle. Jacobs was persistent, though, and leveraged his surfing background to get Warren to agree to make the introduction to Valerie Silk and the Ironman. Warren gave in and the two of them flew to Hawaii in the spring of 1981 to meet with Silk about the possibility of filming the event for a documentary and a TV commercial.

Silk, not wanting to step on the toes of ABC (who had just agreed to give her $10,000 as a rights fee for the February 1982 event) hesitated. At the urging of her ex-husband Hank Grundman, Silk agreed to the deal, with title sponsorship from Anheuser Busch for one year for the grand total of (according to Jacobs) $2500. Jacobs laughs as he recalls what is considered one of his true home runs in the field of event sponsorship. "I had done some work for Anheuser Busch filming commercials and race car stuff that they sponsored. So I sat in Valerie and Hank's apartment, picked up the phone and called Jack McDonough, the brand manager for Budweiser at the time, and I told him I thought it was a great deal. He had given me the seed money to go over to Hawaii in the first place so I felt obligated to offer it to A-B first.

McDonough agreed because they had this new beer coming out that would fit well with the Ironman. And $2500 for a title sponsorship — it was a robbery! I sat at Val's little desk and typed a contract that put all the pieces into motion."

Valerie remembers it a little differently. "Rodney wanted me to sign a three-year deal for $15,000. The check actually came from Freewheelin Films. After that, all my deals with A-B were direct with the company."

There is some dispute on what the original amount was, though it matters little now. Anheuser Busch was betting heavily on triathlon — not because of the amount of sponsorship — it was comparatively small — but they were about to take on Miller Brewing in a battle for market share of the expanding light beer category. Mitch Meyers was heading the Bud Light rollout and needed a tiger to help her do it. She turned to marketing expert Janey Marks. "We looked at the demographics of the sport, the age category, the economic level and decided that triathlon was perfect for Bud Light," remembers Marks. "But what really hooked us on it was the imagery that it gave off, the lifestyle that it portrayed. A-B embraced the entire sport, took a strong position and it worked." And Marks's decision would indeed have a ripple effect throughout the corporate community. Other giants of industry could now look at Bud Light's example and say to themselves, "Hey, if Anheuser Busch is involved, it must be the real deal."

Beginning in 1982, Bud Light would begin a 10-year sponsorship of not only the Ironman, but the USTS, as well as dozens of local and regional

LAUNCHING

events sponsored through the local bottlers and distributors. Triathlon had its first real sugar daddy.

Rodney Jacobs returned to San Diego to get a little upfront footage of Warren, myself and another name on the contender list, my brother, Jeff Tinley. When we got to Kona, the crew at Freewheelin Films had scoped out everything. They knew the best camera angles, the best places for lunch, they had some good background on Warren and the Tinley brothers, and they had actor Bruce Dern there to do the commentary. What they didn't have was the blessing of ABC, who was frustrated by their own lack of preparation and connection with the athletes. ABC was so pissed off that they included a segment on their Wide World of Sports show essentially washing the sport's dirty laundry in public.

It is impossible and futile to affix any blame at this point. Much water has passed under the bridge. For Valerie Silk and the Ironman, though, it was the first of several lessons learned the hard way. She had been led to believe that Jacobs had already cleared the presence of his film crew at the Ironman with ABC, who had paid Valerie for the exclusive television rights to the event. This was not the case. Valerie recalls, "When I mentioned to Bryce Weisman [executive producer from ABC] the week before the event that the Freewheelin Film crew was already here, I could see the hair on the back of his neck stand up." He had heard that this Jacobs was a renegade in the industry. So a meeting was held at nearly midnight the night before the race between the ABC crews, and Jacobs and the Freewheelin Films

MIKE PLANT

TOP LEFT Valerie Silk with a very beguiling smile. Oh, the stories she could tell. **BOTTOM LEFT** If there were any drafting back then, nobody knew that it actually helped. **RIGHT** Nice. The first triathlons in Europe brought out some rare birds.

ABOVE In the early 1980s, people of all kinds were attracted to triathlon.

people. Valerie thought everything was under control. As it turned out, it wasn't.

All day long the two separate film crews jockeyed for position, at times nearly running each other off the road in hopes of getting the best shots. And even as the arguments continued at the finish line, Valerie began to have serious doubts about the future of her race. "They called me into the TV monitor truck at the finish line to show me the footage from the early part of the day," she remembers. "And there in many of the shots was a Freewheelin Films van. Bryce turned to me and said that he wasn't sure if there was enough good footage to make a show and the rights fee was now in question. I knew that without ABC, the future of the Ironman and the vision that I had for it was out of the question. Right about then Julie Moss began her struggle to cross the finish line on her knees. This cameraman came up to the van three times to tell Bryce and me that we had to come out and see this. Well, we both missed the whole show as we anguished over the Freewheelin thing."

Valerie had returned the Ironman moniker to the event, combining the two words, and had it trademarked.

This fact made Bryce Weisman happy, but when the Freewheelin debacle exploded in his face at the finish line, a 22-year-old redhead from Carlsbad, California, provided one of the most dramatic scenes in the history of television sports. In short, the Ironman's deal with ABC was never the same. Each had learned their lesson. Valerie would end up using a well-respected sports agent named Bill Schwartz to broker a multiyear deal. The February 1982 show was so widely received that she could now negotiate from a position of strength instead of the naive race director she was. "It's funny," Silk remembers, "somebody sent

LAUNCHING

me a clipping from the *Wall Street Journal* quoting an ABC executive about their award-winning Ironman coverage. He said that they always knew that they had a really good show. I have to laugh when I recall Julie Moss in the medical tent asking me if second place was good enough to be invited back next year."

Exasperated by poor communication between Silk, ABC and the Freewheelin Films crew, almost everybody walked away a little angry — only to have Julie Moss save the day by her quite accidental finish-line ordeal.

Julie had been an average athlete at Cal Poly with interests in surfing, volleyball and tennis. She had decided to set up her senior thesis as a project that would require her to train for and compete in the February of 1982 Ironman. Always confident of her abilities, Moss had few expectations and had prepared primarily by extending her outdoor interest and lifestyles to include a bit more swimming, cycling and running. She was a virtual unknown, but she provided the most incredible moment ever documented during an Ironman competition.

Her swim time was 1:11, which was quite impressive and good enough to place her almost 20 minutes ahead of her likely competition, Kathleen McCartney from La Jolla, California. After the bike, McCartney had only taken two minutes out of Moss's lead. But Julie was in unfamiliar territory, as most of us were back then, in the area of fluid and glycogen replacement. In the previous two years of Ironman, organizers had required weigh-ins at three to four locations on the course to protect competitors from dehydration. If a

MIKE PLANT

COURTESY USTS

TOP LEFT Grip at Horny Toad 1982 sporting his first sponsor, Rom Mirolla's Phoenix Vitamins. **TOP RIGHT** The Fountain Mountain Triathlon in Phoenix, Arizona, was put on by Rob Wallack of the Runners Den. It was a really cool race and gave out the only trophy I actually keep on display. It's a great statue of an old cowboy sittin' in a chair drinkin' a beer.

competitor lost 5 percent of his or her body weight (determined at registration), they were given a warning. Ten percent and they were pulled from the race. That practice was abandoned in 1982 and Moss probably just forgot or didn't know to eat along the way.

When she was 400 yards from the finish line, the gas tanks went dry and her muscles refused to work. As soon as ABC sensed they had something good, they surrounded and recorded her every move. Unable to stand up and either run or walk to the finish, Moss crawled as McCartney passed her with 30 yards to go. The crowd went absolutely silent. At that moment, I was over on the pier and had been listening to the announcer as the finishers came across. I was trying to hear my friend Steve Perez's name called when the noise just stopped. It was the most eerie thing. Even if you weren't watching it, you could almost sense something electric in the air.

Weisman was happy. ABC had something special and moved the air date up to right after the event and had such good ratings, the show was rebroadcast two weeks later. Moss, for her part, played the whole thing causally, and the sport had its second watershed moment (after McDermott's *Sports Illustrated* article in May 1979)— this time on film for millions to see.

Moss, who has been interviewed a gazillion times since then, can tell the story in any version or with any slant that you like. She has been gracious for the most part and accepts her place in triathlon history with equal parts respect, gratitude and awe. Moss can now wax poetic with the best of them. She's had time to mature and fully comprehend what a simple thing like forgetting to wolf down an energy bar or a couple of bananas can do.

"The final 400 yards of the 1982 Ironman was a defining stretch in my life. It struck an emotional

BOTTOM LEFT Molina, San Diego USTS 1982, thinking he could catch Dave Scott, who beat him out of the transition area. Of course he had to put socks on. ABOVE Racing on a weekday afternoon had a whole different feel to it.

DAVID EPPERSON

LAUNCHING

chord in people who saw the show. I guess they saw the brutal side of sport. It can be unsympathetically impartial. I wouldn't have scripted the finish that way. But for a lot of people who saw that struggle, they were touched, and really, it was a very tough image to grow comfortable with or to really understand the impact. Kathleen was put together and won. I was a mess and crawling.

"Over time, it has become something I see as honorable and actually, very fortunate to have done. It was one of those moments in sport that go beyond the lines of competition and right into the heart of human experience."

The other touching human experience that year was watching my brother Jeff finish third behind my victory. Jeff had done very well in some of the triathlons on Fiesta Island during 1979 and '80 and had won the now defunct Chuck's Triathlon against a tough field, myself included. He was less committed to the sport but posed a talent that was cut short by illness and injury before it could develop. Watching him finish close behind Dave Scott in February 1982 was about as good as it gets for a sporting family. There's a photo of myself, Jeff and Tom Warren hanging behind the bar at Don Drysdale's in Kona. Every time I go to Hawaii I try to get over there and have a beer in memory of Don and days gone by.

NICE BEGINNINGS

After I won the Ironman in February 1982, Valerie decided to move the annual date from October to allow not only a better chance at good TV ratings, but to allow the Europeans and athletes from northern climates to have a chance to train in the warmer summer months leading up to the race. This caught the attention of Barry Frank, head of Trans World International, the television arm of International Management Group. Frank was legendary in sports programming circles for his conception of such off-the-wall but successful shows as "Survival of the Fittest" and the "World's Strongest Man" contest. Frank practically invented the term "trash sports" and had gradually climbed the ladder at various networks.

I ran into him in New Zealand when we were both there for the 1982 Survival of the Fittest competition. Barry was intrigued by this new sport of triathlon and the Ironman in particular. He had a vision of IMG owning and staging a major event of Ironman's magnitude but with a uniquely European twist. Frank approached me at the bar of a little inn at Lake Wanaka, New Zealand, introduced himself and said that he could use some help with this new venture.

Six weeks later I was on a plane to Monte Carlo to set up the first tri-country triathlon. The idea was to swim off a boat into the principality of Monaco, ride into Italy some 60km away, and run back across the border into France. The logistics were horrendous, but Frank and the local IMG people were confident we could do it — or at least set up a hell of a course on the Monte Carlo Formula One loop.

It was never to be though. Princess Grace's untimely death and resultant moratorium on all

DAVID EPPERSON

ABOVE The Alcatraz course is arguably the most scenic course in the world. There are actually very few sharks in the bay … or so I've heard.

LAUNCHING

public events for the next six months forced a move approximately 30km up the road to Nice, France.

IMG was anxious to get one under their belt and invited approximately 12 Americans to Nice during the month of November. Mark Allen was there. Molina, my brother Jeff, Gary Petterson, George Hoover, Kathleen McCartney, Sally Edwards and Lynn Brooks rounded out the mostly American field of 61 competitors. The weather was particularly cool and several of us were gun shy after an episode at the Malibu, California triathlon (loosely titled the U.S. championships, and won by Ferdy Massimino), only three weeks prior, in which 58-degree water had forced more than 40 percent of the field out before they even saw their bikes. This is pre-wetsuit. Allen had been pulled along with my brother, I had crashed on my bike and suffered a broken collarbone, and Molina had dropped out on the bike with a huge lead and two flat tires. Consequently, all of us were hungry for redemption.

Mark Allen was on fire and ran like a man possessed. It was this performance that truly began Mark's reputation as a highly focused competitor. The date was November 20, 1982 and the prize purse was $15,000, the richest ever in the sport. The cold swim was benign enough, but the 75-mile bike ride up into the Maritime Alpes provided good fun. Careening through small, hillside villages, my brother came into one corner a bit hot and bounced off a row of unsuspecting French locals sipping their morning coffee. Jeff apologized, pulled a piece of croissant out of his derailleur, and pedaled away in search of the leaders.

DIANE JOHNSON

ABOVE Big Dave, San Diego, USTS 1982. That corner has a stoplight and a 7-Eleven on it now. **TOP RIGHT** Grip's annual Nice Parade. He was the grand marshal.

The run was a full marathon because Barry Frank was convinced that American television audiences (this was originally a CBS show) would think less of anything else; their thinking was skewed by past Ironman coverage. Mark ended up winning in a time of 6:33, followed by Molina in 6:41, and finally my brother and I in third at 6:45.

Lynn Brooks, won the women's division, followed by JoAnn Dahlkoetter and Sally Edwards.

TRULY A TRIPLE FITNESS SPORT

In 1982, Sally Edwards was 33 and a successful woman on several fronts. She had won the Western States 100-mile running race in 1980. Considered by many to be one of the toughest challenges in all of endurance sports, Edwards used her incredible stamina and mental toughness to place second in the 1981 Ironman. Above all, though, she was a communicator. When a gut feeling told her that this new sport would expand quite rapidly, Sally immersed herself in it, training, competing, politicking and finally, in 1982, writing the first and all-time best-selling book on triathlon. (More than 140,000 copies were sold before it went out of print.) "Triathlon: A Triple Fitness Sport" was self-published by Edwards to the tune of $7500 and 4000 copies. In the fall of 1982, when the second Ironman of the year was held, she took every copy she had to Kona, set up a little table near the pier and sold them for $4 each. A week later they were gone.

When she came back, there was an offer from Contemporary Books of Chicago to take it mainstream. "All of a sudden," Edwards remembers, "people were clamoring for any bit of technical information on the sport they could find."

Edwards would also go on to start a chain of running and fitness stores called Fleet Feet. Before selling the business a decade later, there were more than 50 successful franchises.

TRIATHLON GOES NATIONAL

If the Julie Moss episode provided the inspiration for thousands to take a second look at this whole multisport phenomena, then the inaugural United States Triathlon Series offered the athletes a vehicle in which to experience it. Ever since the first man or women had heard of the Ironman, there have been thoughts and comments of disbelief. "That's insane," they would say, or "Holy smoke, I could never do that!" But when the idea of a shorter triathlon was proposed, fueled by such dramatic publicity like McDermott's *SI* piece and Wide World of Sports's haunting images of men and women going above and beyond the norm, people would start to consider the possibilities, to think, well — maybe.

Enter the USTS. By spring 1982, Carl Thomas, the marketing vice president from Speedo, and Jim Curl, the now ex-lawyer from Davis, California, had not only joined forces to stage the first series of standardized triathlons in the world, they had enlisted every key element they could think of to ensure success. Thomas, who had big plans for the sport, decided to limit the number of races to five in the first year and the geographical spread to the West Coast. The key factors in Thomas's plan were: the same distances for each race to allow people to be able to compare their times with others; safe, organized and fun courses; and lots of publicity to tell the

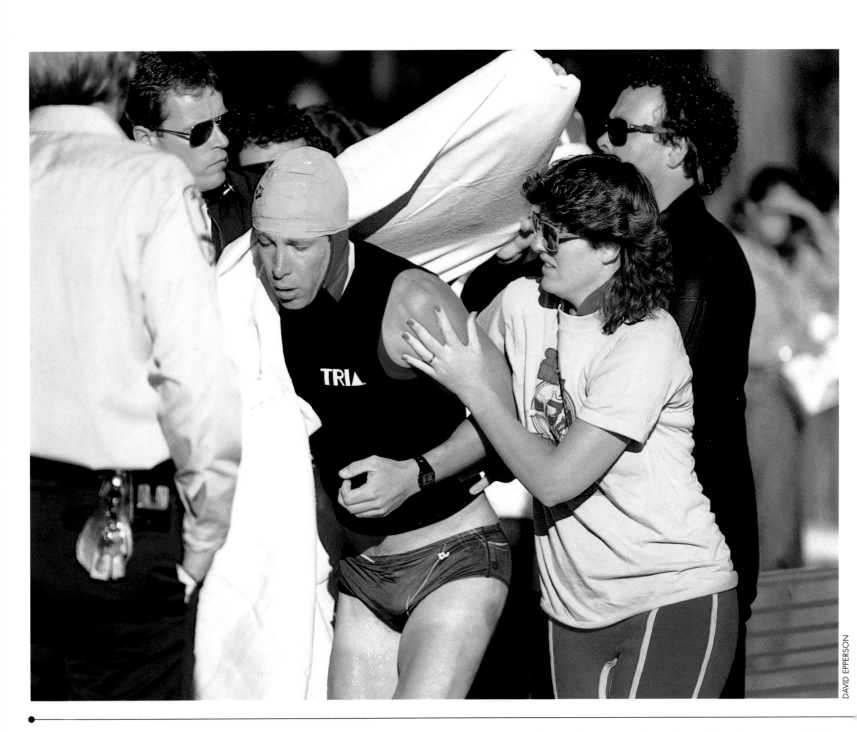

ABOVE Wetsuits really didn't come along in any truly usable form until 1985-ish. These little Neoprene vests were the very first triathlon wetsuits and were developed by Bob Scott at O'Neill. They really didn't do much good though and definitely made you swim slower. **TOP RIGHT** No singing in this shower. **BOTTOM RIGHT** Race promoter Jim Curl in the transition area of the America's Paradise Triathlon in St. Croix. The current organizer for the USTS, the dude has nine lives.

LAUNCHING

world about it.

But first he had to come up with fair distances. For this he enlisted his partner Jim Curl. "Carl was never a detail man," Curl would say. "He had this big vision and he would just assign people to get it done. I was a worker bee. The little things were my specialty." Controversy raged for months about what would be ideal for all parties concerned. I lobbied for a longer run. Dave Scott wanted a huge swim. John Howard made a good case for a substantial cycling leg. It had to be long enough to give it the air of toughness but not so long that the average person couldn't train a bit for it and go out and complete the course without killing him or herself.

In the end, the bike was shortchanged, the swim was a bit too long and the run, much to my pleasure, was the favoring leg — but still too long for the average person.

Speedo enlisted sponsorship partners: Nautilus Sports Medical Industries and Mizuno running shoes. Still, the budget was slim — "in the low five figures," claims Curl.

"In fact, I had to go on the road for weeks at a time up and down the coast, making deals, getting permits and ultimately setting up the cones on race day. We were grossly understaffed." Where they did have excellent support though was in the form of publicity. Speedo America had the Phillips Organization, a small but effective public relations firm in San Diego, under retainer. Their account reps were only too happy to break from the norm and work diligently on the series to help Speedo bring more swimsuit-buying

customers to the market. Cathy Urquart-Hoy and Armen Keteyian worked tirelessly on publicity in each of the five cities (San Diego, L.A., San Francisco, Portland and Seattle).

USTS #1

June 12, 1982 dawned cool and foggy on the beaches of Del Mar, north of San Diego — much like it always does in June. Eight hundred triathletes had signed up for the 1.2-mile swim, 21-mile bike and 9-mile run event (organizers wanted to use the metric standard so it was billed as 2km, 35km and 15km). At the time, wave starts had not even been considered so we all started at once. Including the many bandits (those choosing to race without paying an entry fee) in the start, close to 900 swimmers headed straight out to a buoy that was hard to see, let alone get to without being trounced on by the other 899 athletes. This had never been tried before and quite a few people came out of the water wondering why they had actually paid $25 for this.

Dave Scott was there, anxious to avenge his loss to me at the Ironman in February, as well as a very young, quiet kid from Northern California named Scott Molina who had driven his old 1968 VW Squareback down the coast for a chance at the $2000 purse ($500, $250, $150, $100 — split equally between men and women for the top four places). Also on tap was a skinny lifeguard from up the road doing his first triathlon ever. His name was Mark Allen.

First out of the water was the cofounder of

LAUNCHING

Swim Swim magazine, Harald Johnson. But Dave Scott passed him soon thereafter and came off the bike with a four-minute lead. I couldn't believe this! Dave was supposed to be a swimmer. Maybe he'd die though, and our chase group that included Molina, Allen and Dale Basescu would be able to catch him.

No way. At the turnaround of the 4.5-mile out-and-back course, he had actually increased his lead. It was at this exact moment that I knew Dave would be a formidable competitor for a long time. On the way back, Basescu and Allen fell off the pace and Molina was right on my shoulder. I turned to him and introduced myself. He looked at me like I was from outer space. Here we were, racing along at a nearly six-minute-mile pace, real prize money on the line, and some blond idiot wants to get to know him. To this day, Molina and I always laugh at that one.

With 300 yards to go, Molina took off and outsprinted me for second place, some four-odd minutes behind Dave. Basescu hung onto fourth and Mark was fifth. Over on the women's side, 1982 Ironman champ Kathleen McCartney was running away from the field.

Several weeks later up at Long Beach (the L.A. race), in the absence of Dave Scott, Molina ran away with it. But controversy ensued when Molina failed to wear a helmet on the bike. At the time, rules were not strictly enforced, but the helmet rule was one that stood out. Race director Jim Curl pulled Molina aside and said, "Okay Scott, I can wash it this time 'cuz I'm the boss. But anymore and I'll have to DQ you."

At the next stop of the series, in San Francisco, Molina didn't wear a helmet and was disqualified. But as the final two races in Portland and Seattle rounded out the USTS, it was obvious that Curl and Thomas were on to something. For the first time outside of the Ironman arena, the sport had some legitimacy in the eyes of the mainstream public. No longer was triathlon just a fringe sport practiced by a handful of nuts or a group of marginally talented runner/lifeguards from San Diego who were desperately trying to avoid the inevitable real job. With a few corporate backers, the look and feel of a 'normal' sport (whatever that is) and a small but successful pr push behind them, the USTS catapulted triathlon not only into the homes of the American public, but into the minds of weekend warriors everywhere who felt that for maybe just a brief moment in time, they could be 18 again and push themselves just a bit farther than their day-to-day existence allowed.

For the talented triathlete looking for a reason to trade the normal weekend yard maintenance responsibilities for a 50-mile bike ride, the USTS provided that slight glimmer of hope that somewhere out on the horizon, the door to professional athletics might be opening just a bit. Five hundred dollars for first place is not much, in fact when you compare it to other more widely practiced sports, it pretty much sucks. But in 1982, it was $500 more than what was being offered at any other race. I can remember going into work at the Mission Bay Aquatic Center where I worked in June 1982 after that

ABOVE A kinder, gentler form of a sometimes hectic, stressful situation.

ABOVE Swim start, San Diego, 1983. George Hoover and I with our "secret weapons": Neoprene caps.

first USTS race, and thinking, okay, I made $150 for third place, big deal. But then again, I didn't do it for the money, because there wasn't much. Soon enough that would change.

For Molina, the USTS couldn't have been better. "The distances fit me really well," Molina remembers, "and most of the courses were tough, hilly things. Not a lot of people had open-water swimming experience back then, so I could hang with the best pool swimmers who happened to show up. And there weren't many other races at the time to distract you, so during the summer we could really focus on the series."

Molina would go on to win several USTS events in the next 10 years. He laughs about his no helmet DQ at San Francisco. "I had bent the rules at the previous two races and figured I'd get away with it again. I think Jim felt really bad about the whole thing. He knew how much I needed the money. As I recall, he might have given me a plane ticket up to the final race in Seattle just to make me feel better."

WHAT IS A HORNY TOAD, ANYWAY?

Spurred on by the Ironman's growing legend and by the more recent success of the USTS, new triathlons continued to pop up in forms that were designed to fulfill the need for athletes to simply have enough races. One of those holes would be filled by the new Horny Toad Triathlon. The Horny Toads were a loosely knit group of athletes and business people who would meet at lunchtime every day in San Diego's downtown

Balboa Park. Taking their name as a parody on the Jamul Toads (1978 National Cross-country team champions from San Diego), the Horny Toads would get together, run, drink beer and network among themselves. It was a mostly social group with a strong emphasis on running.

Several of the members were triathletes and had voiced some interest in doing the mostly military personnel run Super Frog Triathlon but for whatever reason, never ended up on the starting line. So in the summer of 1981, the first Horny Toad Triathlon was run. It was a 1.5-mile ocean swim, 50-mile hilly bike and scenic, 13-mile run. Mark Montgomery won that first race, followed by Tom Warren and Scott Tinley. Lisa Gonzales won for the women. In all, 75 athletes competed, exactly the number of athletes who entered.

The following year, interest was even greater. The field would be limited to 100 people only and the interest came from all over California, as well as other parts of the country. Long time Toads Bill Widricks and Conrad Will had designed a course that was both challenging and fun. The prize money was $4000, the largest in the history of the sport at the time. It also received the first sanction by the newly organized governing body, the U.S. Triathlon Association (USTA). Competitors included Mark Allen, the eventual winner, Molina, the Tinley brothers, Dean Harper and a little-known woman from Newport Beach, Julie Leach. (Leach would go on to win the Ironman a month later in October 1982.) Even with all this, the Horny Toad was a wonderful combination of professionalism and old-style, low-key racing. It

would only last a few more years, but it helped launch the careers of several, Allen, Leach and myself included.

THE FALL OF 1982

The Ironman came around again quickly in 1982. Bud Light had signed up to be the title sponsor. ABC, buoyed by the huge windfall brought about by the Julie Moss episode, came back looking for another "human drama of sport," and all the best athletes in the sport were on the starting line.

In the end, Dave Scott led wire to wire, breaking my eight-month-old course record by nearly 12 minutes. Mark Allen, in his Ironman debut, dropped out with a broken derailleur — the first of the many Ironman 'demons' that would follow him until 1989.

Julie Leach, won the women's race in 10:54 over a hard-charging Joann Dahlkoetter, who was only 4:13 behind in the end. She was the first women to go under the-then elusive 11-hour mark.

I got second, my brother third, Molina fourth and Gordon Haller finished in 94th with a time of 11:19:05.

Three weeks later, Allen, Molina, myself, Mark Montgomery and 200 others lined up on the shores of Zuma Beach, California, in a dense and cold fog for the start of the first U.S. National Championship. Organized by a former Nike employee and Dave Scott's agent at the time, Hans Albrecht, it featured a 1.5-mile swim, sans wetsuits, in a 58-degree ocean. It became appar-

LAUNCHING

ent from the start that the swim was closer to two miles, and if anyone would make it out of the water, they were going to have to want it really badly or subject themselves to one of the lifeguards that swept the course, pulling hypothermic bodies like salmon from the sea. Allen was pulled and John Howard, too. As my brother Jeff and I sprinted to one lifeguard on a paddle board, it became apparent that he could only handle one rescue at a time. Jeff got the board, I finished the swim, then climbed on my bike and two miles later was sitting on the side of a steep downhill, clutching a crash-induced collarbone. Molina did not finish with two flat tires, and Dr. Ferdy Massamino went on to become the sport's first national champion.

Three weeks after that, we all went to Nice. Crushed bones, crushed ego aside, we were professionals now and that is what pro athletes did.

CHAPTER SEVEN

"The less justified a man is in claiming excellence for his own self, the more ready is he to claim all excellence for his nation, his religion, his race or his holy cause." — *Eric Hoffer, 1902-1983*

LAVALAND

DAVID EPPERSON

Ironman. The name conjures up a host of varied images. To the uninitiated it brings to mind either a musclehead weight lifter or a fictional cartoon character. To the slightly informed, channel-surfing couch potato, it's a momentary glimpse of lava landscapes, funny-looking bikes and sweaty bodies attempting seemingly insurmountable distances. And to the triathlete, it is mecca, heaven and the Holy Grail rolled into one on a full moon Saturday in October. The visions that present themselves in the minds of people everywhere are probably equal parts real and imagined. Indeed, it seems that the event itself has taken on a life of its own, creating in its wake an aura that transcends multisport athletics.

Some people divide their year on a calendar, looking at each January 1 as the start of something new. Others have a fiscal year, whereby the books begin and end, usually along with profits and losses. But for the serious athlete, the year begins with preseason base work and ends with "The Big Event." Each sport has its year-end spectacle — a tournament, a series, a playoff, however it's labeled. It's a time and place for all the athletes to dump their eggs and

local merchants to hawk cheesy T-shirts. Above all else, it's a way to mark another year, a cusp of old and new. And there always seem to be some ripping parties afterward. In the sport of triathlon, that sport is the Ironman. Since its inception on February 15, 1978, it has been the Top Dog. Ironman has withstood a barrage of tactical assaults over the years, but still retains the *numero uno* slot. The folks standing on the corner in Trenton, New Jersey, have never heard of the ITU, but somewhere, some time, they saw something about the Ironman. That is not simply a byproduct of good public relations.

The event has humble enough beginnings. Interesting maybe, but not quite the stuff of legends. Commander John Collins, by admission, was no visionary. Like most endurance athletes and military personnel, though, he was a doer, a person who came up with an idea, and good, bad or ugly, got the thing done. Collins's now infamous "challenge" at the Perimeter Relay Awards Ceremony in January 1977 has been told and retold so many times, most of them incorrectly, that he's almost resigned himself to giving the listener what they want.

"The television people in particular want an outrageous quotation," he said. "So far I haven't given them the appropriate one so my interview with them always gets cut." Several years ago the woman broadcaster for ABC television said, "Now let me understand how this started. A bunch of you sailors were drunk in a bar in Honolulu...." Collins stopped the women and said that wasn't how it happened. "But there was a lot of beer, was-n't there?" she persisted. "Yeah," said Collins. "It was

PREVIOUS PAGE Okay, so it's hot. Just throw a little water on your head and deal with it. ABOVE Mark Allen, Kona '90, aero', focused. Nice background scenery, too.

from the beer manufacturer who owned the Primo Gardens." (Primo was a locally brewed beer.)

"Then there was a lot of beer."

"Yeah," said Collins.

"So, then, you were all drunk," the women said.

"No," Collins said sorrowfully, "we weren't."

Eventually the woman gave up and walked away, frustrated that the tale of Ironman's beginning was a relatively benign affair. So much for a melodramatic birth. But the Ironman would certainly fulfill that need with its own brand of human drama in the years to come.

For years, race directors, promoters, television producers and corporate heads have tried to reproduce the magic that is Ironman. There are better organized races. There are safer races. There are more beautiful courses and there are, no doubt, much easier triathlons of the same distance. And none have been able to reproduce the feeling that one gets from Kona. It's not that the event is flawless. It is not the fact that all of the best athletes from around the world partake, or that entry is limited to a fraction of those who really want to race. It's not TV. It's not even the fabled aloha spirit that thousands of local volunteers graciously bestow upon the competitors.

The magic of Ironman is a perplexing, baffling, and seemingly inexplicable desire in the hearts and minds of its competitors, both real and imagined. When men and women hear about the event, it strikes a chord, waking a sometimes dormant primal instinct to do battle. Perhaps war has become slightly less popular of late, but the innate need to challenge oneself, to explore one's physical and mental limits, has remained an integral part of the human experience.

The Ironman has mystique. It has mystery. Even if other triathlons have their own versions of personal heroism and intrigue, none have provid-

TOP LEFT Valerie Silk placed leis on almost every competitor in the nine years she owned the race. Imagine having to pick all those flowers. **TOP RIGHT** Nineteen ninety-three was the first year of my precipitous slide at Kona, and the second time I finished out of the top six. I'm sure it was because of the number they assigned me. **BOTTOM** Every little bit helps, eh?

LAVALAND

ed so many, so long, with so much exposure telling the world of these tales ... as the Ironman.

It is the seemingly inconsequential yet personal acts of valor, chronicled in newspapers and magazines, that spark the interest of the athlete's "everyman"; the obligatory "day in the life" segment that sends a message to triathletes everywhere, initiating a little voice inside that says, "I want to ... no, I *need* to do that race!"

Maybe some of the tales are blown out of proportion by the authors and editors taking poetic license with the story. For example, there was this little piece on one of the television segments about a competitor who was diagnosed with cancer, but went on to race anyway because she just had to do it before she died. Well, to make a long story short, she didn't really have cancer and someone somewhere had mud on their face.

Still, real world tales with real world soul abound. One of my favorites is the story of a young, inexperienced competitor in the 1979 Ironman. During the final portions of a particularly long day (and night), he hailed a passing paper boy during the early morning hours for a peek at the day's sport's page. It seems that he wanted to check the results of the race that he was still competing in and had begun nearly 24 hours ago. Can you imagine what was going through his head at the time? And few people recall the time that a pig carcass was tied to the turn-around buoy of the swim by a disgruntled local fisherman; or when an equally unhappy boat captain drove his 35-foot fishing vessel right into the start of the swim, later to be arrested by local

authorities. I actually remember seeing the prop of that boat going 'round and 'round under water as I swam by and thought, "Damn, that would hurt to get sliced up by that thing. And you'd probably have to drop out of the race, too."

If that sounds normal to you, then you would fit right in. Barry McDermott, the *Sports Illustrated* writer whose spring '79 piece on the race baptized millions into the ranks of triathlon believers, says this of early Ironman competitors: "They were all characters. They were all crazy, obviously certifiable. Even the guy Cowman, who is bizarre, you know, in that group he was 'normal.'" If by accident or sheer intuitive genius, McDermott had hit upon a small but growing subculture of unique endurance athletes. "I thought it would be a good story," McDermott said, "but when I got there I knew it would be great." And the colorful characters, even if there were only 15 of them in 1979, were what made it great. And none greater than that year's winner, Tom Warren.

"To me," McDermott continues, "there was always this one Ironman of Hawaii contest, and there's always going to be just one Ironman — Tom Warren. These other guys, yeah, they can do it. And they beat his time by three hours and all that stuff, but so what?

"If you can do the Ironman in eight hours and 30 minutes, great, but no one in my mind can ever approach the spectacle that I witnessed. The way Tom Warren won that race was incredible. And to do what he did for a silly little trophy made out of nuts and bolts — that to me was special. He'll always be the Iron Man. He did it in

Little Welchy placed third in 1989, the year of the epic Mark/Dave dual. He passed Kenny Glah with a mile to go on his way to an impressive 2:56 marathon. Greg was now a "name" to watch.

LAVALAND

a way and for a reason that will never exist again."

True enough.

At times the very word Ironman seems in danger of becoming generic (for example, you're a triathlete, hence you're an Ironman). But I doubt that will ever diffuse the event's stature. After all, take away the franchise races, the merchandising applications, the media hype, and it is still one race a year, one personal forum for 1500 lucky individuals. Oddly enough, that number could be 15,000. Why? Who knows? The lack of other great personal challenges in this day and age? Maybe. To experience some sort of self discovery along the way? Possibly. Because, then, they too would be Ironmen and Ironwomen? Absolutely.

After I had won my first Ironman in 1982, I went to the awards ceremony with my wife, Virginia, my brother Jeff (who had placed third that year), and our friend and competitor, Steve Perez. When we got to the door, we were informed that it was sold out and no more tickets were available. "Okay," I said, "but can we just go in and collect our hardware?" "Sorry, brudda. You gonna be waiting long time here," was the man's reply.

In the meantime, Steve had disappeared, Virginia was mumbling something about poor planning, and Jeff just shook his head. For a moment I was pissed but figured if they wouldn't let us in, well, screw it. What are they going to do? Disqualify me? It was just another episode in an ongoing tiff between the elite athletes and the organizers, and the lack of any preferential treatment whatsoever for us. So I headed off on a

TOP The finish line awaiting the winner in 1982. It looks a little more like the "Gates of Babylon" now. BOTTOM Period shot of bikes on the pier the day before the race. You just drove up in your car, pulled the bike out of the trunk, set it in the rack somewhere and split. A kinder, gentler transition area.

ABOVE Kurt "Mad Dog" Madden, an El Cajon boy who went on to do good things as a high school teacher and ultra-distance runner. He also held the course record for the Ultra Man for awhile.

reconnaissance mission to the alley behind the convention center, and spotted Perez holding a case of a strange-looking new beer they were calling Budweiser Light. He had been handed this stuff by an Anheuser Busch guy trying to "get the word out." Things were looking up.

We then found a back entrance from the alley, through the kitchen and onto the stage. So we sat on the curb in the alley for awhile, talking about anything but triathlons, drinking some of the first Bud Light ever brewed, and half-listening to the awards presentation unfolding inside. When our names came up, a cook was handed a six-pack and we slid right through the kitchen piled high with dirty dinner plates and onto the stage.

The Ironman is like that — a place in which preparation meets opportunity, where emotional swings are constant, and where tenacity and perseverance are king. There are few events in which pleasure and pain are so integrated. You have to ask yourself if the Little Rock, Arkansas, bowling league offers the same opportunity for self-knowledge. And maybe it does, though I have always thought that the harder you work for something, the more you appreciate it. Granted, it's easy for people to get teary-eyed when discussing their personal experience with Ironman. After all, it's a very emotional event to be a part of. Still, beyond the faces of pain and tears of joy, there lies something more, something abstract. It's almost like people use the race to create an indelible image of one long day; a memory that supersedes less powerful imagery. To think that it all came about quite by accident, too.

· · · · ·

The first Ironman, in February 1978, was won by Gordon Haller, a 27-year-old Honolulu taxi driver, former Naval officer and successful military pentathlete. Haller was a self-admitted fitness fanatic and one of the only people involved in the original Ironman who knew that the Around-the-Island Bike Ride (Oahu), from which the cycling leg of 112 miles was drawn, was always held over two days. Started in the 1920s as the Honolulu Star 'Round-the-Island bike ride, this 112-mile course was actually a group ride. But local cyclists would congregate each Wednesday to train on the course and occasionally hold a club race on this circumnavigated loop. An offshoot of this "ride" was the Sea Spree series of two-day races in which the cyclists overnighted in Haliewa, approximately halfway around the island. There is also another "ride" called the Perimeter Ride that follows the entire perimeter of the island, including off-road sections and excluding military installations. It's a two-day event that stops for the night at Turtle Bay on the North Shore.

When it came time to choose a course for the Ironman in 1978, the 112-mile course favored by the local cyclists was a natural. In 1982, one of the island's best cyclists, Dick Evans, was killed and the ride became known as the Dick Evans Memorial from '83 on. Haller, confident in his abilities to win this event from the very moment that Collins proposed it, failed to disclaim this fact to the other organizers and competitors, being afraid they might reconsider the monumental task of combining the Waikiki Rough Water Swim (2.4 miles), the Round-the-Island Bike Race (115 miles cut down to 112 for logistical reasons) and the Honolulu Marathon (26.2 miles).

In 1986, triathlon writer Mike Plant interviewed Haller for his seminal book, "Iron Will," on the first 10 years of Ironman. Haller told Plant, "We just kind of put it together. I don't know why I didn't mention that the bike race took two days. I knew I could do that. I used to do bike camping trips where I'd do as many as 140 miles in a day with full packs and everything."

Haller's main competition would come from an ex-Navy SEAL named John Dunbar who, like Haller, was a self-confessed training nut. Dunbar was blond, good-looking and equally eccentric in his own right. He is also one of the main individuals who, when he originally heard Collins's challenge at the Primo Gardens, *knew* he could win. At the time, he was a student, living off the G.I. Bill in his van. Dunbar was a SEAL to the core. "I wasn't about to be beaten in an event that incorporated a number of activities," said Dunbar. On the morning of the 1979 race, he showed up in a Superman outfit.

Dunbar had been stationed in San Diego between 1972 and 1976. "If you understand what the SEALs are all about," says Dunbar, "then you know why the sport of triathlon has always been attractive to them." Dunbar knew of the early Fiesta Island events and competed when he could. He also met Collins, another Navy guy, but not a SEAL. "That always bothered Collins," laughs Dunbar, "that SEALS used triathlons as part of their training and preparation for sea, air and land military combat."

For my own part, I remember when the SEAL teams would show up at the early races on Fiesta Island. They looked tough, sitting in the back of those gray, four-wheel drive trucks in their cut-off

Masters competitor Ron Smith came up with the name "Dig Me Beach" in 1983 after returning from a swim there one morning. He said, "Boy, you should see all the people strutting there stuff, saying 'dig me, would you' down at that little beach on the pier."

fatigues. I always felt bad beating them though, because I knew that any one of them could kill me with a credit card. Besides, if there were ever a far-off war like Vietnam again, they would go and risk their lives so that I could hang out in Mission Bay and train for triathlons.

In December 1977, Haller needed a job and ended up at the Nautilus Fitness Center on King Street in Honolulu. The owner, Hank Grundman, told Haller he couldn't hire him, but would let him work out for free if he would do a few odd jobs around the place from time to time. Haller and Grundman became friends and Grundman sponsored him for that first race in February 1978. (Grundman would also end up sponsoring the race in 1979 and '80). The interesting connection here is that upstairs at the King Street location worked Grundman's wife, Valerie, doing the books and occasionally complaining about the money the centers were putting into this "crazy-assed" sport.

• • • • •

The Mother of all Ironmen and Women, Valerie Silk (Valerie Grundman when married to Hank), was a working, married bookkeeper who emerged into a near-icon of Ironman's first decade. From 1978 through '80, Valerie watched her husband's Nautilus Fitness centers pour more and more resources into the Ironman triathlon. As the accountant lacking the vision of a marketer, she questioned the promotional investment. "After the 1979 race, our entire staff was burned out from the efforts that essentially supported 15 people," she said. Race founder John Collins was transferred to the mainland in 1979 and "bequeathed" the race to Hank and Valerie after failing to get any of the local running or cycling clubs to take it. Remember: In 1979 the race had no value. Valerie knew this, but figured that maybe it would be profitable soon enough. "I was really naïve in the beginning," she said. "I really thought that every sporting event made money."

John Collins had charged a $5 entry fee for the first race in 1978. After all was said and done, he lost $25 on the event and tried to make it up the next year by raising the entry fee to $8. Nautilus was his only "sponsor," primarily because they helped pay for the T-shirts for 15 athletes and let them shower off at the club after the race.

The 1980 race brought 108 entries at $25 each, but Valerie's marriage to Grundman was in trouble. Even with the presence of ABC television filming a show for their Wide World of Sports program, neither of them really wanted to take the race in the divorce settlement. But Valerie was destined to do some good for others and ended up getting the Iron Man (the way it was spelled then) in the amiable split. And this is where the mystique of Ironman gets another windfall.

Valerie (now back to Silk) was not so much interested in the profitability as she was in "helping others realize their dreams." Sparked by a speech by a Honolulu Lutheran pastor, Rev. Doug Olson, she set about rearing the race as a child. For Valerie, who never had kids of her own, the opportunity to treat hundreds of athletes as if she were completely responsible for their well being

DAVID EPPERSON

ABOVE Hasn't this guy heard of marker pen poisoning?

was perfect. What she lacked in business acumen and long-term vision she made up for with compassion and thought. "I had a lot of business advisors over the years," Valerie told me. "Some gave me good advice and some gave me bad advice. But in hindsight, I always went with my gut feeling. I wouldn't change much."

People question whether the Ironman would have achieved its mystery and mystique if it had been run as a well-oiled corporate machine from the early days. The only answer I can give to that is to question whether that company would personally sign 400 birthday cards every month, as Valerie did.

While Silk will not live in the past or dwell on her mistakes, she does acknowledge some of her failures, as well as her successes. In 1980 and '81, the "official" title was The Nautilus International Triathlon. Loyal to a fault, Valerie continued to use the Nautilus moniker partially to repay her ex-husband for supporting the event even after she moved it to the Big Island, and partially because she truly believed that a large sponsorship from the Mainland-based national chain of health clubs was forthcoming — which it wasn't. After a successful move to a less-crowded, less-dangerous venue, Silk returned to the Ironman name, trademarked it and incorporated the race. She was also relieved when ABC agreed to raise their rights fee to $35,000 in 1982 from the $20,000 they paid in 1981 (no rights fee was paid in 1980.) Throw in the title sponsorship from Anheuser Busch for use under the Bud Light Brand and the $85 entry fee from the 800-plus entrants and *voilà* — The Hawaiian Triathlon Corporation had a nice, workable budget.

DAVID EPPERSON

HARALD JOHNSON

TOP Aid station mirage. BOTTOM After I won in 1985, I started training for my next career as a moto-crosser.

This, however, never gave Valerie the same satisfaction as standing on the finish line and placing a lei around each and every finisher's neck from 4 p.m. until well past midnight. Still, while she doted on her 'Iron Children,' cynics, slick profiteers and even members of the original Ironman race were lining up to criticize her. Even though I tried to stay as neutral as possible, eventually I gave in to a growing group of professional athletes who were frustrated by Silk's refusal to offer any prize money when we continued to come, paying all our own expenses, and receiving a trophy for our efforts. Other events were quickly beginning to usurp some of Ironman's prestige by courting the elite competitors. In my first six Ironman events, I placed first twice, second three times and third once. My net financial loss for the period, specific to those results, was in the thousands. In experience and other arenas, I was growing rich with knowledge. Valerie knew that I knew that. It was simply a waiting game, with the athletes threatening to race elsewhere, and Silk, in her typically slow but methodical style, pondering how to introduce the crassness of prize money into Ironman without losing the "everyman" appeal.

In 1986, an "anonymous" donor named Steve Drogan offered to put up $100,000 for prize money, no strings attached. Steve was a successful and extremely kind businessman from La Jolla, California, with a home and interests in Kona. Valerie accepted the donation and put the entire lot into prize money that went 10 deep, split equally. Only Drogan knows for sure why he put the money up. Maybe it was a foray into his interest in the Ironman, maybe it was purely philanthropic. By the

time 1987 rolled around, Valerie could not go back and would assign portions of the sponsor commitment to a minimum prize purse of $100,000. Steve Drogan was never publicly acknowledged or thanked and to my knowledge, was never approached about putting any more money into the race. To this day, I doubt that the significance of his gift is truly understood or appreciated by more than a handful.

By then, though, Silk's battles were only beginning. A failed sale to a British company brought the first of what amounted to seven or eight different lawsuits. Marvel Comics would join in with a claim against the name "Ironman," and Gordon Haller, John Dunbar (who finished second in 1978 and '79) and several others from 'the first 14' would claim that Collins assigned the Ironman without permission of "The Hawaiian Iron Man Triathlon Organizing Committee," a group set up by Collins to ward off litigious claims by competitors and others to follow. By the time Silk had fought or disposed of all the lawsuits, the lion's share of her 51-percent take in the sale, on December 4, 1989, of the Ironman to Dr. James Gills, (a renowned ophthalmologist and successful investor from Florida) was gone. What she was left with was a decade's worth of memories, some bad, mostly good and all of them intense.

• • • • •

Nineteen-eighty became Ironman's year of transition. One hundred and eight competitors showed up to start, influenced by the intangi-

RICHARD GRAHAM

TOP In 1988, the Ironman people brought back some of the finishers of the first race in 1978. On the right are Gordon Haller, first winner, and John Collins, founding father. Haller lives in Colorado now, and Collins is on a boat somewhere in Panama. **BOTTOM LEFT** Rob Barel finished fourth in Kona 1990. That was the year the Europeans began dominating the event. Along with Pauli Kiuru (4th), Henry Keins (6th) and Jürgen Zäck (8th), they put four in the top 10.

RICHARD GRAHAM

ble attraction that was chronicled in Barry McDermott's *Sports Illustrated* article. One of the 108 was a swim coach from Davis, California named Dave Scott, who had heard of the event at the Waikiki Rough Water Swim the year before. Scott, a graduate of UC Davis with a degree in exercise physiology, was a technical whiz with training principles. He had looked at Warren's splits from the year before and had told a friend that they were "incredibly soft." Scott arrived on Oahu in February 1980 better prepared than any athlete before him. His victory took almost two hours off the course record.

Also showing up was a former Olympic and national team cyclist named John Howard. Howard was very confident of his ability and like Scott, thought that Warren's times could be slaughtered by a "real" athlete. Howard would go on to find that even though his cycling skills were legendary, his swimming was barely adequate and his running only slightly better. He would finish third in 1980, more than an hour behind Dave Scott's new benchmark of 9:24. Second place would go to another former Navy SEAL named Chuck Neuman, whose unique claim to fame was that he fell asleep during a post-race, finish-line interview with ABC. Warren, almost 35 that year, would finish fourth.

The fact that Collins was now gone as race director and Silk would move the race to Kona the next year somehow washes the historical significance of the 1980 race. Dave Scott was incredible — maybe too incredible. His athletic performance helped to establish the validity of

Ironman. This wasn't just a survival-fest for the oddball and the eccentric. This event could be raced!

But what happened to the Dunbars in their Superman outfits? Or the Cowmans with there cow horns sticking up out of the water in the swim? Or even the quirky bar owner with the soft-spoken determination of a nuclear bomb? How would they survive against guys like John Howard who had been to the Olympics? ABC television would take care of those who marched to a different drummer.

Another one of the many readers of McDermott's *Sports Illustrated* article was a director for sports at ABC, a 33-year-old wonderkid type who had a feeling that the Ironman would appeal to American television viewers.

"It was just a hunch," Robert Iger recounted from his New York office, "that the potential human drama that athletes put themselves through to go to the absolute limits in endurance sports seemed to fit into the mold of Wide World of Sports. And it was an event that our viewers had never seen before."

What Iger had was vision. What the rest of ABC didn't have was a clue as to how to cover the event. Should it be a race, a human drama deal, a show of masochistic freaks and wannabees? Over the years, all of those "angles" were used. It has been difficult for ABC, then CBS and now NBC, to tap into the mystique of Ironman. Not everyone wants to bare their souls and share their memories just to get their mug on the box for a fleeting moment. Memories are paramount. They are the only thing that can't be taken away from us.

BOTTOM CENTER Mike Reilly, going on 10 years as "the voice of Ironman." **BOTTOM RIGHT** The very first winner of the Ironman (1978). How'd you like to have that on your resume! Gordon Haller before the start of the 1979 Ironman.

LAVALAND

Still, the television cameras roll on, trying to seek out and find the next Julie Moss Crawl, the next Mark and Dave Showdown, the next "human condition" that can be airbrushed with mood lighting and highlighted with a haunting Tim Weisberg flute. For some, the media's quest for canned emotion is an intrusion into their own quest of another type. They don't want, or need to be, a celluloid hero. But television and print exposure mean sponsorship dollars that should trickle down to the very nuts and bolts of a race. They are strange bedfellows indeed. Professional athletes need exposure to "fund" their chosen profession, but only in recent years have all parties involved figured out how to work together. For the first 15 years of Ironman, the lead riders received some type of "draft" off the many camera trucks that stationed themselves in front of them. Some years were worse than others and some of the athletes who benefited would downplay the scenario. In reality, the situation affected the race results in both the men's and women's field on more than one occasion.

Now that vehicle drafting has been alleviated and time has softened hard feelings, most parties agree that the media overstepped their boundaries, well aware that Ironman organizers, in their thirst for exposure, would turn the other cheek. It would be difficult in any circumstance to ask a media giant such as ABC Sports to "stay clear" of the lead cyclists, but there are those of us who believe it should have at least been given a greater effort, considering the way vehicle drafting could affect the outcome. And we could say that

TOP LEFT Tony Richardson has his priorities straight. TOP RIGHT Scott Molina beat Mike Pigg by two minutes in 1989. The day after he won, somebody from Triathlon Federation leaked the fact that the French federation had decided that his drug test taken at Nice three weeks prior was not in compliance with their standards. There were a lot of strange circumstances, including the fact that some athletes claimed that their urine samples were "sealed" in glass jars with a

piece of cellophane and a rubber band. Even though Scott was eventually cleared of any wrongdoing, it still spoiled his Ironman victory. **BOTTOM LEFT** When you see the swim finish, for a brief moment you are ecstatic — until you realize what lies ahead. **ABOVE** "When we come to the place where the road and the sky collide, throw me over the edge and let my spirit fly." — *Jackson Browne*.

maybe the TV folks never truly understood how an athlete could benefit from their vehicles. In fact, much of the responsibility could and should have fallen to the athletes to avoid the assistance when it occurred. After all, that responsibility has always been on the cyclists' shoulders when it pertains to drafting off of other cyclists. It is a small, but sad episode in the sport's past.

My own memories of past Ironman races are a powerful and permanently etched collection of bittersweet days under the hot Kona sun. They have provided me with more than a graduate degree from the school of hard knocks. I wouldn't trade them for anything. Still, anything done in repetition changes; it is a learning process, a method to mastery. And as familiarity induces skill, it also breeds contempt. Sometimes I think that my best Ironman races are behind me, not because of my age, but because I have raced in so many of them. I know what it takes to win and it's not all pretty. As great as the layman believes the sacrifices to be, it's hard to fully comprehend putting your life on hold for three or four months so that all possible energy systems can focus on one Saturday in October. Just to have the means, the opportunity to do this once in your life, is both a blessing and a curse. In all my years of triathlon, I have known only one person who did it right once and then walked away for good.

By no means am I trying to raise the Ironman to global proportions. Far from it. One day, one sporting event. No more, no less. There is a reason for the magic though, a correlation between an individual's hunger for personal triumph and John

C.J. OLIVARES

ABOVE Erin Baker. Those Giro helmets were fast, but geez were they big.

Collins's challenge to a handful of Honolulu athletes. Ironman has given me and thousands of other competitors opportunities to experience a multitude of feelings in a few short hours. And while those feelings were at least 50 percent painful, I know that I, as well as others, have become better people because of it. For that, I am grateful.

Could something else have provided us the same forum for personal growth? Probably. It could have been another triathlon, maybe another sport. But it wasn't, and Ironman lives on. For a growing subculture of endurance enthusiasts, it remains the Holy Grail, one of the last bastions of elite, world-class sporting events that reserves a spot or two for "everyman."

Each goal, each dream is different. But the thread that weaves the winners with the group that finishes in 16 hours is the same desire to do something that will allow them to stand a little taller, with a little more confidence. And in this crowded, confusing day and age, when a chance like that comes along, you've just got to run with it.

KATHLEEN McCARTNEY

As soon as the walls of preconceived notions were struck down by early Ironman competitors Lyn Lemaire, Robin Beck, Linda Sweeney, Sally Edwards, Lynn Brooks and Ardis Bow, women everywhere took up the Ironman challenge in increasing numbers. One of them was a 22-year-old college coed from Orange County, California, named Kathleen McCartney. McCartney befriended her eventual husband, Dennis Hearst, in a bar on Mammoth Mountain, a ski resort in Northern California. She

DAVID EPPERSON

was intrigued by his discussions of an event he was training for that was to be held in a few months time, in February of 1981, on the Big Island of Hawaii. It would be a stretch to say that McCartney's attraction to Hearst was overly founded on his athletic prowess; McCartney had a limited sporting background, with negligible experience in swimming, cycling and running, however, it was safe to say that when Hearst quietly spoke of 26-mile runs and 24-hour bike races, it piqued her interest.

McCartney began dating Hearst and accompanied him to Kona, in 1981, for his Ironman event, which had a profound affect on her. She knew that she, too, could train with Dennis, run with him and ride with him. She had just finished college at the University of California at Santa Barbara, and didn't have a particular career yet, and she knew that the athletic lifestyle could be hers.

And so began one of the most meteoric rises in athletic skill in the history of women's endurance sports. One day, McCartney was sitting on the curb watching Hearst compete against 317 other competitors, 93 percent of them men, over a rugged stretch of roadway, and the next moment she was asking bystanders what type of bicycle she should get in order to enter in next year's event.

She began training soon thereafter, setting her sights comfortably low. "At first, Dennis said I had the chance to finish in 17 hours or so," McCartney recalled, "but then I ran a marathon and it came quite easy. Then I stayed with Dennis on some of his long, arduous training rides. Pretty soon we were talking 15 hours, and then 14 and so on." The training that McCartney, Hearst and a few of his buddies did was challenging, even by today's standards. "Basically, we would train all day. My body just kept assimilating, soaking up the miles and improving. It was such a rapid evolution into the sport that it all seems like a blur at this point."

McCartney's first real test toward the February 1982 Ironman was the Santa Barbara Triathlon, in July 1981. I happened to be at that event and finished first, and when I was watching the first woman come across the line, I thought, "Whoa, that gal isn't all that far behind me." Six weeks later, McCartney won the Navy SEAL-based Super Frog Half-Ironman. "It was all so primitive," McCartney said. "Changing clothes, trying to figure out what to eat, riding these heavy 10 speeds, but I kept improving."

When the 1982 Ironman rolled around, McCartney had few expectations. She was confident

TOP Paula in Kona 1988, on her way to a convincing win.

that she could finish, buoyed by her two half-Iron-man races, but this was a different gig. Her swim was disappointing, leaving her a long way behind the front-running women. But that was okay; all she wanted was to finish in a strong position.

As the bike ride unfolded, though, it became obvious that she was moving up through the field. And when she climbed off her bike and into the run, she was surprised to find that it really wasn't so bad. Up front, the ABC-TV crews had stayed with a red-head from Carlsbad named Julie Moss, who had a commanding lead. It wasn't until very late in the run that McCartney was even considered as a potential threat. Not only was McCartney in second place, but was closing in on Moss. Moss's lead, though, was substantial, even as she entered Kona.

That's when McCartney realized that she was closer than she thought. "When I looked up during the last few miles of the run," she said, "I saw the TV helicopter over where I took Julie to be. I also saw a helicopter that seemed to be hovering over me, too. At first they seemed to be a mile apart, but then they kept getting closer and closer together. Then a van with a couple of media-looking types showed up."

With a quarter-mile to go, drama was unfolding in a very big way. As the TV producers and race director Valerie Silk argued over the effect of Rodney Jacob's Freewheelin' Films crew, who was there to film a short documentary for the event's new title sponsor, Bud Light, Julie Moss fell 200 yards from the finish line, got up, fell again and finally walked the final yards to victory. When Moss fell a third time and couldn't get up, the film-crew haggling became a moot point, and the helicopters

were nearly on top of each other. As Moss was crawling the final 20 yards, McCartney, incredulously came around the final corner to witness this unfolding before her eyes.

McCartney ran by the fallen Moss and into the arms of a waiting Hearst. Maybe she barely noticed Moss on the ground, shielded by cameras, officials and medical people as she ran right by and won the Ironman. Consequently, her victory paled to the limelight that was garnered by the Moss episode. Of course, McCartney never begrudged Moss for her accidental theft of the spotlight. They became close friends, did a media tour together, and raced each other for the following two seasons until McCartney's exodus from the sport. She had accomplished what she came to do.

CHAPTER EIGHT

"When the will and the imagination are in conflict, it is always the imagination that wins." — Emile Coué, 1857-1926

ENCOUNTERS

DAVID EPPERSON

Have you ever noticed children encountering a new area or a new toy? Their face is bright with curiosity, their movements inquisitive. The unexplored presents an opportunity for discovery and knowledge. The new object is a means to understand how things work. To sit and watch this wonderful exploration is to witness the learning process in its purest form.

As we grow older, our egos prevent us from experiencing new situations with innocence and naiveté. Society has taught us to exercise caution; to open new doors slowly and never too wide. And yet through athletics we can reverse that trend, turn back the clock, and go into the room with wild-eyed wonder. Whether or not we realize it, each encounter we have in this sport has the potential to either become a footnote of our career or slip silently into the past, never to be recalled or relived. Each little thing that we come in contact with — a place, another competitor, a strange or unique situation, becomes part of our collective, living résumé.

ENCOUNTERS

For many people who entered triathlon in its first decade, their first encounter with the sport was Barry McDermott's *SI* article on Tom Warren and the 1979 Ironman. What started out as a working vacation turned into one of the most notable windfalls in the history of any sport. "All I wanted to do," says McDermott, 19 years after the article came out, "was go to Hawaii. You know how the East Coast can be in winter. You see, this guy I knew told me about the Ironman in 1978 and thought it might make for a good piece. He sent me a little newspaper clipping and I figured that maybe there was something there. But when I got there I *knew* it would be great." And great it was. To this day, people still get chills when they read the article. "I just became enamored by this Warren character. Nobody gave him a second thought. The whole deal was supposed to be a contest between the two Navy guys, Haller and Dunbar. Warren just sort of sat in the corner and kept to himself. And as we followed him during the event it became apparent that this guy had no talent, but a heart as big as Kansas.

"I remember on the way back from the marathon turnaround, he had a commanding lead, and there was this huge head wind. I couldn't help myself anymore and decided to run alongside of him. I asked him if that would be okay and all he said was 'Fine, just don't block the wind.' He didn't want to be accused of any cheating, even though his lead was substantial."

McDermott took the story back to New York and when it came out a couple of months later, he was besieged with letters and calls for more infor-

PREVIOUS PAGE "So are you gonna' have the burrito especial No.3 or the chile relleno plate for lunch?" ABOVE This bunny rabbit is worth three minutes off your time at the Easter Ride and Tie, well worth Murphy Reinschreiber's effort.

mation. He finally had to make up a little info sheet and give to his secretary to send out. Strangely enough, even Hollywood had shown some interest. "Warren and I went with this guy George Wallack, who was Bruce Jenner's agent at the time, to meet this producer at one of the big studios. At about the same time, the movie "Running" with Michael Douglas came out and flopped big time. That put Hollywood off of fringe sport flicks for a long time," remembers McDermott.

. . . . .

As I look back on my years circling the globe, first in search of athletic victories and more recently in search of something else, I can't help but ponder the different encounters that I've had. Many were positive, some negative, some strange and all — as stories become with time — very funny to look back on.

Here are a few of mine, in no particular order or significance that I can think of, followed by those that belong to some of my contemporaries:

. . . . .

For awhile in 1988 it became popular to rub my daughter Torrie's head for good luck just before the swim start. I think Kenny Souza started the tradition when he did it before a big event and went on to have the race of his life. We had to put a stop to it when the age-groupers began to line up for a quick rub of her one-year-old head.

I went to a race in Brazil in 1984 with Mark

TOP Dean Harper, Rob Roller and Julie Moss. Why do I get the feeling that this was Julie's idea? Early Brazil tour. BOTTOM At the core of triathlon are the volunteers. Without them there would be no pros, no governing body, no TV crews, no sponsors. Each time we encounter them at an aid station, remember this.

ABOVE Back when triathlons were considered primarily a Southern California counterculture activity, swims in the surf were a weekly occurrence. You're not a complete athlete until you've raced two or three kilometers in a six- to eight-foot surf.

ENCOUNTERS

Allen and Mark Montgomery. A few days before the race we did a training ride with some of the locals. I couldn't help but notice the car following in close proximity for the entire ride. It turns out that when you ride through certain locations on your bike, an armed escort is necessary to discourage the less-fortunate locals from "acquiring" your bike while you are still sitting on it.

• • • • •

There was a triathlon in Tasmania, off the southern coast of Australia, years ago that included a swim in the Antarctic Ocean. Quite cold, I understand. An Aussie competitor, Marc Dragan, was so hypothermic at the end of the swim that he decided to start the bike ride with his wetsuit on, even though he was in the lead. You'd be surprised how fast you warm up wearing a wetsuit while riding a bike.

• • • • •

In 1983 I did a race in New York City where we swam from the Statue of Liberty to Battery Park at the south end of Manhattan. This necessitated pre-race injections as a precaution for typhoid, hepatitis and dysentery. Three of us decided to ride our bikes to the start from our hotel near Central Park. Riding south through a pre-dawn New York, dodging taxis, drunks, late-night partiers and homeless individuals, we arrived at the swim transition to watch the coroner pull a dead body out of the Hudson River.

• • • • •

I remember master's star Ron Smith training for a 24-hour bike race by waking up at 3 a.m. to ride his bike around a well-lit parking lot of a local grocery store. What do you say when a good friend asks you to go for a bike ride with him and casually mentions that you will be finished with a 60-miler before the sun comes up?

• • • • •

My brother Jeff and I once waited on a road alongside a golf course for Scott Molina and Gary Petterson to pick us up for the pre-race meeting at the 1984 Kaui Loves You Triathlon. Molina saw us sitting on the wet grass and decided to power-slide his rental car right up to our feet. Unfortunately, his brakes didn't work on the slippery grass and his car slid over a 10-foot embankment into a sandtrap. As the car came to rest on its side, Gary found himself pinned in and unable to extricate himself from the passenger side. Molina climbed out the window and tried to push the car back on its wheels. Jeff and I couldn't help because we were laughing so hard we couldn't stand up.

• • • • •

During a particularly hot USTS championship race on Hilton Head Island, South Carolina, Bill Leach overheated during the run and jumped into one of the water-filled canals that wound along the course. He was then told it was against the law due to the presence of alligators.

. . . . .

In the 1985 Ironman, I was leading the run with six miles to go when a guy in the lead vehicle starts to give me splits and encouragement to break the course record. Two miles later, I realize that the guy is Dave Scott providing the incentive, even though it was his course record.

. . . . .

During the 1990 Tug's Swim-Run-Swim Biathlon, I noticed this rough-looking guy walking toward the starting line wearing a bathing suit and carrying a small handgun. I was a little concerned until he pointed the gun skyward, shot it once and started running toward the water. I realized it was Tom Warren starting his own race just before joining it.

. . . . .

Ken Souza and I arrived in Surfer's Paradise, Australia, in the spring of 1987 to compete in the World Cup Gold Coast Triathlon. After the long flight, we decided a short swim was in order. After 15 minutes of hard swimming, I noticed that the current had slowed my progress considerably. I turned around to check Kenny's progress and saw him being sucked out the mouth of the river, into the ocean and out to sea. I still don't know how he made it in.

RICHARD GRAHAM

. . . . .

After the 1984 Chicago Bud Light USTS, race director Jim Curl got married. The reception got pretty wild, but what was more interesting was ending up at a bar in downtown Chicago with 50 triathletes, and entering a twist contest with Colleen Cannon. We won solely based on applause.

. . . . .

The first time I saw Cowman was at the start of the 1981 Ironman; he was warming up for the swim wearing his horns. I thought that was pretty cool.

. . . . .

Some time ago I asked several of my friends to share a few "encounters" with me for an article I was writing. What I received was some memorable stuff that was never used — until now. Check these out.

From Dave Scott

"My position of leading the pack on the bike was just where I wanted to be at mile 25 of the Ironman in October 1982. I received a report that the second man was slowly closing the gap, and at mile 33 he pulled alongside me. We both turned our heads and introduced each other. 'Hi I'm Dave Scott,' and 'Hi, I'm Mark Allen.' We had raced each other twice but this was our first formal introduction. I knew even then that Mark and I would meet each other in future Ironman races.

TOP A free, autographed copy of this book to the first reader to identify the Olympic backstroker interviewing Dave Scott and I after the 1989 St. Croix Triathlon. **BOTTOM** Glen Cook, Andrew McNaughton and Tony Richardson just hanging out on the Great Wall of China after a race.

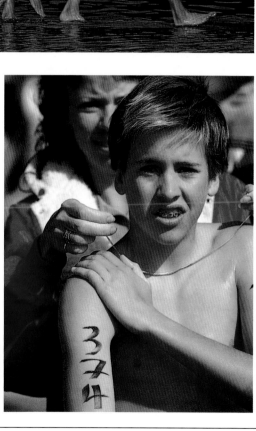

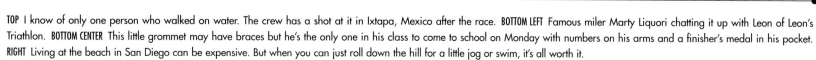

TOP I know of only one person who walked on water. The crew has a shot at it in Ixtapa, Mexico after the race. **BOTTOM LEFT** Famous miler Marty Liquori chatting it up with Leon of Leon's Triathlon. **BOTTOM CENTER** This little grommet may have braces but he's the only one in his class to come to school on Monday with numbers on his arms and a finisher's medal in his pocket. **RIGHT** Living at the beach in San Diego can be expensive. But when you can just roll down the hill for a little jog or swim, it's all worth it.

ENCOUNTERS

"At mile 107 of the October 1983 Ironman, Scott Tinley pulled up next to me on Alii Drive. He was cool and casual as if he didn't even feel the effects of chasing me down. Very politely he turned and offered his water bottle, a great sporting gesture. Riding slightly behind Scott, slightly off to his left, I received a second gesture of his passing. Unfortunately, the spray was not from his water bottle. Scott had mastered the fine art of urinating while riding — and unexpectedly, I was the recipient of his relief. A memorable encounter indeed.

"Two days prior to the 1989 Ironman Japan in Lake Biwa, Murphy Reinschreiber and I decided to ride an easy 40 miles to loosen up our legs. But after a few turns on the small confined countryside, we were lost. The mountains moved, the map served no purpose and our Japanese language skills were nonexistent. For the next six hours Murphy and I traversed, followed canals and crossed mountains in hopes that our hotel would lie ahead. I had left with no money, no food, just a water bottle. Thank God Murphy had brought along some yen.

"When race day came I was unsure of what to expect. We hadn't gotten home until after dark on that 'easy spin.' I wasn't thinking about the race because my wife Anna was due with our first child. As it turned out, I went an 8:01, my fastest Ironman ever. Strange."

From Scott Molina

"The World's Toughest Triathlon in Lake Tahoe had a first prize of $10,000 in the mid-1980s. I won the thing easily and they paid me in cash — 100, $100 dollar bills."

"USTS Baltimore, 1985, flying down a hill at 40 mph and coming around a corner to see a fire truck coming at me."

"Standing in front of a hotel elevator in Provo, Utah, after a major triathlon in which I'd won and having Erin Baker walk out of it and into my life."

From Tom Warren

"I was a kid in San Diego in the early 1950s and I used to race this 'triathlon' every day. I would get up super-early and do my paper route as fast as I could, run down to the beach and body surf a few waves and try to be at school by 8 a.m."

"Bill Phillips and I used to train together in Pacific Beach two days a week. We were equally matched and good friends. The idea was to 'sand bag' until the other guy really thought that you didn't feel good or were out of shape. One time I was trying it on Bill, complaining of this and that, and he was matching it word for word. Finally we both talked ourselves into feeling really shitty when we were both fine."

"Tinley and I used to sneak in to the old Mission Beach Plunge through the boiler room (I had borrowed a key) on Sunday mornings and swim long course in the odd-shaped pool. The

HARALD JOHNSON

TOP Penny Marshall during the filming of a made-for-TV movie about a housewife that trains for and competes in a triathlon. She doesn't look too comfortable, does she? BOTTOM A group of runners "escaping" from Alcatraz.

old building was 60 or 70 years old and there used to be bats hiding up in the rafters. One time we got caught by the manager and ended up buying our way out of trouble with Tug's Tavern T-shirts.

From Ken Souza

"I had moved to Scott Milliner's house up in the mountains above Boulder just to train with him. He had just split up with his wife and was in a bit of a funk. Well, I called him up and said, 'Hey dude, I'm coming out to train with you.' He said, 'Okay, bring it on.' Anyway, I get there at 10:00 p.m. and he's already in bed, but there's a note that says, 'I'll wake you up and we'll go run early.' I get up at 7:00 and he was already gone. So the next day I get up at 6:00 to make sure I didn't miss him and he is already gone. This goes on for a week and each morning he's up earlier and says that he just wanted to let me sleep. Finally, I get pissed and confront him. 'Hey man, I drove 1000 miles to hang out with you and you keep stiffing me!' He just smiled and walked away. The next morning I got up at 4:30 to run with him and he slept in until 9 a.m."

From Ron Smith

"I did this little obscure event in Mission Bay called a ride and tie. Basically it was two people and one bicycle alternating turns running and cycling in a leapfrog mode. The race director, Bob Babbitt, hooked me up with this guy who used to be a runner, but was starting to get into mountain biking. I think we won largely based on his skills. I didn't

DAVID EPPERSON

RICHARD GRAHAM

TOP Joanne Ernst encounters a lunchtime crowd oblivious to her ways. BOTTOM Cycling technology stayed relatively the same for 50 years under the strict rules of cycling's hardline bureaucrats. It took triathlon six or seven years of experimentation to radically alter the way a bike slices through the wind. Gary Hooker designed this 1989 prototype Hooker Elite, and found that it descended like a shopping cart, but squirted across the flats like a bar of soap.

ENCOUNTERS

RICHARD GRAHAM

know who it was until I read about him later on when he won the mountain bike world's in 1990. It was Ned Overend."

"When I first read Barry McDermott's article on the 1979 Ironman in *Sports Illustrated*, I knew I had to do that race. I told a friend about it and he said only a few people in the world could do that. I re-read it and began training for the 1980 event the next day."

"I once watched Kim Bushong eat 56 papaya slices, three full plates of scrambled eggs and 22 large pancakes at the Kona Surf Buffet. After that, he got on his bike and rode to Hawi and back. That guy was strange."

From Todd Jacobs

"I had a chance to race in Ixtapa, Mexico several years ago. I figured that I'd go down the day before the race and then stay a few days after the race and hang out on the beach. Well, there ended up being several canceled flights, more delays and a shuttle bus ride from the airport that more or less scared me to death. I ended up at headquarters hotel around midnight only to find that my reservations had been canceled. The place was full and I didn't feel like camping out in a foreign city in Mexico. So I decided to share some of my discomfort with a competitor. Looking in the hotel register, I found the fastest guy there and woke him up asking if I could sleep on his floor. Kenny Glah was more than accommodating. By 2 a.m. I had my bike together and was ready to grab an hour or two of sleep.

RICHARD GRAHAM

RICHARD GRAHAM

TOP Avignon, France. A classic European city with a long, colorful history and host of a really classy race in the late 1980s. It was the site of the first ITU world championship in 1989. We used to swim downstream through this centuries-old bridge. **BOTTOM LEFT** Quite a few probably chased, but never caught these two. **BOTTOM RIGHT** The Allen Trio, Gary, Grip and their dad.

"Since I was staying with Glah I figured I might as well draft off him in the swim. When we came out of the water, Molina and Mike Durkin took off on the bike with Kenny and I chasing. I was barely hanging on to the group when we came around a corner smack into a bunch of chickens in the road. Everybody hit the brakes but me. Feathers went flying, guys were dodging potholes, it was total mayhem.

"On the run, the sun came out and it was 200 degrees and humid as hell. When we all sprinted for the finish, people were seeing double. Ten yards from the line there was a huge pool that we all dove into to cool off."

From Sally Edwards

"My first triathlon was Verne Scott's Davis Triathlon in 1979. I was a poor swimmer, average cyclist and actually quite confident of my running abilities, having won the Western States 100 mile run several years prior. The swim wasn't that long, maybe 1200 or 1500 yards. But like most of the races back then, the swim was last. I came off the five-mile run in first place, held my own on the bike and started the swim first. Unfortunately, the water was something like 55 degrees. My whole body cramped up, I started to sink and had to be pulled from the race. I fell in love with the sport though."

From Harald Johnson

"We were criticized by the Europeans in the early days as the 'power elite' and the 'California Clique.' Too much control in too few hands. Maybe it was true, but I believe it was necessary. I mean, who else but those with a vested interest were going to spend their Sundays holed up in some San Fernando Valley conference room trying to figure out how to form a governing body for this goofy new sport. The fact is, it was the entrepreneurs, virtually all Californians, who gave triathlon its uniquely American flavor, and who helped put it on the road to success."

From Peter Read Miller
(*Sports Illustrated* photographer)

"I was taking pictures of Tom Warren as he went into the final few miles of the 1979 Ironman and we pulled up alongside him in a car. I asked him how he felt, you know, just to get a rise out of him. He just stared straight ahead and began to whistle the USC fight song."

From Bob Bright
(Ironman Athlete Liaison, 1986-88)

"The IOC needs sports it can market, and TV likes the Ironman distance. Don't forget, sports is show biz."

From Mark Montgomery
(Old-time triathlete competitor)

"The other guys who did really well for a short period didn't always enjoy the lifestyle like I did. Just being out there training was a treat for me. I ended up getting paid to compete in the 350-plus races I did for 12 years. It was great." (Mark started the Ironman 15 times, finally finishing on the ninth try. He ultimately finished three more and claimed a record 11 DNFs.)

ABOVE If you ever get a chance to race in an old town in Europe, do it.

CHAPTER NINE

"The person who has a 'why' to live can bear almost any 'how'..." — *Friedrich Nietzsche, 1844-1900*

MIDTERMS

When 1983 rolled around, it was obvious that the sport of triathlon was picking up steam. No longer would people give a blank stare when you told them what you 'did.' No longer would the semi-knowledgeable ask you if fencing was still included in Olympic triathlon. No longer would everyone ask you 'why?'

Key elements needed to secure the sport's future in a form somewhat larger and more recognizable than a San Diego Track Club swim/run/barbecue were being put in place. On the media front, Valerie Silk hired a full-time public relations person named Jeanette Foster. Foster would work tirelessly for several years trying to tell people that the Ironman triathlon was not about weightlifting or lifeguard beach competitions. Over at the Bud Light USTS group, Speedo America hired Cathy Hoy away from their PR firm to work primarily on the series. And down in San Diego, Mike Plant, who would go on to be the most productive and creative journalist in the history of the sport, had expanded his *Running News* (an offshoot of the former San Diego

Track Club newsletter) to include major stories on triathlon. *Running and Triathlon News* became the timely resource for the sport in Southern California. Plant, a former high school All American springboard diver from Connecticut by way of the University of Nebraska, first came to San Diego on a bike trip from the Canadian border to his sister's house in Tucson, Arizona. "I came down that big hill above La Jolla Cove, saw the ocean and knew I'd be back to stay."

Plant had served in Vietnam under the Medical Corps from 1969 to '70. When he finally landed in San Diego to stay, he ended up managing restaurants and running to stay fit. A self-taught writer and photographer, he began editing the track club newsletter in 1978. Three years later, he and partner Ed Oleata began the *Running News* and until his exit back to the restaurant business in 1990, he was considered one of the most reliable and professional sources of journalism around the emerging multisport industry. His 1987 book about the inner workings of the Ironman, entitled "Iron Will" (Contemporary Books, Chicago, currently out of print) is considered a classic and is one of the most well-written pieces that claims multisport as its genre.

One hundred miles to the north, in the "offices" of *Swim, Swim* magazine, the first issue of *Triathlon* magazine was about to be launched. Quite by accident, three swimming fanatics came together to create a small, but interesting publication devoted almost entirely to fitness and age-group swimming. Penny Little, Harald Johnson and Mike Gilmore put out *Swim,Swim* for several

DAVID EPPERSON

PREVIOUS PAGE If you just wandered down the street at 6:30 a.m. and saw all these people in Lycra suits standing at the water's edge, what would you think? ABOVE Our swim coach would say "too many bubbles." So what?

years before Harald and Penny were bitten by the triathlon bug. "We were on our way back from one of the Waikiki Swims when Penny and I came up with the idea to put out a swimming 'newsletter,' maybe write a little story about our trip to Hawaii," Johnson remembers. "I had been doing freelance work for magazines and by the time the plane landed, we had plans for an entire magazine on swimming. Mike Gilmore sort of caught on to our idea and he came on board with his MBA from USC to help out on the business side. We set up shop in the fall of 1977 and produced our first issue in the spring of '78. I think we printed around 5000 copies." *Swim, Swim* ran for five years until being sold in 1983.

Operating out of Santa Monica, California, Johnson, 31 at the time and a former varsity swimmer from the University of Texas, was intrigued with the Ironman ever since a chance encounter with Dave Scott back in 1979. Johnson recalls: "It was the morning after the Waikiki Rough Water Swim and I was having a leisurely breakfast next to the Outrigger Canoe Club, looking out over the bay. Near the end of the meal, I saw a lone swimmer in the distance. I went down to the beach and saw Dave Scott (who had beaten me the day before in the race) get out of the water. 'Hey Dave, waddaya doin' out there?' I asked. 'Oh, just training for this thing coming up in a few months called an Ironman. I think swimmers might make the best triathletes,' he answered. After that, I knew I had to do it one day."

In the spring of 1982, influenced by the growing interest in multisport, Johnson, Little

DAVID EPPERSON

TOP "Well, I don't feel like dancing." Grant Boswell. BOTTOM LEFT Long-distance swimmer and television commentator Diana Nyad interviewing women's leader Jennifer Hinshaw at the one-off Ricoh Ironman in '83. BOTTOM RIGHT *Triathlon* magazine staff circa 1987: C.J. Olivares, Rich Graham, Harald Johnson, Terry Mulgannon. This was the first string when the mag was at its peak.

and Gilmore produced 35,000 copies of a 'booklet' containing primarily applications to biathlons, triathlons and rough water swim events. It was called *Swim/Bike/Run* and featured a glossy cover shot of the Tinley brothers coming out of the water. For those expecting a full-blown magazine, it was a huge disappointment. But it fulfilled a need and was a smashing commercial success.

The group from Santa Monica then went over to Kona for the fall 1982 Ironman, where Harald Johnson competed, and pitched a group of potential investors into underwriting a full-scale magazine about the sport of triathlon. Over the next month, nearly $250,000 was raised, much of it from well-to-do triathletes like Conrad Will from the Horny Toads running group. In the spring of 1983, the first issue of *Triathlon* magazine was launched, featuring a photo of Dave Scott winning the October 1982 Ironman taken by Pulitzer prize-winning photographer Skeeter Halger. It included articles and information by Mike Plant, Sally Edwards, Pat Hines, Carol Hogan, Bob Babbitt, John Howard and myself. It also featured a listing for 56 different multisport events, every single one of which was to be held in the United States.

THE OTHER TRI MAG

Five hundred miles to the north, a most unlikely individual had almost beaten the Santa Monica group to press. William R. Katovsky, a former U.C. Berkeley political science teacher, Ph.D. candidate, and self-described "double episode of 'Gilligan's Island'-watching couch

COURTESY USTS

MIKE PLANT

TOP "Okay, the rabbit goes around the tree and then back into his hole." **BOTTOM** When was the last time you were in a race and could see no one ahead of you and no one behind you? It used to happen a lot. Mark Montgomery with a titanium chin strap/drool collector.

ABOVE I count no fewer than 14 people with their mouths open. Hope the flies were still asleep for this Pigg/Wells duel.

potato" had become enamored of triathlon. Katovsky had, in the previous few years, begun to live an outdoor, multisport lifestyle that he found not only invigorating, but also interesting from a sociocultural outlook. A non-athlete as a child, he had begun to ride his bike, run and swim longer and longer distances. It made him feel better and allowed him time to analyze the things that he found interesting, in particular, the "human condition." Katovsky reflects: "In 1977, I took some time off of grad school and rode my bike across the country. In all these places that I stopped, I ran around and looked at things or I swam in lakes and pools. I was 21 then and that trip changed my life. I realized that a lot of what sport was about was finishing what you start, and having an experience that transforms your life, you know, how it affects all the things you do in life." What Katovsky wanted to do in his life then was keep riding his bike.

A few years later he had planned a trip from the Canadian border to Mexico when he happened to see the Ironman on TV in February 1982. "I thought to myself, hmmmm, maybe I should try this. So I found this ad in *Bicycling* magazine and taped it up to my refrigerator. I called over to Kona and a lady named Valerie Silk answers the phone and tells me today is the last day to sign up. I sent her $100 and started to learn how to swim more than one lap at a time without stopping. By the time the Ironman rolled around in October of 1982 I wasn't sure I could make it through the swim. I was petrified.

"I was an alien standing on the pier. Here

were all these incredibly fit people, and I was not like any of them, I had never associated with athletes before in my life. Listening to all these people talk about how they had trained and I'd not done a fraction of what they did. I was bewildered. But during the race I started to associate with these people … just totally relating to the whole process of us being out there and doing this thing. And to finish it was so incredible, that I had been able to achieve what I had set out to do. When I got back to Berkeley, I started to think how I could transform this experience into something positive for others, too, because the reason I was in political science was to make a difference in the world, to change things for the better. Then one day I realized I could effect more people through sport, through triathlon. That's why I started *Triathlete* magazine."

Although he had no idea that *Triathlon* magazine was a keystroke away in Los Angeles, Katovsky sold all of his IBM stock, raised some $16,500 and printed 20,000 copies of a tabloid style paper called *Triathlete* magazine. The May 1983 paper featured an interview of Bay Area athlete Dean Harper, a look behind the scenes of the Ironman, and a very insightful commentary by Katovsky on the emerging fascination with triathlons by society. The advertising revenue was a paltry $2700.

Katovsky didn't fit the mold. Here was this goofy poli-sci dude from up north who had only done two triathlons, one of them being a very pedestrian 15-hour affair in Kona, and now he was owner and publisher of a nationwide

DAVID EPPERSON

DAVID EPPERSON

TOP For a couple of years in the mid-1980s, New Zealand marathoner Allison Roe competed and did quite well. Here she crosses one of the many bridges on the Kauai run course. BOTTOM Jonathon Boyer, the

triathlon magazine. I was skeptical myself. In fact, I can remember being on a bike ride one day and having this short, thick curly-hairdo guy with crooked glasses flag me over from an old, funky car. It was Bill, and when he introduced himself as the publisher of *Triathlete* magazine, it was hard not to laugh. But Bill was always true to his quest to hunt down and find the part of triathlon that reflected society, the part that no one else had the desire, nor the courage to explore. Sometimes he was way off base. For instance, in November 1985 he put Julie Moss on the cover dressed up in a seductive looking halter top, carrying a golf club and looking into the camera more like you'd expect a downtown hooker to, rather than a courageous and talented athlete. It was an embarrassment to the sport as well as Moss, but Katovsky wasn't fazed. Other times, he was insightful and right on in his unique observations. He could dig up something no one else could and bring it to light in a way that made the sport much more than the dry, technical 'how to' it was becoming. In one fascinating piece on Scott Molina, he assigned him the moniker "The Terminator." That stuck.

Together with his partner and girlfriend Theresa Taylor, they drove up and down the coast, distributing their free publication to anyone who'd care to read it.

OH, WHAT A TANGLED WEB WE WOVE

The American Triathlon Association began as the U.S. Triathlon Association, which began as

first American to ride the Tour de France and Eric Heiden, Olympic speedskater and now team doctor for the NBA Sacramento Kings, share color commentary duties at one of the televised triathlons. A lot of famous athletes have worked on the shows before. I liked these guys the best because they didn't have a Hollywood attitude. ABOVE Klaus Barth, the first German to come over to the states and race, maybe 20 years ago. He finished fourth at the 1986 Ironman, at age 40.

ABOVE Kenny Souza, star duathlete, sometimes triathlete, always neat and tidy.

the United States Triathlon Federation, which began as Tri-Fed, which became USA Triathlon — for now, anyway. If you understand any of this, then you have spent way too much time following the bureaucracy of the sport.

Every major sport (defined by any number of factors ranging from Olympic inclusion to prize money and participant base) has some type of national governing body. They exist for a variety of reasons, some having to do with safety, fairness and promotion, others having more to do with greed, power, money and profit. I cannot speak for all of the NGBs from the many countries that practice triathlon now, but I can say unequivocally that the U.S. has had an incredibly complicated, convoluted and embarrassing history behind its NGB. As Carl Thomas said recently: "A lot of deals were made, compromises taken and feelings hurt, more than people will ever know, nor should they." And in some ways I agree. The background is there for those who want to dig it up, and things are better now, for the time being.

When the first triathlons were held in the early 1970s, the formation of a national governing body was the furthest thing from the minds of competitors. The races were held, in part, as a byproduct of their desire to escape the rules and bureaucracy of traditional swimming, cycling and running. As the sport grew, those with a vested interest, primarily race organizers, sponsors, media types and to a lesser degree, the athletes, felt a need for standardization of distances, rules, and the need for a 'central clearinghouse' of information and services such as race sanctioning

and group insurance rates. If you're interested, here's how USA Triathlon was conceived.

In the fall of 1981, a triathlete from Burbank, California, named Jim Gayton, decided to start a small association of triathletes, primarily to give future decisions to the athletes. Gayton had had some experience with the morass and heavy-handed United States Cycling Federation (USCF, the NGB of cycling in America) and was concerned that this new sport stood the chance of being "swallowed up" by another NGB. Together with two other triathletes from the area, John Disterdick and Walt Cannon, they incorporated an entity known as the United States Triathlon Association (USTA) and drew up bylaws that would be acceptable within international athletic circles. They made their first pitch at the February 1982 Ironman and soon had 100 members.

At approximately the same time, unbeknown to each other, Carl Thomas of Speedo and Mike Gilmore of *Swim, Swim* magazine began a dialogue. They decided that the sport was moving at too fast a pace and badly needed some direction. Thomas and Gilmore were also versed in the politics of sport and came to the same conclusion that Gayton did — the sport of triathlon would someday be organized, but by who and how were yet to be determined. A meeting was held at a seaside restaurant in Santa Monica that included Thomas, Gilmore, Harald Johnson, Penny Little, Sally Edwards, Dave Scott, Rick Delanty (a top triathlete at the time), Jim Curl and myself. Together we formed the American Triathlon Association, with $1500 seed money:

MIKE PLANT

TOP Dave, Dave, Dave … you told me that you never got a draft off the camera vans. And now this. BOTTOM Verne Scott and Dave Curnow. Two guys who worked tirelessly for the U.S. Federation, basically for free.

MIDTERMS

$500 each from Speedo, Edward's Fleet Feet and *Swim, Swim* magazine.

Within two weeks, the two groups discovered each other and meetings were held, first in Sacramento and then San Diego, to merge the groups. Committees were formed, duties assigned, blah, blah, blah, we were on our way.

The Federation has gone through some tumultuous times, and has had half a dozen presidents and executive directors. The underhanded deals that were made, the gross conflict of interests and the good people run out by their own doing or by their opponents shall remain buried. It is the author's opinion that to go into detail about the varied workings of an organization that has for the most part been run on a volunteer basis, would not only open up a can of worms, the likes of which I might not be able to close, but also unfairly indict by association a number of individuals whose hearts were really in the right place, tainted though the actions may have been.

USA Triathlon has now recorded a streak of nearly eight years of solid, well-intentioned growth. It is profitable and respected by many a triathlete. It still has yet to ultimately define its role in the field of international sporting politics and has been both at odds, and in bed with, the controversial workings of the International Triathlon Union. At times USA Triathlon finds itself caught between a rock (the USOC, ITU and the pro-drafting sect) and a hard place (the vast majority of American age-group and pro athletes who abhor drafting and want an organization that will not bow under intense political

COURTESY USTS

ABOVE Marc Surprenant. Mizuno stopped making running shoes not long after he had that tattoo put on his chest. Knowing Marc, it was worth it.

pressure). It is not an enviable position for the board of directors and the executive director. Only time will tell if the correct decisions are made and good alignments forged.

TRIATHLON GOES HIGH TECH

By 1983, athletes had discovered that to go fast in a triathlon, you needed the "right stuff." Not only did you have to train long, hard and smart, but when you went to your equipment, it had to be good to win. This reality brought with it some discussion on whether people could 'buy' a victory with the fastest wheel or the lightest shoe. Ultimately, the consensus was that the items needed to go fast were widely available and reasonably priced. I don't know about that. The first disk wheel I got was 'loaned' to me and valued at $2500.

Wetsuits were not in vogue yet, primarily because people hadn't figured out that they made you swim faster. And aero' bars were still several years away. What was the cool thing, though, was tri-suits — one-piece Lycra Spandex body suits that allowed a competitor to skip the change of clothes in transition, tone down any 'excess baggage' around the middle and serve as a moving billboard for any potential sponsors. They came in a variety of colors and seemed to embody the sport of triathlon perfectly; the sport's first piece of equipment it could call its own. (Later on, that list would grow to include aero' bars, clipless pedals, lace locks and Dayglo-colored running shorts.)

Triathlete Mark Montgomery would wear them, Dave Horning, even Molina sported a tri-suit from time to time.

Triathlon-specific shops began to spring up all over. Bikesport in Canoga Park, California was probably the first to cater directly to the

triathlete. Sportech in Irvine, the Transition Area in Seal Beach, the First Tri in Berkeley, Fleet Feet in Sacramento and TriSports in La Jolla, all followed within a year or two.

Gradually the price on high tech stuff went down and triathlon became a valuable niche market that gave birth to a number of small, but creative companies. Steve Hed nearly invented the aero' cross section rim and cut the cost of a disk wheel to within the budget of almost every triathlete. Dan Empfield forged the swimming wetsuit market a few years later with his Quintana Roo suits, and added a steep seat angled bike to complement the aero'-shaped bars when they came. Oakley sunglasses put a pair of their revolutionary Eyeshades on Scott Molina in 1984 and has owned the sport sunglasses market ever since. Not long after that, Timex slapped an Ironman moniker on a newly designed watch and it became the largest-selling timepiece in history. Jim Gentes designed a lightweight, comfortable and aerodynamic helmet that was perfect for triathletes and their mandatory helmet rule. The Giro brand is now one of the best-selling bike helmets in the world.

All these companies and more used triathlon as a launching pad for several reasons. First, the demographics of triathletes were very appealing; two, there were few restrictions with rules; and finally, tri-geeks would try anything if they thought it would make them faster.

BIG RACES, BIG MONEY, BIG FUN

Nineteen eighty-three and 1984 not only brought politics, media and organization to the sport of triathlon, it brought some high profile, well-paying races to the scene. People were starting to take notice. The Reagan

TOP "That's two Bud Lights, not one. You got it?" Colleen Cannon, days of future past. BOTTOM Molina at the 1982 Long Beach USTS. That was the last race he did without a helmet.

administration's supply-side economics had put confidence and cash in the coffers of companies wanting to associate with the upscale demographics of triathlon, as well as the unique, confident image it radiated. Those who couldn't get on the L.A. Olympic bandwagon considered spending money in the new sport of the 1980s.

The Japanese company Ricoh put a considerable amount of money into the first Ironman franchise race in Los Angeles. Valerie Silk had granted Ricoh the exclusive right to host an official Ironman race on the mainland, smack in the middle of one of the most densely populated areas on the planet. There would be no prize money, but CBS was on hand to film the race for a later air date. It looked as though the battle would be between 1981 Ironman winner John Howard, and Oxford Triathlon (Maryland) winner Dave Horning. At the last moment, encouraged by his early-season competitive success, Scott Molina entered and ultimately crushed the field. The surf was huge, the water cold, and the bike course hilly — everything that Molina loved. "After the way I lost to Howard in Kona two years ago, I had to stomp him," remembers Molina, "and running the marathon down a fully closed Wilshire Boulevard was incredible." He had won by more than 10 minutes over Howard and Dean Harper. Julie Leach won for the women, finishing 10th overall, but not before a truly gutsy performance by Jennifer Hinshaw. Hinshaw was a 21-year-old swimmer from Saratoga, California. When she maintained a fourth-place overall placing during most of the bike ride, people

COURTESY USTS

MIKE PLANT

TOP This was the cover shot of SWIM/BIKE/RUN, the precursor to the first triathlon magazine. That's my brother Jeff on the left. **BOTTOM** I love this shot of Kathleen McCartney passing Charlie Graves. Never forget the power of the pen, Charlie.

ABOVE Dave at the first San Diego USTS in 1982, starting the run with a 3:30 lead over the field.

began to shake their heads in wonder.

Unfortunately, the event was never held again, the TV show never aired and the entire episode is lost to someone's fond or failing memory.

TEAM JDAVID

At the February 1982 Ironman, Ted Pulaski, a salesman from an investment brokerage firm in La Jolla, California named JDavid, after its principle, Jerry David Domenelli, met and eventually helped sponsor women's Ironman winner Kathleen McCartney. At the same time, one of Domenelli's partners, Nancy Hoover, found that her 20-year-old son George was enthralled with the sport. George had a lot of natural talent and developed his skills quickly. So with Pulaski's urging, the firm decided to sponsor an entire team of triathletes under the JDavid banner. George's friend Gary Petersen was signed up; next came Mark Allen, who had known George from their beach life guard days; I was enlisted because I was a local and had won the Ironman in February 1982, and Scott Molina was recruited down from Pittsburg, California to the warmer climes of Del Mar, California.

Within the next six to eight months, Ironman winner Julie Leach came on board, as well as her husband Bill Leach, investors such as masters athlete Ron Smith, Gary Masako, and Conrad Will were given spots, along with John Howard and my brother Jeff. It became a well-financed and tightly organized group of most of the best triathletes in the country at the time. There were group workouts, the team traveled and stayed in the best places together and for the most part, I think, everybody truly enjoyed each other's company. Throughout most of 1983, Team JDavid was the dominant group in the sport. But by January

1984, it became obvious that something was very wrong. It turned out that the entire firm was a Ponzzi scheme — most of the investments never existed. Hundreds of people, including some of the athletes and elderly individuals, lost their entire savings, victims of the firm's lavish spending and poor trading records.

The triathlon team was just a small piece of Dominelli's fallen empire. He had sponsored a race car team, owned luxury cars, jets, homes — you name it. It was gross excess and white collar crime at its worst, and it sent DomInelli to prison for more than 10 years. The athletes survived though, went on to get other sponsors, and more importantly, learned a valuable lesson in the sometimes treacherous ways of the world. An interesting footnote to a sport that indeed has a few skeletons in its closet.

· · · · ·

The USTS expanded their schedule to include 11 races across the country and a national championship in Bass Lake, California. Scott Molina and I dominated the series, winning seven of the eight races that we entered, including a one-two in Bass Lake. Over on the women's side, a pair of identical twins from Montreal, Canada burst onto the scene. Patricia and Sylviane Puntous, 22 at the time, were charismatic with their broken, French-accented English, their penchant for giggling and their come-from-behind running speed. They would quite often compete together, and, much to the chagrin of their com-

petitors, would pass them in unison, dropping the women not one, but two places in one fell swoop. They finished one and two in the Tampa, Atlanta, San Francisco and Bass Lake events and two and three behind Linda Buchanan in Los Angeles.

Buchanan, who would go on to win the 1983 Nice Triathlon later in the season by more than 11 minutes, together with collegiate running star Colleen Cannon, were the Puntous's main competition. Buchanan was from Redondo Beach, California and Cannon from Huntsville, Alabama. On any given day, it seemed, one of the Puntous's, Buchanan, Cannon or the fading star, Julie Moss, were the women to beat.

Women's triathlon racing was much deeper in terms of competition. Other names included Diane Israel, Ironman winner Julie Leach, Anne Dandoy from L.A.'s South Bay, Jann Girard (who, like the Puntous's, had a competitive twin), Leslie Maurer from Del Mar, Julie Olson and Anne McDonnell from Minneapolis, Molly Barnum from Coronado, Jenny Lamott from Pacific Beach, Joanne Ernst from Palo Alto, California, and Sue Latshaw from Boulder, Colorado. For all of these women, as well as the growing field of competitive men, the race opportunities would also expand.

Monterey County Parks and Recreation Supervisor Terry Davis was looking for a way to expand the 'lake season' at Lake Macimiento in central California. Davis approached a local Fleet Feet store owner about sponsoring a 10km running race. He kicked it upstairs to franchise owner Sally Edwards who said, "No, but we will support a triathlon." That fall of 1983 in a pour-

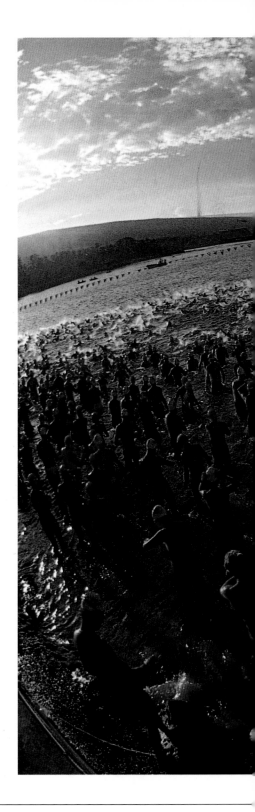

ABOVE After 1984, the Ironman got a little crowded.

ing rainstorm, 86 people raced the approximately half-Ironman distance inaugural Wildflower triathlon. Competing for what was then the second-largest prize purse in the sport ($3000), was perennial short course star Mark Montgomery and Bay Area triathlete Dean Harper. With minor but laughable course confusion, both men finished the race at approximately the same time coming from the opposite directions. "The only reason we did the race the following year was to prove that we could do a better job than the first year," remembers Davis.

Both Ironman and Nice grew in stature in 1983. Nice, however, was positioning itself for a showdown with Ironman. Nice was owned by IMG [International Management Group], and they had a great network television contract, as well as the largest prize purse in the sport: $50,000. The problem was, nobody wanted to run another marathon at the end of a long swim and ride. Even though Ironman had zero prize money, it was still the big enchilada of triathlon. Nice's founder, Barry Frank of TWI (the TV arm of IMG), scheduled a meeting with members of Team JDavid to discuss how to work out the "differences" on the current race distances. Nancy Hoover, a partner in JDavid and mother of George, authorized me to offer Frank up to $50,000 towards the prize money if the Nice organizers would shorten the run distance. Nancy was doing this only to help us. She understood that the marathon distance was particularly taxing and wanted a creative way of addressing the problem. There was never any intended malice on her part.

She was looking after her son and his training partners. Nevertheless, I was flabbergasted. How much money did these people have that they were not only able to pay each athlete a monthly "training stipend," but could afford 50km to get a race organizer to shorten the run? Frank, in the meantime, knew that he needed Allen, Tinley, Molina, John Howard and McCartney at the starting line. He could probably sell NBC on the shorter run distance. We offered to add $25,000 of Dominelli's money toward the prize purse. I don't know if Nancy Hoover ever paid IMG, but the run did end up being shortened to 20 miles, which it was contracted to be. We were young and naïve at the time and all we were looking for was a compromise and a place to earn a living as a professional athlete. It was a strange and fast-paced time for the sport and for all of us involved with that team. And Barry Frank is to be given great credit not only for conceiving the Nice event, but for facilitating the differences between a small group of young endurance athletes and the television empire that it needed for growth, but failed to understand.

I have no regrets. I did the best I knew how at the time and I think most of my peers did the same. Things happen for a reason and even though a lot of people were hurt in that episode, Team JDavid was just a tiny piece of a large and convoluted ball of string that unraveled in people's faces. Our sport would survive and it would some day become stronger for this episode, and others of even greater tragedy, because and in spite of them.

TOP JoAnn Dahlkoetter — a very intimidating competitor.
BOTTOM Take away Mike Plant and a lot of the recorded history of this sport would not exist.

"....and stare into the vacuum of his eyes and say do you want to make a deal?" — Bob Dylan, "Like A Rolling Stone"

FACES

From the beginning, triathlon has had its share of colorful characters. It's hard to say why certain types of individuals are attracted to a particular sport or event. That's a question for the sociologist, not me. I always thought it was easier to look from the inside out as opposed to the outside looking in. And after awhile you want to know why you want to hang out with some people, and why others drive you nuts. A little insight into what makes your peers tick is not only natural, but healthy.

When I look at the sport of triathlon, I try to see people, unique and individual unto themselves. It's too easy to wipe the faces away, put them all in the same pot and generalize about the sport — or anything for that matter. After all, what is a particular sport but a group of different people gathered to share in competition and gamesmanship? It's like the guy who has a bad experience at a restaurant and says, "I really don't like that city."

Ah, but it's the different faces that give a sport its character — not equipment or playing fields or rules. We know now that triathlon has its roots in the collection of unique individuals

FACES

who flocked to San Diego's Fiesta Island. In fact, not only was the sport born on the backs of these colorful characters, it was born *because* of them; because of their quest for something new and different, for a sport they could call their own.

You met some of these people in Chapter One. But there are others; others who constituted the early races and are lost forever to some ancient competitor list or race results. They know who they are, however; that much will never change. It's like my friend Todd's grandfather used to brag: "Remember that great right-handed pitcher Satchel Paige," he'd say. "Well, I batted against him when I was coming up in the Bigs. He was just another young guy with a decent fastball if you ask me." Time makes legends out of the "also rans" as well as the great ones.

The face of an endurance athlete ages differently than others. The sun carves deep crow's feet around the eyes. The wind sucks the moisture out of the skin like a high desert afternoon in September. And the pool chlorine changes hair to green straw. But the eyes are clear and the look of contentment in a muted smile is a frequent occurrence.

Triathletes can look older than their age and younger than what their driver's license says. But mostly they are walking contradictions; living, breathing oxymorons without pot bellies, clogged arteries and sagging biceps. It's the training, they say, that keeps the body young. It's the endless laps back and forth that torture each unnecessary ounce of fat into nonexistence. I think it is the mind, though — the mind behind the face that thinks young, and therefore is young.

You can spend a boatload of money on facial

HARALD JOHNSON

PREVIOUS PAGE "Okay, who let one go?" **ABOVE** King Ron Smith, a gnarly guy, gets more done by six in the morning than most people do all day.

TOP Horning and Tinley, the "odd couple." **BOTTOM LEFT** Dave McGillivary with President Carter after running from Florida to Boston. Triathlon has people like that within its ranks.
BOTTOM CENTER New Zealand's Allison Roe: marathoner, mother and businesswoman. **BOTTOM RIGHT** Jeff Tinley, two top-three finishes at Ironman.

FACES

creams to slow the inevitable. Or you can just shortcut the whole deal and pay some Beverly Hills plastic surgeon to rebuild your old one. But consider for a moment that your face is like a constantly evolving story, a topographical map of all that you have seen and done. To change it is to submit to societal pressures to "look" young. Why not spend your time and effort slowing down the internal clock? I'd much rather have a smooth, tight ass and a weathered face than the opposite.

The face of triathlon will change through the years. Like many things, it must do so to survive. And the faces that make up the starting line will also change. But there will always be similarities between past and future, common denominators among the individuals who face every challenge with this, their chosen vehicle of athletic expression.

CHARACTERS

Some sports are about speed. Others exist in the context of power and skill, maybe chance. And many others are focused on the course that exists as a medium for one's dare and speed. But endurance sports are about people. They are about colorful, interesting, sometimes outrageous people. And while the average triathlete may have become a bit deluded in his or her penchant for the extreme, you can still stereotype an endurance athlete and come up with a human being way left of center.

And none were more unique than the characters of early triathlons. You had to be just a bit off the wall to even consider participating in a sport

DAVID EPPERSON

ABOVE The face of Barbara Dunbar, my longest and most consistent training partner. We have shared the same lane at UCSD pool for 15 years. No matter how much I improve or how old she gets, she is still a better and faster swimmer. She used to bring her infant sons onto the pool deck to sit in a stroller while she swam. Now they are star high school runners.

RICHARD GRAHAM

RICHARD GRAHAM

RICHARD GRAHAM

C.J. OLIVERAS

DAVID EPPERSON

TOP LEFT Erin Baker and longtime friend/coach, John Hellemans. "It's over now." **TOP RIGHT** Gordon Haller below a photo of himself and John Collins, "the face that launched a thousand ships."
BOTTOM LEFT Erin Baker looking buffed, bitchin' and happy. **BOTTOM CENTER** Friends and training partners Brad Kearns and Andrew McNaughton at the Desert Princess Duathlon near Palm Springs.
Existing just within reach of stardom, they were true journeyman athletes. **BOTTOM RIGHT** Colleen Cannon never liked to think too hard; much too disruptive to her play time.

FACES

with not just a sketchy history but no history at all. Take Tom Warren, for example. He went out and built a 4000-square-foot custom home with only one bedroom and an 800-square-foot cocktail lounge, complete with little tables and a 20-foot bar. He often wouldn't say anything to anybody for days, and then would corner any living soul who'd listen and tell stories for three hours at a time. He can't use a fax machine or a video player, but he is wealthy enough to be retired at 50 and can remember names and dates of old girlfriends from 25 years ago.

Or take the case of Dan Hendricksen. As a Navy SEAL and friend of naval commander John Collins, he had participated in a few triathlons on Fiesta Island in the early 1970s. As a part of the group who sat at the Primo Gardens during the awards ceremony for the Perimeter Relay Race on Oahu, discussing which athlete was the fittest runner, cyclist or swimmer, he innocently became part of triathlon lore. "We were sitting around mumbling about how the young guys had shown us up in the race, and John was talking about combining the longest endurance events on Oahu into one race. No one had even considered doing that before. I left to go to the head for a minute and by the time I got back, Collins was up on the stage challenging the Marines — 'Boys, I've got a real race for you,'" remembers Hendricksen.

By the time Collins had organized the thing, Hendricksen would not be able to back out. The night before the race he bought a new Free Spirit 10-speed for $89 from Sears. When he went to Collins to ask for help in putting it together, Collins couldn't help because he was still welding

TOP Mark and his mom, facing the emotional fruits of victory. **BOTTOM LEFT** Norm Paul Huddle, just back from shopping at the Big Dog Factory Outlet. A core guy, salt of the Earth. Good athlete, outstanding backgammon player. **ABOVE RIGHT** *Triathlete* magazine publisher Jean Claude Garot, journalist Thierry Dekatelare and Ann ... editorial meeting/lunch. **BOTTOM RIGHT** Sometimes, no words are necessary.

DAVID EPPERSON

DAVID EPPERSON

DAVID EPPERSON

HARALD JOHNSON

the finishers' trophies together.

Maybe you'd like to hear the story of Howard Moody, a former Hell's Angel who was either going to end up in prison or on the starting line of a marathon. Howard was incredibly intense, but kind to a fault. He trained like his future depended on it — which it did. I could never get his whole story out of him and haven't seen him in 20 years. I hope he had a good life.

One of my favorite out of all these odd sorts is Ken Shirk, alias Cowman. If you've been to the Ironman or maybe another major race in some remote place, then you've seen him dressed in his legendary horns. As a construction worker in Tahoe City, Nevada, Shirk first saw the horns in a mountaineering shop in Truckee, California. "They reminded me of the pictures of Indians I've seen," remembers Shirk. " 'Wow,' I thought. 'Do I have enough nerve to wear those things?' " In 1976, a friend told him about a running marathon. At 6-feet 3-inches and 220 pounds, he is no natural on his feet. So for no particular reason at all, he picked up a pair of deer antlers and ran the entire distance in his cut-down basketball shoes." I wanted to make a statement about the Bicentennial," he said. "Everyone was saying how great the country was. Well, it is, but we have made a few mistakes. Look what we did to the Native Americans, and the Japanese during World War II. So I had some friends paint my body in red, white and blue stars and stripes. I put on the horns and carried a big Bicentennial flag and streaked through downtown Lake Tahoe."

Three years later, while in Honolulu for the marathon, Cowman stumbled onto the Ironman in February 1979. He entered the race never having swam more than 400 yards and not having been on a bike since he was a kid. He also finished eighth.

The most bizarre of all the characters, though, was Chip Salaun. A nature photographer by trade,

LEFT When you see Cowman out on the course, you just have to smile, no matter how much you're hurting. If you don't, there is something wrong with your motivations. TOP RIGHT The big guy has aged better than most — in fact, better than any of us. SECOND FROM TOP RIGHT Scott Molina, sporting that year-round tan of his. THIRD FROM TOP RIGHT Now if you take the square root of 68 and divide it by the circumference of pi times X ... Okay, just trying to get my mind off of the race. BOTTOM RIGHT Longtime triathlete, race director and friend Rick Kozlowski. He carved those glasses frames out of a tree in his backyard. Not.

FACES

Salaun was an avid mountaineer who regularly spent days at a time pinned to the side of a cliff, unable to go up or down. He could handle hardship like most people deal with a bruised banana. After he had entered and completed his first Ironman in 1981, he was so enamored with the sport, and the Ironman in particular, that he moved from the mountains of Colorado to Kona. Problem was, Salaun was probably the poorest person I was ever associated with in this sport. When he couldn't afford to pay rent anymore, Salaun moved out onto the lava fields north of Kona and slept in a tent. He had an infectious laugh, would always remember your name and owed money to everybody in town. During the mid-1980s, Salaun got back into climbing and was spending a lot of time in Australia and New Zealand. On his last climb he fell into a deep crevasse and his partners never could find his body.

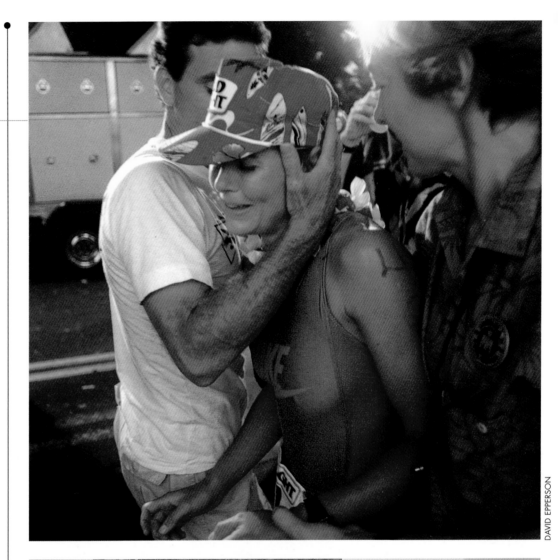

DAVID EPPERSON

C.J. OLIVERAS

TOP Joanne Ernst is faced with a heavy moment at the 1985 Ironman finish line. BOTTOM *Triathlon* magazine co-founder Harald Johnson, trying desperately to find a buyer for his 1973 Ford Pinto while magazine deadlines loom.

CHAPTER ELEVEN

"Women have served all these centuries as looking-glasses possessing the magic and delicious power of reflecting the figure of a man at twice its natural size." — *Virginia Woolf, 1882-1941*

SALAD DAYS

By 1984, we were on a roll. I was so confident that the professional opportunities in the sport would continue to grow that I quit my full-time job, took on a part-time position as a marketing consultant for a chain of athletic shoe stores and trained like a madman. Scott Molina had moved his wife and three-year-old daughter to San Diego on the back of his JDavid sponsorship and when the house of cards folded, he decided to remain in Del Mar. Together, we began to log the big miles— regularly riding 400 miles, running 80-plus and swimming 25,000 yards in a week. If a lot was good, a lot more was better. Who knew? There were no coaches or clinics or videos and barely any concept of what "cross training" was all about. The two magazines existed (Bill Katovsky had sold the majority interest in *Triathlete* to Frenchman Jean Claude Garot late in 1983, but continued to function as editor-in-chief), but most of the technical articles were being written by people like us who only had experience to go on. It would

SALAD DAYS

still be a few years before the exercise physiology types would take the sport "into the lab" and develop some harder training data.

So we trained. And we raced. The first big event of the year was on January 3 in Kauai, Hawaii. It was the brainchild of local resident and ex-husband of tennis star Billy Jean King, Larry King. Together with his "partners" Bill Leach and Mark Montgomery, they secured McDonald's as a sponsor, CBS for television and a stellar field of athletes. The Kauai Loves You Triathlon was also the first in a new professional series of events entitled the ATP Super Series (Association of Triathlon Professionals — not to be confused with the USTS or the USTA). This was an effort by King and Leach to organize the pros into a working coalition of individuals with a common goal of advancing the professional opportunities within the sport. Molina won in a time of 3:49 over myself and Dave Scott on the 1.3-mile swim, 12.4-mile run and 51-mile bike course. Linda Buchanon won the women's race over Jann Girard and Joanne Ernst.

In March, the Diamond Triathlon of the Stars would mix B-level celebrities with triathletes in the Bahamas over a beautiful, well-run course, but in the end, organizer Bruce Portner would leave in his wake unpaid bills and low-grade diamonds passed off as a prize money alternative. Race director Jim Curl was actually pulled off a plane by the local authorities and placed in jail before he could explain the Portner situation and exculpate himself from the islands. The next week I took the diamonds I had won for finishing first

PREVIOUS PAGE Harald "Stretch" Robinson, winning his first USTS race in front of a capacity crowd. ABOVE Todd Jacobs and Tony Richardson overcome by their good fortune to have chosen a path that puts them in a tropical environment while half the world freezes its tutus off. They both work in the "real world" now. Good things don't always last forever.

RICHARD GRAHAM

(supposedly worth $10,000 and then appraised at $2500) and sent them to Portner for replacement. That's the last I ever saw of them.

The U.S. Triathlon Series, after two years of wrestling with new distances, settled on the current 1.5-kilometer swim, 40-kilometer bike and 10-kilometer run because, as Jim Curl claims, "It was perfect. Those distances already existed in the Olympics." Curl, in a brilliant strategic move for the sport, conceived the idea for wave starts. "I was thinking about how we could put more people on a course safely when I thought about the Bolder Boulder 10km race, where they send off 100 or so at a time until 10,000 people are running a 10km through the streets of a big city. Why couldn't we do that with triathlon?" Curl remembers. There were 10 USTS events in 1984 not including the championship at Bass Lake. The big addition was a course in downtown Chicago. No longer would triathlons be relegated to the backcountry. Chicago showed the world that you could put two or three thousand people safely through a course in a major metropolitan area. This was key to the attraction of new sponsors.

Other ATP events included a race outside Las Vegas with a purse of $50,000, and a race in downtown Manhattan that began with a swim from the Statue of Liberty and concluded with a run through Central Park. Mark Allen won this race and had his picture on the cover of the *New York Times* newspaper the next morning. Trouble was, he was in such a hurry to get out of the transition area before Molina that he had forgotten his Nike singlet. As I recall, Nike wasn't too happy.

SALAD DAYS

MORE MONEY, MORE MONEY RACES

With a record five events on network television that year, it appeared that the prize money and the professional opportunities would continue to grow. In July, Molina and I went to Austin, Minnesota, for another mainland Ironman distance race. By 1984, not everybody who wanted to get into the Ironman in Hawaii could, though it was still easy by today's standards. Dave Standiger, a businessman and triathlon organizer, decided to put on an Ironman right smack in the middle of the country's bread basket. There was $25,000 at stake, $6000 for the win.

Molina led over myself and Kurt Madden until I caught him at the 16-mile mark. He looked pretty stiff, and I went through an easy 2:54 marathon to win. The overall time of 8:50 was the fastest Ironman to date and immediately escalated the argument of what a "record" really meant in the sport. After all, the Ironman's distance was historically based, and each course and condition could alter the time substantially. The pressure to standardize the rules and regulations increased all year long and the fuel behind this seemed to be coming from abroad.

The last Dixie cup had not been picked up at the Nice International triathlon in November of 1982 when the European nations who had witnessed the race or maybe only *heard* of the event, began laying the groundwork for triathlon to spread across the Pond. On the political front, some of the Euros may have carried a chip on

RUSSELL MOORE

ABOVE The venerable Trisha Cadden, "power walking" at Ironman if only to avoid the dreaded "Kona shuffle."

their shoulder for getting in the game a decade late, but the athletes, and maybe more importantly the seamless support system behind them, were beginning to gear up. Cycling had existed as a national pastime in parts of Europe for decades. Running was quite big in the major cities and Olympic swimming had created swim clubs and coaches all over the place. It would not be hard for the European athletes to excel in this new sport from America.

But while European countries did many things right, they did many things wrong. America had established one central national governing body. Several European countries had three or four battling for control. America discouraged drafting from the beginning. Europeans couldn't seem to get the cycling peloton mentality out of their heads. Americans offered prize money and corporate sponsorships. Europeans like to support their athletes through small clubs, teams and town groups — just like in cycling. This system ultimately produces a better crop of athletes (proven in the late 1990s), but takes some time to get in place and develop youth talent.

European athletes just hadn't won any big races yet so people tended not to look too closely at them. But some of us did. In early 1984 Rob Barel from the Netherlands came over to San Diego and trained with us for several weeks. It was not hard to tell that he had what it took to make it big. (Barel has been the longest lasting, most successful triathlete from Europe over the past 15 years). And then in August of that year, three Dutch athletes, Axel Koender, 24, Gregor Stam, 22,

TOP "Quick, take the shot, I've got a weight-loss class to go to." "Oh, be quiet Dave, you're lucky we let you hang out with us." "Listen, you little twerp, I'll break you in two." BOTTOM Wolfgang Dittrich. Quiet, unassuming German. A survivor and Californiaized Euro dude.

SALAD DAYS

and Barel, 26, all posted impressive times in the two-year-old Almere Ironman in the small city of Holland. Ardis Bow, the perky 28-year-old from Sacramento, California, had also come across to "spread the word." "There is fever for triathlon in Europe," she would say, "but not so much for the women." Ardis won easily against the five other females entered and placed 47th overall.

By the end of the summer, many of the European countries had banned together to form the European Triathlon Union (ETU) to help forward the cause. This organization also floundered for a year or two before retaining some semblance of stability, not unlike Tri Fed's early days.

• • • • •

Back in the states, Molina and friends were lining up for the inaugural World's Toughest Triathlon — arguably the hardest triathlon ever staged. Set in the Sierra Nevada range outside of Lake Tahoe, the race is formidable on three accounts. First, the 2.4-mile swim is held in average water temperatures of 57 degrees. Second, the 120-mile bike climbs over three mountain passes between 6000 and 8500 feet. Finally, the 26.7-mile run is mostly rough trail with climbing and descending throughout. Molina liked it because of the difficulty and the $10,000 cash first-place prize. When it was over, he was holding an envelope with 100 $100 bills in it. His reaction, "I knew then that I had made the right career choice. Difficult, but rewarding." Second place went to Grant Boswell while Julie Olson won the women's division. Moli-

TOP Marc Suprenant at Tampa Bay USTS circa 1984. His seat pack contains a tent, a Swiss army knife and C-rations for two. BOTTOM A kinder, gentler starting line.

ABOVE "All hands on deck. This is not a drill." But I said Bud Light.

na's time for the day was 10:28 and Olson clocked a 12:31, slow by Ironman standards but good enough to win the hardest race known at the time.

Molina would go on to win *Triathlete* magazine's inaugural Triathlete of the Year award by compiling a season that included 23 triathlons. Now critics will no doubt say that the competition was not as deep back then and they will be correct. But remember that the sponsorship was not as prevalent, the knowledge of training systems was weak and the equipment was archaic relative to today's standard. For the record, Molina won 18 of those races including the USTS Championship, finished second four times and fifth once when he went off course.

By November, the season was almost over and I was looking for one more race. Along came an opportunity to compete in one of the first triathlons ever held in Australia. Unfortunately it was another Ironman, but the prize money was good. I didn't say anything to my peers and flew down to the Sydney Triple M triathlon to race Australia's best, an affable tennis pro named Marc Dragan. When it was over, I had only five minutes on Dragan. The next day he took me out and beat me 6-0, 6-0, 6-0 in tennis. Nice guy, Marc is.

1985

Besides the influx of bigger and richer races, triathlon also started to develop some of its own unique personality. The equipment forefront grew as companies began to develop "go fast" goodies for all three sports — especially cycling.

Clipless pedals showed up from AeroLite and Look, lightweight frames from Vitus and Peugot, racing flats from Reebok and Nike and all sorts of little oddball parts that triathletes devoured in their search to slice a few grams of weight or a few seconds of time. Competitors still struggled with what to wear. One piece tri-suits proved to be a bit slow in the water (still no wetsuits yet) and nobody really thought that racing in only a bathing suit was acceptable. There was this one kid from South Africa who did the entire Ironman in a little Speedo-type suit. We all called him "screaming crotch." His transition times were fast though.

There also seemed to be a growing "power base" in San Diego. More and more athletes moved into town to train with residents Allen, Molina, Gary Pettersen, Shannon Delaney, etc. Pretty soon some of the workouts looked like a local gathering for a 10km. Murphy Reinschreiber, a former attorney who now represents many of the sport's top triathletes, was quoted as saying to *Triathlon* magazine editor C.J. Olivares, "We're going to have to put a limit on it soon or the spring will be crazy. We don't mind if they come down here to train, as long as they are willing to contribute to our community." Reinschreiber himself would contribute to several aspects of the growing sport. He was a cofounder of the Horny Toad Triathlon, the first executive director of the United States Triathlon Association, and a decent swimmer in his day.

The USTS office moved from northern California to Encinitas, just north of San Diego. *Running* and *Triathlon News* was here, and so were a

LOIS SCHWARTZ

COURTESY BUD LIGHT USTS

TOP Dale Basescu waiting for his buddies to show up for a run. Dale went through some hard times, but pulled his life together through music and sport. **BOTTOM** Houston USTS, a choppy, freshwater swim. Tough conditions, good volunteers.

growing number of triathlon shops. Pretty soon you could look around on a group ride and see six out of the top 10 finishers, male and female, from the last Ironman. Dave Scott remained up in Davis, California, training on his own, fueling his reputation as a loner and eccentric by choosing to race only when he was 100 percent on his game. A May 1984 article in *Triathlete* magazine on Dave entitled "It's lonely at the top," raised a few eyebrows in the sport. Dave's quote, "I like the mystique of being a loner," only pushed the image farther. Truth was, though, Dave simply liked the small town of Davis. He had all his family and friends there, he knew how to train hard by himself and there was no compelling reason to go anywhere else. Dave's folks, Verne and Dorothy, were his biggest fans and they were only two blocks away. At one point the town even held a "Dave Scott Day," complete with proclamations and all sorts of official hoopla. And he deserved every bit of it. He had won the Ironman by 24 minutes the previous October. That counted for a lot.

The year 1985 also marked the last time the Ironman failed to offer prize money. The Nice race had continued to raise the stakes by offering more prize money, airline flights and hotel rooms. It was getting increasingly difficult for Valerie Silk to refuse the growing need to "turn professional." When I won the Ironman that year, it was against a field that did not include Scott, Allen, Molina or John Howard. A course record helped to calm the critics, though not much. Chris Hinshaw, who led until mile five of the marathon, proved that there was now a growing crop of young newcomers

RICHARD GRAHAM

ABOVE "I never thought exercise could be so much fun."

SALAD DAYS

ready to step in if any of the Big Four should make the slightest of mistakes.

Joanne Ernst, the 26-year-old former Stanford scholar, hung on to win the women's division in Kona by a slim margin over Liz Bulman (1:33). Ernst's victory would give women a huge boost in the sport. Not only was she smart, talented and beautiful, she could speak well and began to take a stand on issues that plagued the sport.

Ernst was particularly critical of the ongoing drafting problem. The race organizers of many events still had not figured out how to properly control drafting. In the early days of 50 to 100 competitors, peer pressure alone would help. But when the fields grew exponentially, the faces were blurred and one had to rely on draft marshals to pick up where integrity stopped.

The sport continued to grow on the international front, with an increasing number of events in South America, Canada, Europe and Japan. (The first Ironman Japan was held in June 1985 with Dave Scott and Julie Moss the victors). Other countries would send athletes and social "delegates" to Kona, San Diego, or anywhere they could learn about the sport. They in turn would bring back bits and pieces of information to disseminate to the local athletes hungry for any tidbit or scoop about what America was doing.

You could see the change, though. Eight weeks after my first trip to Australia I returned to find five new events, a local newsletter and hundreds of budding triathletes all gearing up for the next event. The world was a triathlon sponge; every bit of technical, competitive and social news was gobbled up regardless of its source or content. It almost became an incestuous mix of the 50 or 60 people who worked, trained and raced on the "inside." In an eight-month period, there were four separate articles in the triathlon press on "the San Diego Brigade" or the "North County Mafia." Fortunately for all of us, though, the new crop of athletes came in and shook things up. Competitors like Paul Huddle, Jimmy Riccitello, Tony Richardson, Ken Glah, Todd Jacobs, Sean Molina, Ray Browning, Clark Cambell, Rick Crawford, Ruben Chappins, Mike Durkin, Marc Surprenant, Jody Durst, George Hoover, Emilio De Soto, Charlie Graves, Lance Armstrong (yes, *that* Lance), Glen Cook from Britain, Jeff Devlin from the East Coast, Harald Robinson, Brad Kearns, Andrew McNaughton and a phenomenon from Arcata, California, named Mike Pigg would all have a shot at the podium on any given day.

For the women, even though the field was always a bit more open; women like Colleen Cannon, Jacqueline Shaw, Joy and Joan Hansen, Linda Janelli, Kirsten Hanssen (who would rule the USTS events in 1987), Julie Brenning, Carolina Heins, Beth Mitchell, Lisa Laihti, Laurie Samuelsen, Liz Bulman, Jan Ripple, Anne McDonald, Elaine Alrutz, Lynn Brooks (the only person ever to compete in 18 Hawaiian Ironman events — and counting), Karleen Crowell and three newcomers, Erin Baker, Paula Newby-Fraser and Karen Smyers, would begin to show up in the placings of races big and small.

TOP "Something's lost, but something's gained in living every day." — "The Circle Game," *Joni Mitchell.* Julie Moss after dropping out of an Ironman. BOTTOM Carol Montgomery. I wish I had a few more photos of her to

put in the book. Canadian speedster extraordinaire. **ABOVE** And the first pig built his house out of straw.... Kiwi rooting section, you've got to love 'em.

SALAD DAYS

THE WOMEN OF TRIATHLON

In many ways, women have not been given their fair due in the sport of triathlon. In some circles, the sport has a macho, survivalist reputation. You can blame it on the media, blame it on our society or just blame it on the boys. But the female contingent has been key to the development of the sport from day one. Consider these contributors:

Valerie Silk

"My identity has been wrapped up — my way of life has been the Ironman." As one of 10 children from St. Petersburg, Florida, Silk, married at 19, set off to see the world with her thumb and a backpack. When she and her husband landed in Honolulu, their fitness clubs became the first sponsor of the Ironman. Three years later, Silk divorced, moved to Kona, and became the owner/race director of what would become arguably the greatest endurance event in the world. For her the race was her mate, her child and her lifestyle.

Sally Edwards

"Women have to worry about beauty and sweat and muscle. In sport, though, they learn that their bodies are capable of doing things that they've been role-modeled to think impossible." Edwards's contributions to the sport of triathlon are vast and varied. Three top-five finishes in Kona, author of the first book on the sport, cofounder of USA Triathlon, cofounder of Fleet

TOP LEFT "Oh the stories they could tell..." TOP RIGHT Katie Webb, top female triathlete, sometime dental hygienist, loyal Tinley Performance Wear devotee. BOTTOM Journalist and PR man extraordinaire Mike Plant with women's winner Julie Brenning.

Feet stores, camp director, motivational speaker and visionary. A staunch feminist without being cynical, she once said, "I see human beings, not men and women." She will walk her talk all day long, evidenced by the fact that she spent 18 months in Vietnam at the height of the war working as a Red Cross volunteer.

Lyn Lemaire

Was the only female entered in the Ironman in 1979 when it was unclear if anybody could finish. She finished in 12:55.

Robin Beck

Took an hour-and-a-half off of Lemaire's time the following year to win the 1980 Ironman in a time of 11:21.

Penny Little

Little was a fitness swimmer and avid open-water competitor from Santa Monica, California, whose creative flair and hard work helped launch *Triathlon* magazine in 1983 and *Swim/Swim* magazine before that.

Lynn Brooks

As a top finisher in the sport's early years, Brooks tied for third in Hawaii in 1982 and went on to win the first Nice triathlon six weeks later. She was the race director for USTS Baltimore for several years and worked tirelessly on many governing body committees to improve the state of women's racing in the sport. Brooks is also the current record holder for the most number of

consecutive Ironman finishes at 18.

Julie Moss

"I portray a very average girl who pulled off something incredible." Moss's story will be told for decades. It should also be footnoted that she entered the 1997 Ironman as an amateur and finished second in her age group to Kirsten Hanssen, who also made a comeback of sorts. Her legacy is secure and self-evident.

Ardis Bow

Bow's record in many early races is somewhat lost in that she failed to win the Ironman or any other big event at the time. But a closer look will show that she was the first female to compete successfully at a variety of distances all over the world. Ardis was confident and creative. Her appearance at any race was a shot in the arm for any race director.

Janey Marks

"Different management teams like to embrace different marketing tactics, maybe use different sports as promotional vehicles. We liked triathlon and it worked." Marks can be credited with directing the flow of hundreds of thousands of dollars over a seven-year period into the sport of triathlon. In her position at Anheuser Busch, she not only oversaw the Bud Light brand's involvement in Ironman and the USTS, she helped advise and direct many of the individuals who struggled to make a living in the thin and fragile economic arena of triathlon.

TOP Female pro from the mid 1980s, Beth Mitchell. **BOTTOM** Dave Standiger, organizer and competitor of the Midwest Classic, an Ironman run through the country's bread basket. Thanks, Dave.

SALAD DAYS

Kirsten Hanssen

"It was scary, but I thought if it lasted just a month, a week, it would be worth a try," speaking about her decision to quit a full-time job and have a go as a pro triathlete. Hanssen was probably the first woman of the "modern era" — 1984 to 1989 — to completely dominate the sport. In 1987 she raced 22 times, winning 16 of those races and finishing second four times. She also earned more than $100,000 in prize money and endorsements. And she did it on her own terms, more often than not, training by herself, racing off the front and thanking God when handed the microphone at the awards. Mike Plant, the pre-eminent triathlon journalist of the 1980s once said of her, "The other women roll their eyes, but it is Hanssen with the trophy, the paycheck. When you race the way she does, you can thank whomever you like." Kirsten, more than anything, gave other women the incentive to have a go at the fledgling side of professional women's sports. She enjoyed a full-time job in 1985, making decent money at a Denver telecommunications firm, before a friend convinced her to try the local USTS event. She finished fifth in her debut, but still had to be at work Monday morning at 8 a.m. When she quit six months later to go pro, she gave a lot of others the motivation to follow their dreams.

Sylviane and Patricia Puntous

"We are not terribly talented. It's just that we have a high threshold for pain. I don't even like running too close to Sylviane because I feel her pain too acutely" — Patricia Puntous. The contri-

ABOVE Jimmy Riccitello crusin'.

butions of the Puntous twins are difficult to measure. Often misunderstood because of their thick French accents, they provided a kind of bubbly, mirror image to some hard-core racing experiences. Once victims of poor fiscal management, they had to wipe the slate clean of past wrongdoings and essentially start their careers over again. You cannot argue with their tenacity nor their drive. And everything they did was times two. Above all, the media loved these two hard-running, giggling and affable twins.

Flo Bryan

Epitomized the dedicated, hard-working entrepreneurial spirit that helped launch the sport of triathlon. She began working for CAT Sports in 1985 as an assistant coordinator of two events on the East Coast, the Baltimore USTS and the very first national championship at Hilton Head Island, South Carolina. Six years later, she was more or less running the whole show as vice president and series coordinator. For Bryan, it was always an interesting and unique challenge to go into a new city, convince the authorities that they "needed" a triathlon in their town, and oh, by the way, can we close down a few main streets for the morning?

Beyond her commitment to the sport, Bryan also had a pragmatic and realistic vision of triathlon that others under the employ of its ranks often failed to possess. She knew that we were a "small pond" and that to thrive in coming decades we would need to take the occasional reality check. When triathlon flattened out in the

RICHARD GRAHAM

early 1990s, she had this to say: "Triathlon was a yuppie sport — it paralleled the interest in serving one's personal desires that was so prevalent then. When those people grew up a bit and had kids, guess what? The time and the money allocated for triathlon went away." Bryan continues to stay involved with sports organization though you won't find her setting up traffic cones at three in the morning. She works Disney's Orlando-based sports event complex as one of the key individuals running the entire organization.

ABOVE The confidence to know that you've done the work and are ready. Wellsy.

"That period was a wonderful time in my life," she recalls. "If the people involved with the sport didn't have the passion for it that they did, triathlon wouldn't be what it is today."

Karen Smyers

Three-time *Triathlete* magazine "Triathlete of the Year," 1995 world champion and Ironman winner, 1990 ITU World Champion, Pan-Am gold medalist, U.S. national pro champion 1990-95, one of the only women who can win the big ones at any distance. Princeton graduate in economics, public speaker, writer, relaxed attitude and humorous outlook. And to think that she did all this living east of Interstate 5. Certain to be around for a long time. A solid, hard-working, no bullshit, funny person — even if she is from Boston, I like her.

. . . . .

Still, however, there exists a small gap between the genders within the confine of certain aspects of the sport. One cannot start a sentence saying, "All things being equal," because they are not. Men and women have unique physiological differences. And thank God for that. When it comes to athletics, though, men have an advantage. Women usually have a higher percentage of body fat, lower muscle mass and less aerobic capacity. And yet they regularly finish ahead of men their own age.

In triathlon, due to the efforts of early female stars like Erin Baker and Joanne Ernst, the prize money is almost always equal. Yet women make

SALAD DAYS

up anywhere from 12 to 17 percent of the fields. This was discussed only briefly in the sport's development and was usually endorsed by the men as well. Yet the "encouragement theory," as Erin Baker would call it, never really worked like it was supposed to. There were events being held with 60 male pros fighting for seven or eight paying slots while on the women's side, sometimes not enough pro women showed up to even race for a paycheck. Even Baker, a staunch fighter for equal prize money, has changed her tune over the years. "Women have had all the help and support they could be given and they have not stepped up to bat," Baker said. "I can no longer see the value of a women being paid to go 10:30 for an Ironman while men go 8:50 and don't make a dime." This might be easy for Erin to say, now that she no longer relies on prize money to pay the bills, but it is a valid argument nonetheless. The larger picture is that the women race just as hard as the guys. Maybe there are not as many of them, but they should be compensated equally. Whether or not it should go as deep is a discussion *not* for these pages.

MAINSTREAM MEDIA

In 1986, the majority owner of *Triathlete* magazine, Jean Claude Garot, merged his publication with *Triathlon* magazine (Harald Johnson, Penny Little and Mike Gilmore). The Frenchman Garot, basing his operations out of Belgium, would then acquire all of *Triathlon's* assets two years later. Little had departed in a dispute with Gilmore a year

earlier and Johnson left to start his own PR firm soon thereafter. Gilmore stuck around trying to keep the Santa Monica-based operation profitable while C.J. Olivares and Rich Graham ran the editorial side.

There was a lot to write about. The sport was booming. USTS had 12 events in 1987 and a new professional series entitled the Tri-America Series, combining a number of key quality events under one banner. Races included the Kauai Loves You, Catalina Triathlon, Las Vegas Olympians Tri, Cascade Lakes Tri, Wildflower, Monterey Bay and probably one or two others I can't remember. Mike Durkin from Tucson, Arizona, won a brand new Jeep in 1987, and Mark Montgomery recalls winning in 1988, but doesn't remember what the bonus pool was.

The USTS Chicago Tri split up into two races soon thereafter and each race would succeed with huge numbers. Eighty percent of the participants in this Lakeshore Drive venue would do only one race each year and it was Chicago.

ABC, anxious to piggyback on its Ironman coverage success, created a made-for-TV movie loosely based on the stories of Julie Moss (who served as technical director and stunt double) and one Millie Brown, a housewife-turned-Ironwoman who was featured on one of the Ironman telecasts. Penny Marshall played the part of the woman while Dave Scott had a hilarious cameo part where he was supposed to "drop by" a triathlon party. Dave does his best dime store Indian imitation and gives us ample ammunition to rile the six-time Ironman champion.

But in real life Dave plays the part of the reluctant yet graceful champion like no other. His demeanor is akin to a parish priest; he will sit and listen to the "everyman" triathlete's recent interval workout until the line to get his autograph is around the block. I never had quite the patience. Scott never raced as much as Molina nor I, and didn't have the following in Europe like Mark did, but he was Mr. October in Kona like no other. He became an icon despite his multiple "retirements" and occasional competitive flop.

His greatest feats, though, were his second-place in Ironman in 1994 at 40 years old and his fifth place in 1996. In those races, in front of his growing family, Dave would have to employ all of his knowledge, stamina and personal courage learned over an entire career.

Things cannot always remain the same, though, and quite often the present becomes "the good old days" in a blink of an eyelash.

CHAPTER TWELVE

"When you were born, you cried and the world rejoiced. Live your life in such a manner that when you die the world cries and you rejoice." — Traditional Native American saying

SMILES & ECHOES

I love my garage, not only because I can organize it anyway I like, but because it's a sanctuary of sorts — a place of refuge for a person like me to escape to. It's a fairly typical garage for Southern California, as crammed full of toys as possible. There are three motorcycles, a moped, six surfboards that I know of, and between 20 and 30 pair of athletic shoes, including my new Reebok wrestling shoes I just got to race go-carts in. There is a veritable plethora of kids' toys — at least enough to keep the Toys R Us shareholders happy for another quarter — and believe it or not, 14 bicycles. Okay, Before you jump to conclusions and start asking for a hand-me-down, realize only eight of those belong to me. So there are another four or five in varying stages of disrepair ... but hey, I *use* them all. And it's taken me 20 years to get my quiver just about where I want it.

As far as all the other stuff, well, let's just say that if I used everything on a regular basis, even once a month, I wouldn't have time for much else. That would be fine with me if I won the lottery, which I won't hold my breath for. Suffice it to say though, that I'm like a lot of other guys and gals who are into a bunch of different sports — I just feel better knowing they're there. In fact, every once in awhile, even when my gear sits around going unused, it comes in handy. A new family moved into the neighborhood recently and the mother wandered into my garage to say hello. She couldn't take her eyes off the rows of bikes hanging from the ceiling and said out loud, "You have everything in this garage but your own personalized bowling ball." Not wanting to seem pretentious, I just nodded while I pulled out my ball and wiped off the dust.

Triathletes remind me of garages — at least male triathletes. Women may or may not have the same garage fetish as guys, but this is simply a metaphor, not a sexist observation. When we were kids, much of our outdoor activity began and ended in the garage. It was our cave, our home base, our playhouse and our airplane hanger. The garage was where we stored our kickballs, our skateboards and yes, our bikes. My sisters would drape old blankets from the rafters and create haunted houses. Out in the garage, you never had to be clean, quiet or well-behaved. We could be kicked out of the living room, banished from the kitchen, bored stiff in the den and even expunged from our own bedroom. But once we were in the garage, things seemed to be okay. I guess some of my fondest memories are of hanging out in our old wood, one-car garage, playing ping-pong with the Perez brothers, listening to Jackson Brown on a warm summer night.

Years later when I got my own home, I immediately set about duplicating that scenario. Besides the requisite sports gear, I had to have a world map with little pins stuck in each of the countries I'd

RICHARD GRAHAM

PREVIOUS PAGE Gary Clark. Check out the scar on his chest. That's because his old heart busted and he got a new one. And you're pissed because you can't find your wetsuit. Right on, Gary. **ABOVE** This little yampster is smiling big-time inside. He just made it all the way across without stopping. And for all of us at one time or another, that's a big deal.

MIKE PLANT

DAVID EPPERSON

BETTY JENEWIN

HARALD JOHNSON

TOP Hey, a thumbs up to you too, Ted. **TOP RIGHT** Golden smile. **BOTTOM** Hanssen and Hoover after the pool heater broke. **RIGHT** Karen Smyers, Ironman winner, outspoken, and solid beer drinkin' gal. Good credentials.

SMILES & ECHOES

been to and a row of glass jars above the bench holding all the odd sized nuts and bolts. My garage had to do more than just remind me of my youth, it had to actually transport me there every time I took out the garbage. Even if the sink was backed up and my wife sent me out for the plunger, I wanted to be able to glance up at one of my big wave guns and feel a smile come over my face remembering an epic session in Fiji; I wanted to hear one little echo of life's simpler past as my daughter's Barbie head lodged deeper and deeper into the kitchen's bowels. Maybe that's why garages are like triathletes. They have become vehicles that connect us to our youth yet allow us to move forward with some understanding and control. Am I reaching here? Have I gone a little too far in search of a philosophical tangent? Maybe. On the wall opposite that big world map, right between my son's pogo stick and a snowboard with a skull and crossbones on the deck, sits a poem that was given to me when I was 18 by a 14-year-old who wanted to be 21 in the worst way. It goes like this:

So the years pass by like parallel rails, and it
seems like only yesterday you were too old to
play or too young to remember.
And you sometimes wish you had the time to
stop the train and save one day for tomorrow.
But it wouldn't at all be the same ... if you stayed.

I have no idea who wrote it or how it has stayed with me all these years through all the moves. But I like its message and every once in awhile I read it when I'm out in the garage, tinkering with a busted VCR or washing my muddy shoes out in the sink. I guess I just appreciate the

TOP LEFT A young Lance Armstrong, smiling at the thought that a life in professional sports will eventually get him out of auto shop class at Plano High School in central Texas. **BOTTOM LEFT** *"Con mis amigos en la playa."* **TOP RIGHT** Shannon Delaney grew up with the sport. I don't know if that's good or bad. She turned out all right, though. Actually, more than all right. **BOTTOM RIGHT** Eney Jones. She still looks this good.

harsh reality of its lesson. Many of my triathlete friends are like that. We plow ahead with our linear training, putting one foot, one pedal, one arm in front of the other, day after day. We think about the next training session, maybe the next race and everything else we do is necessary filler, stuff that keeps us afloat. We are beyond the basics of learning our skill, but we refuse to stop and reflect. There will be time enough to talk about the "good old days" when our knees won't carry us through a blistering track workout anymore. But inside somewhere we know instinctively that what we are doing is a good thing, a thing that we should enjoy with a passion as it unfolds. You can't stop the train and save just a little time for when we really need it, like when we are very old and very unathletic. No, Thomas Wolfe was right. You can't go home again. But you can live in the moment, savoring its presence without ignoring the past or forgetting the future. How? Hell, I don't know. But smiling always seems to help. Finding the lighter side of each and every situation (and they do exist) will allow us to keep the path clear, to keep the blood flowing through conduits.

Go watch a triathlon sometime. Go look into the faces of the participants as they move along the small but compelling journey that takes an hour or so a day. See the intensity, the force of nature beyond their understanding or control, see the killer instinct in some, the submissive sigh of resign in others. But open your own eyes and look for the common denominator, look for the smile. What you will see is people, competitors, workers, spectators, passers-by — all with an ear-to-ear grin like

ABOVE Sweden's Magnus Lunquist, a great competitor and a really nice guy. Left the sport to sell Porsches.

no other. Why? Because they won. Because they lost. Because they moved quickly, because they ran slowly, because they didn't drown. Because they didn't crash. Because they didn't flat. Because they lost five pounds. Because they could now gain seven pounds in one sitting. Because they're feeling sexy. Because they're finished working out for the day. Because they achieved what they set out to do. Because they now have even loftier goals. Because it doesn't hurt anymore. Because they know that the pain will go away. Because they will get a finishers T-shirt. Just because. Triathletes like to smile.

But being happy is something that many of us have to relearn. As a kid, that comes naturally. What do we have to worry about? Homework? Come on. Try a tax audit, you say. Strangely enough, we fail to realize how good we have it. As we grow a little, we suddenly yearn to grow a little more, start to sample a few of the treats of adulthood. Then we reach adulthood. We can now drive a car, order a drink, stay up late, eat all the candy we want. What happens? We slam on the brakes and long again for the innocence of youth. We will do anything to be young again, to be happy and carefree, to smile willfully and without reservation. When it doesn't happen overnight, we try to give ourselves a little primer to help the wheels reverse direction. Pour ourselves into size 5 jeans, pay a bit more for facial cream, join a new health club. I went out to buy a new car last year, something practical for the family. I came home with a 1967 VW Bug convertible — the very same car I bought when I was 16 years old. Twenty years later, I paid nearly 20 times as much as my first one

DAVID EPPERSON

ABOVE "Hey, I'm just happy to be here; besides, I'm going to kick your 20-year-old ass!"

HARALD JOHNSON

HARALD JOHNSON

COURTESY OPTIMUM HEALTH LABS

TOP LEFT V.T. in Sater, Sweden. It's about 10 o'clock at night here in the land of the midnight sun. You can rack up some serious mileage when you don't have to come home when the streetlights come on. **BOTTOM LEFT** Author, businesswoman, all-around good chick (sorry Sally) Ms. Edwards. **LEFT CENTER** Doctor Ferdy Massimino — that's right, Doctor Ferdy — the first "national champion" in 1982. A great competitor. **RIGHT** USTS cofounder Jim Curl, "Hey, where are all the groupies?"

and four times what it cost when it was new. But it was bitchen' and it reminded me of a less complicated time. The day I sold it six months later, I regretted it deeply.

Nothing will remind us of the passage of time like athletics. You can color your hair and suck in your gut, but when you go out and play a rowdy game of touch football at 40, well, things don't work like they did when you were 15. Without the regular participation in athletic activities, though, the clock will continue unabated. Being a triathlete will not stop it — as I'm sitting here though, it will slow it down. Yeah, it's a battle. But what are you going to do? Act your age? Submit to sometimes heavy societal pressures to measure one's self worth in terms of material wealth, employment status and political clout? A long time ago I decided that I wanted to associate with people whose satisfaction was congruent with health, lifestyle and the ability to ride a skateboard to the store for a quart of milk. Which brings us back to your garage or sitting room or garden or any place, whether it exists in your house or in your mind, that you can go and relearn what we are born with — the ability to be happy, to smile. Yeah, yeah, easy for you to say, you're a pro triathlete. Hey folks, we all struggle for the balance of freedom and responsibility. But never forget that you have a responsibility to be free. What will it take? The untimely death of a loved one? An epic religious experience? Maybe the catalyst is out in the garage. Maybe your wake-up call will come in the form of a spider's web. Look at your favorite bike, your favorite No. 3 iron, your fastest pair of inline skates. Do they have

HARALD JOHNSON

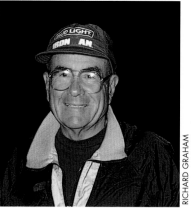

RICHARD GRAHAM

LEFT Ex-patrioted Kiwi and founder of Perfection Sport, Jim Reilly smiles at the prospect of finishing. **TOP RIGHT** One of the best female triathletes ever, Linda Buchanan. **MIDDLE RIGHT** Joy Hanssen, triathlon's Easter bunny. **BOTTOM RIGHT** Irongent Bill Bell smiling at the thought that most people his age have to play golf.

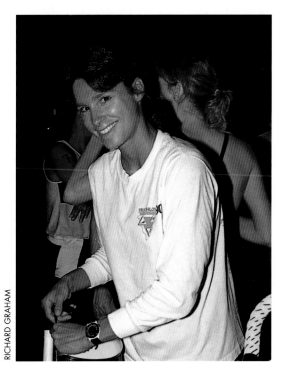

TOP LEFT Mark Sisson, top 10 Ironman finisher, former exec at Tri-Fed, and businessman. Not everybody agrees with him, but you can't argue with his contributions to the sport. **BOTTOM LEFT** Lisa Laihti — a take-no-prisoners gal, fast, hard luck, good person. **RIGHT** "Okay, so I don't have a lot of money to spend on sponsors' products. But at the 2012 Olympics you're going to want me to win a gold medal for the U.S. How about a few more kids' races now, people?"

a thin layer of dust, a cobweb between the handle-bars and the frame? Do they make you smile when you walk by to take out the trash or do they call out your name, "You know, I could use a bit of fresh air, young lady." You have a responsibility to your toys too. When they are happy, you will smile. Easy enough.

Or you can set your professional sights on the moon, work your fingers to the bone to get there. Nothing is wrong with that. Ask yourself though, what is the cost — because nothing comes for free. If you make a million bucks but lose all your friends stepping on them getting to the top, are you really a rich man? Correct me if I'm wrong, but you can't take it with you when you go.

Fifteen hundred years ago we knew that the Earth was the center of the universe. Five hundred years ago we knew that the Earth was flat. Fifteen minutes ago you knew that you would wake up again in the morning. Imagine what you'll know tomorrow.

This whole thing may have little to do with the sport of triathlon over the past 25 years. But I think it does. If we all had a clearer picture of why we train and why we race, well, we'd proba-bly win more — or at least we'd smile more. And isn't that winning?

RICHARD GRAHAM

ABOVE Bob Babbitt trying to let the water out of his wetsuit so people don't think he is 10 pounds overweight. Notice anything else? Like, there's no one behind him in the swim?

CHAPTER THIRTEEN

"A new philosophy, a way of life, is not given for nothing. It has to be paid dearly for and only acquired with much patience and great effort." — *Fydor Dostoevski, 1821-1881*

FINAL ACCEPTANCE

From 1985 through 1989, the sport of triathlon succeeded on all fronts. It was finally accepted by not only the various parties within the realm of more traditional sports, but became an icon of sorts for the growing phenomenon called "cross training." Spurred on by the shoe companies' desire to create and market to an entirely new niche, the simple yet complex concept of training in multiple sports became the fitness craze. Never mind the fact that triathletes all over the country had embraced cross training and its resultant benefits years ago. When the topic makes headlines in the Wall Street Journal ... it truly has arrived.

At the top of the cross training heap was triathlon. Even if your exercise program consisted of weightlifting, jogging and inline skating, somewhere inside you existed a desire to seek out and compete in a triathlon. If for no other reason than to say that they had, enough individuals of all shapes and sizes were certainly drawn to the new sport of the 1980s."

ACCEPTANCE

INTERNATIONAL WILDFIRE

In 1986, I competed in no fewer than seven different countries. The sport had arrived everywhere, it seemed. My passport was filled with stamps from Australia, New Zealand, France, Germany, Sweden, Canada, Japan, Mexico and Bakersfield (okay, so it seemed like a foreign country). The opportunities to race abroad came fast and furious to anyone with a résumé that included more than three or four victories. It was an incredible opportunity to see the world on someone else's meal ticket. And the best part about it was that the competition abroad was still in the developmental stages. Once in awhile an up-and-comer would sneak in ahead of you, like Dirk Aschmoneit from Germany or Rob Barel from The Netherlands or Stephen Foster from Australia. But for the most part, in 1986 and '87, the top dogs were still Americans.

By 1987 all of that was beginning to change. The European Triathlon Union was gaining strength and in its wake was a whole host of competitive opportunities. France had not only the self-titled Nice World Championships but also a Le Coq Sportif-sponsored series of six triathlons held in France and its territories. Japan had its Ironman franchise race organized by Dentsun as well as the new USTS licensed and modeled Japan Triathlon Series of short distance Olympic events. In 1987 there were JTS events in four major Japanese cities, each one organized in true Japanese fashion — perfectly. Canada had four or five events mostly around the Toronto area organized by Graham

Fraser and his family. Out on the west coast in Penticton, Lyn Van Ert was staging the Canadian Ironman Triathlon Championships, won by local hero Dave Kirk. And just a bit to the east of them in Vancouver, Don Andrews was hosting the first Vancouver International Triathlon at English Bay.

New Zealand also had an Ironman event in full swing and American Ray Browning put together an incredible string of victories in this as well as the other non-Hawaii Ironman events. And up on the Gold Coast of Australia, Barry and Juli Voevodin organized a three-quarter Ironman distance event with a Japanese sponsor (Daikyo) that would become the richest event in all of triathlon. Mark Allen ran away from me at the 8km mark of a 30km run to earn close to $30,000 for his efforts. Other athletes who scored big time that day were Ken Glah, Pauli Kiuru from Finland, Tim Bently from Australia, the duathlete from San Diego, Ken Souza, and a newcomer from New Zealand who most of us hadn't seen race in the states yet — Erin Baker.

Baker had been arrested in New Zealand years before while demonstrating against the presence of nuclear warships in Auckland Harbor and was subsequently labeled a terrorist. Denied a visa to come to the U.S., Baker raced well and often in Europe, gradually building up her skill and strength without all the distractions of the U.S. triathlon scene. In Voevodin's World Cup Gold Coast, she beat the No. 1-ranked Puntous twins by over 20 minutes. Baker would later say, "If I would have arrived in the U.S. sooner and realized the women were not any good, I may not have trained so hard in Europe." Bold indeed, but Baker was to become one of the most

DAVID EPPERSON

DAVID EPPERSON

PREVIOUS PAGE On any given weekend you could find a triathlon within two hours of your house, no matter where you lived. This is the Neptune Triathlon in Virginia Beach.

DAVID EPPERSON

TOP LEFT Masters triathlete Hans Deidein, bridging the gap on Kauai. **BOTTOM LEFT** okay, so the bike was two sizes too small for me. It weighed 13 pounds, honest. **ABOVE** Greg Welch, raising his hands in third place victory, Ironman 1989.

misunderstood individuals in the sport.

Indeed, if one was to look at a calendar of events in 1987, starting with the self-titled World Sprint Championships in Perth, Australia, followed by high profile races in Mission Viejo, California; Avignon, France; Sater, Sweden; Bermuda; Hilton Head, South Carolina; Ironman; and ending with Nice ... one would have thought that the opportunities for triathletes were endless. Soon enough the competition would follow.

THE NEW BREED

If one is to try and find the best athletes who bridged the gap between old and new, between the Big Four and the current fire-breathing crew, between the Moss/McCartney/Buchanan days to the Karen Smyers/Heather Fuhr period, one has only to look at four individuals: Mike Pigg, Greg Welch, Erin Baker and Paula Newby-Fraser.

In 1985 Mike Pigg was a 21-year-old part-time student from the cold confines of Arcata, California. A moderately successful track and cross-country runner in high school, his try as a steeplechaser at College of the Redwoods was less than spectacular. Pigg was, however, a jock of all trades and was attracted to the sport of triathlon as early as 1983 after watching one of the Ironman telecasts. His first foray into the triple sport lifestyle was aggressive as he placed fourth at the New Zealand Ironman, sixth at the World's Toughest, and seventh at Ironman. But it wasn't until 1987 and the 12-city United States Triathlon Series that Pigg began to put his stamp on the sport. You see, up until 1986

Pigg had been a mechanic's helper at the Redwood Coast Construction Company. There, and as part of supportive family structure, he had developed a work ethic like few have ever possessed in the sport. When he finished seventh at Ironman in his freshman season, in front of his entire family, he knew this sport was for him. "I was ready to cry at the finish line," he said. "Pigg power was born."

Pigg would go on to win the Coke Grand Prix (a bonus pool for the best overall competitor at all the USTS events) a record number of times. Between 1987 and 1991 he won 55 out of 88 races he entered, including 30 USTS victories. His hard work and playful go-for-it attitude was his secret weapon. Pigg still embodies the devil-may-care spirit and competitive zeal that was the fuel for many of the sport's early figures. His place in triathlon's history is well secured.

Greg Welch, like Pigg and Newby-Fraser before him, came into the sport from a full-time job that he was quite happy with. As a journeyman carpenter in the Cronulla Beach suburb of Sydney, Australia, Welch competed only for fun and fitness in the odd beach lifeguard competition that is so common in that country. But he processed a natural running speed that raised more than a few eyebrows when he jumped in to support the local Cronulla Beach Club that many of his mates belonged to.

When Welch first came to the U.S. in 1989, it was with his friend and training partners Brad Beven and Simon Skillokorn. They landed directly in the thick of Triathlon Central — San Diego's Encinitas. North San Diego was similar to Cronul-

RICHARD GRAHAM

ABOVE No longer an American sport alone, triathlons began popping up everywhere, the most popular of which were in warmer climates.

ACCEPTANCE

la but what it had that Welch's hometown lacked was an infrastructure in which to motivate and educate the Aussie trio. Unfortunately, Simon was hurt in a car accident and had to return to Australia, and Beven, after a year or so, moved back to train near his family. But Welch stayed and in 1990, won the second world triathlon championships at the Olympic distance. All of a sudden he was a sought-after commodity. And he was ready for it. Welch began to alternate from one country to the other, competing nearly year-round while following the alternating competitive seasons. His crowning achievement came in 1994 when he became the first non-American to win the Hawaii Ironman. He remains one of the only athletes of the modern era who can compete successfully at both the short and long distances. Besides all that, he is fun to be around.

Erin Baker was perhaps the fiercest, most determined female competitor to ever compete in triathlon. When she was on her game and hungry for a win, she rarely, if ever, lost. But what Baker possessed in athletic skill, she lacked in diplomacy. Never one to mince words or pull punches, Erin would call them the way she saw them, which more often than not, was the way everybody else saw it but was afraid to say.

Baker comes from a large, tight-knit family in Christchurch, New Zealand. She is a 5-foot 6-inch woman and approximately 120 pounds. Her first big win came in Perth in January of 1987 where she won $25,000. She also won Nice that year but was disqualified for taking water from her sister — a rule that most of the other competitors had also

HARALD JOHNSON

COURTESY USTS

TOP How I wish I had had this kind of opportunity as a kid. **BOTTOM** Mike Plant interviews Molina and a new kid from Phoenix who almost beat him. Jimmy Riccitello has gone on to become one of the most consistent short-course triathletes ever. He has been racing at or near the top for 15 years and he is still in his early 30s (there you go Jimmy, I said something good about you. Now about that $50 you borrowed ...).

ABOVE Sharing with those a lot less fortunate than us. This guy should get a head start if not a few chips to be cashed in at the Pearly Gates.

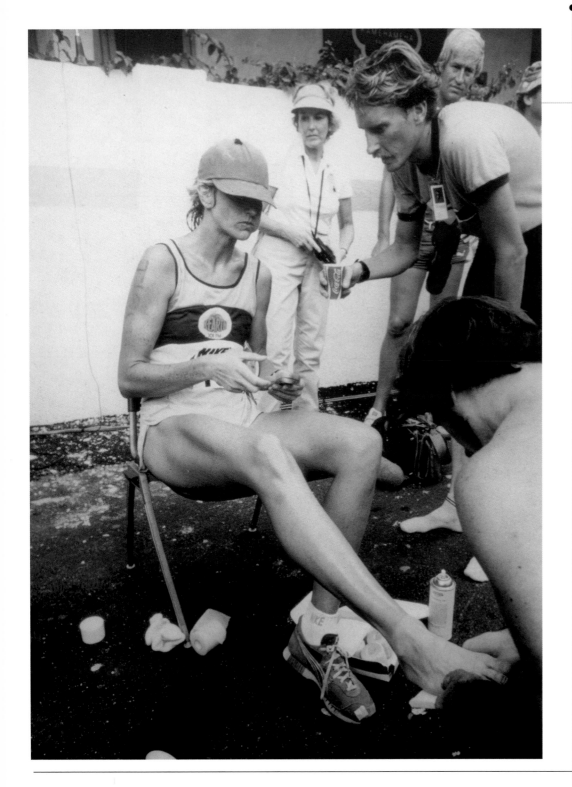

ABOVE Competitor Pat Hines has a pedicure while adoring men bring her rum and Cokes.

violated that year. Baker could appear to be gruff and unyielding, but when you break through the veneer, she is considerate, kind and as loyal as a puppy dog. When she beat Paula Newby-Fraser in the 1990 Ironman, it was a woman more at peace with her place in the sport than we had seen before. Ultimately, she was one of the only top women, other than Kathleen McCartney, to have a number of children and settle down into a quiet family life after her retirement.

• • • • •

Paula Newby-Fraser needs only one calling card — eight-time winner of the Ironman. When you consider how difficult it is simply to get to the starting line of that race, how much one has to endure before the gun is even fired, it is simply amazing that one person can win it more than once, let alone eight times.

As a former dancer, gymnast and swimmer, Paula did her first race in her native South Africa in 1985. Realizing that it would be nearly impossible to compete from that country at that time, she moved to Encinitas, California — ground zero for the sport. When one looks at Newby-Fraser's career, they see a progressively advancing commitment on a nearly incremental plane. In other words, she very gradually added more distance and intensity to her training, more races to her schedule and more sponsors to her résumé. In 1986, when she won the Ironman as Patricia Puntous was DQ'd for drafting, Newby was employed part-time working in a travel agency. At that point, she considered a 200-mile bike week overtraining. Each season would bring with it a few more long races, a few more intense track sessions and with it, competitive success.

But it is her streak of Ironman victories and the way in which they came where Newby's story can be told. Each year she would have to look for a new edge, a new system and a new motivation to stay ahead of the women who chased her relentlessly. At the same time she was able to mature as a person and apply life's little lessons to each race, regardless of the outcome.

SHOOTING STARS

Along with Pigg, Welch, Newby-Fraser, Kirsten Hanssen, Baker and the original Big Four, other athletes were coming out of the woodwork. A 16-year-old Lance Armstrong from Plano, Texas, would have his mother drive him to races in the Southwest after he got out of school on Friday afternoon. The kid was a bit cocky, but he was fast and determined.

Guys like Clark Campbell from Coffeyville, Kansas; Nick Radkewich from Florida; Steve Fitch from Pennsylvania; Nick Taylor from Houston; Todd Jacobs from El Paso (who would finish third in the Coke Grand Prix rankings for 1987); Brad Kearns from Malibu (who had one of the longest, most consistent careers of any of these guys); Andrew McMartin from "the Valley"; Garrett McCarthy from Los Angeles; Peter Cazalet from Palo Alto, California; Greg Stewart from Australia; Dirk Aschmoneit, Klaus Barth, Wolfgang Deitrich

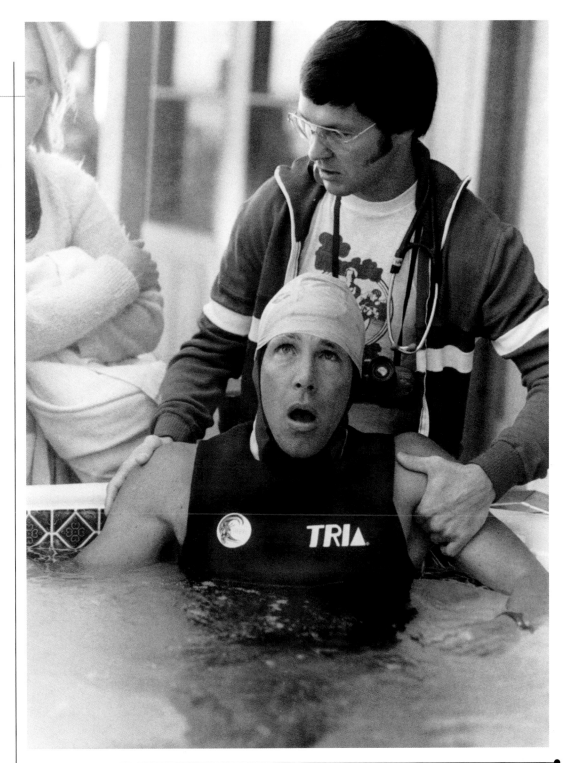

ABOVE The dude in the tub is saying (choose one): 1. "I paid $120 and all I get is 10 minutes in the Jacuzzi;" 2. " If you squeeze my armpit any harder, Doc, I'm gonna kick your ass;" 3. "This is the cold pool for overheated competitors, you idiot."

ACCEPTANCE

and a young Jürgen Zack, all from Germany; Tony Richardson from La Jolla, California; and Harald Robinson from Santa Rosa, California, all threatened to topple the status quo. And at the top of the heap in the late 1980s was Mark Allen.

Allen came to San Diego in 1976 from Palo Alto to attend UCSD and swim on the college team. He first entered the USTS San Diego when he was inspired by the Julie Moss episode. With incredible natural talent, his apprenticeship lasted but a few months.

Allen had graduated from college and was wrestling with the idea of applying to medical school, biding his time as a lifeguard. When he scored a free trip to the Nice triathlon in November of 1982 and actually won, he figured he'd take a year off and see what happened. He was picked up by the JDavid organization in 1983, won Nice again, a few other races and *voilà* — Allen was a star pro triathlete. His true talents came, like Dave Scott, in being able to win the big ones when it counted. Frustrated at Ironman for several years in a row, he was still able to win Nice 10 years in a row. After working out the bugs in Kona, he began a streak of six victories there also. Possibly Mark's greatest athletic achievement came in 1988-89 when he won 20 races in a row.

For the women it was still as exciting as ever. On any given day, six or seven women could emerge victorious. Linda Buchanan could be unbeatable, Jan Ripple from Louisiana, Liz Downing from Portland, Oregon, Lisa Laihti from El Paso, Texas, Karen Rainey from Canada, Sylviane and Paricia Puntous, Debbie Kauzlarich, Jann and

ABOVE Boy, that reconstructive surgery on your nose is coming back nicely. This is Edson Sower at the 1985 Ironman. We should all be so lucky to live this long.

MIKE PLANT

ABOVE The Brown brothers, Barry and Colin, from La Jolla. Two smart guys, Barry is now a neuro-surgeon and Colin is big wave charger at Maverick's. **CENTER TOP** Get a room. **CENTER MIDDLE** Señor Cristian Bustos, *fuerte y bueno amigo. Mas rapido.* **CENTER BOTTOM** Scott Zagarino, triathlete, businessman, father and founder of several wonderful programs within the sport, including Triathletes For Kids. **TOP RIGHT** "Save yourselves from the evils of overtraining. Stay away from that distance devil Tinley, he will tempt you with longer and longer runs." The Reverend Bob Babbitt, preaching the word of conservative exercise. **BOTTOM RIGHT** Mickey Mitsumiro wonders why Paul Huddle is so confident at the start. He looks forward to passing him with one mile to go on the run.

ACCEPTANCE

Dian Girard, Liz Bulman, Julie Moss, Julie Brenning, Beth Mitchell, Sarah Springman from London, England, Carolina Heins from Ontario, Canada and one of my favorites, Colleen Cannon from Boulder, Colorado (winner of the Nice Triathlon in 1984), all were in contention at any point in time. More often than not, they were chasing Kirsten Hanssen of Denver or Erin Baker or ....

TRIATHLON STYLE

By the late 1980s, triathlon's key events, key players, key sponsors and peripheral media were well in place. What developed next was a resulting style to go along with the cross-training that more and more people were emulating. The look of a triathlete became unique unto itself. Spandex in the form of DuPont Lycra was quickly embraced as it was aerodynamic, non-binding and form-fitting. If you had the goods, Lycra allowed you to show them off. Color was important, the brighter the better. In fact, the whole neon running shorts craze was fueled by triathletes wanting to spice up their runs, if not their lives.

Equipment became a big part of looking like you were a triathlete. After Brad Kearns introduced Scott USA's new aero handlebar to the sport at the 1987 Desert Princess Duathlon, every triathlete *had* to have them. When demand exceeded supply, people would make them out of PVC pipe. They looked like a sprinkler system on wheels. Disc wheels were a must. Steve and Anne Hed created and marketed the first affordable aero wheels to triathletes in 1987 and have upped the ante with better stuff every year.

When Scott Molina first raced in a pair of Oakley eyeshades in 1984, people laughed. Six weeks later, they *had* to have a pair. Sport sunglasses were functional, fast and different — much the same as the athletes themselves. The same went for Giro helmets and the ultimate triathlete fashion icon — the Timex Ironman watch.

TRIATHLON FOOD

It soon became apparent that one of the last areas of undeveloped knowledge was that of sports nutrition. We all wanted to train hard, train long and race fast. But we knew that we needed to refuel the tanks at regular intervals. But with what? When? How much? Triathletes became human guinea pigs, ingesting anything that had the slightest possibility to give them an edge. Bud Light may have been the choice of post-race libation, but out on the course it was either Gatorade or Exceed or Pocari or ERG or Coke or Cytomax or even water. And that's just the legal stuff that we knew about. Lots of people liked to experiment, mixing up their own concoctions like some high school science project. For the most part, these home brews had a placebo effect at best and at worst, screwed up a few potentially good performances.

A few people got it right. Bill Gookin, a San Diego teacher, created the very first electrolyte replacement drink in the mid-1970s. Never properly marketed, it went as far as the local 10km. Up north in Berkeley, California, though, Brian Maxwell, a 2:14 marathoner from Canada, cooked

RUSSEL MOORE

RICHARD GRAHAM

TOP Chuckie V, fast dude, personality, knows his rock bands.
BOTTOM "Over here ma'am. I ordered the boat drink."

ABOVE By the early 1990s, even the googy parade became a fun thing to do.

ACCEPTANCE

up the first real sports nutrition bar in his kitchen, creating an entire new food category in the process. Some of the early triathletes were "samplers" of test batches and helped get the word out on Maxwell's new PowerBar.

NATIONAL MEDIA

By the mid to late 1980s, *Triathlete* magazine had merged with *Triathlon*, and soon therafter, Jean Claude Garot acquired the rest of the original Santa Monica company's assets. Harald Johnson was gone to form his own communications company, Terry Mulgannon came in as editor along with Rich Graham and after that followed Tim Downs, C.J. Olivares, Gary Newkirk and Jeffrey Justice. Each put their own spin on the publication, sometimes uniquely creative, other times technically dry and mundane. For the most part though, it was *the v*oice of the sport. The national governing body, Tri Fed, had its own newsletter, *Triathlon Times*, that covered mostly age group results. But in 1988, in a huge dispute over how much the federation was paying the publisher of *Triathlon Today* to be the official Tri-Fed newsletter, executive director Verne Scott quit. Claiming conflict of interest, the federation was turned on its ear in turmoil, nearly disintegrating in the process and only surviving on the back of new executive director and former top-10 Ironman finisher, Mark Sisson. It was a terrible period for Scott, who had worked tirelessly for the sport, and for the many people who felt betrayed by the dissention that erupted at the highest ranks. Nobody will ever know the whole story — what's done is done. Sever-

ABOVE Golden girl Wendy Ingraham, former landscape designer, sets her designs on first place wherever she races. Well-rounded and talented woman who will party until the last dog is dead and get up and run 20 in the morning.

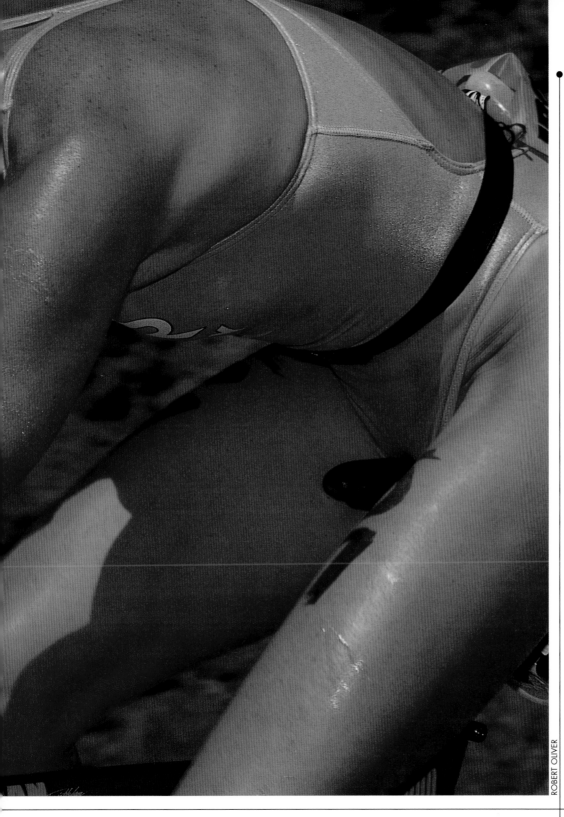

ROBERT OLIVER

al years later, *Triathlon Today* was bought by Inside Communications of Boulder, Colorado, and became *Inside Triathlon*. The sport now had two separate and complementary publications.

Of even greater interest, though, was the growing number of articles in national mainstream press about the sport. The *New York Times* had a piece in 1984, *People* magazine did a blurb, mentions of the sport appeared in *Time* on several occasions, the *Wall Street Journal* ran a two-page diatribe in September of 1982, and *Sports Illustrated* seemed to sneak in a column or two around Ironman time. Hell, even the *Hollywood Reporter* did a piece on the ill-fated Bahamas Diamond Triathlon of the Stars.

What this meant was that with widespread acceptance of triathlon, people, sponsors, city officials, etc., who may have been "on the fence" about this new sport would now give it the proper attention and respect it deserved. It just made everybody whose job it was to get the word out a bit easier. No longer were we masochistic freaks. When well known and respected athletes from other sports began paying attention, even competing, whammo — instant credibility. I mean, here was New York marathon winner Allison Roe finishing in the top three at the Mighty Hampton Triathlon, or Frank Shorter and Greg LeMond doing commentary for the Nice television show, or Kathleen McCartney on the Johnny Carson show discussing the cross training concept — talking like an exercise physiologist, looking like a model. All this helped take triathlon into the hearts and homes of millions worldwide.

CHAPTER FOURTEEN

"Fate chooses our relatives, we choose our friends." — *Jacques Delille, 1738-1813*

COMRADES

Someone once said, "Athletes aren't the kind of people to wear their hearts on their sleeve." When referring to endurance athletes, there is some truth to this. But when the anonymous sage made this comment, diagnosing the physical types as introverted and withdrawn in the area of outward affection, they failed to include the language of friendship. It may even seem natural for individuals in ultradistance sports to lose their ability to communicate openly, to "bubble with love" as it were. I like to think though, that if the years and miles have somehow altered the way we share ourselves, it is for the better, a natural and developing process that was fine-tuned by the hours alone on a bike seat or in a tree-covered single track, listening to the sound of our footsteps.

Quite honestly though, it's difficult to speak of my personal relationships with my athletic peers. I would say that it is true of them also, at least the guys. That macho thing is just so hard to let down. The women are much better, as they are at most things personal and intimate. It is easier to write about however, hiding behind the safety of the keyboard, knowing that a computer will never reject or judge you. And while I'm not going to heap lavish praise on my friends from triathlon, nor mask my feelings with a trite joke, no introspective look at the sport would be complete without some commentary on personal relationships.

As far back as I can remember, sports have always been a way to simultaneously stand apart from the crowd and be a part of it. We are taught at a very young age that teamwork is important, that it takes a minimum number of people to make things work. If you want to play basketball, you have to find five guys or gals to do it right. At least for the American male youth, joining a team was of paramount importance.

As we progressed, we realized that just being on the team was not always enough. If you were good (or the coach's son), you played. If you weren't, you warmed the bench. This was my first lesson in Darwin's theory of survival. It seems though, that at least some of what we did was because we wanted to be accepted, to be liked, to be one of the guys or gals. To gain that esteemed position, we labored to be quicker, faster, better than the next guy. To gain respect we had to win.

It doesn't appear to be something that we out-grow. You can see it on the neighborhood tennis courts when a friend calls you up to play a set or two but treats the game like the Wimbledon finals. You can see it at the company softball game when a coworker calls you out on strikes. More than once I've walked off courts, fields and courses when a friendly game has degenerated into a club-

PREVIOUS PAGE Karleen Crowell and her dad, I think. TOP LEFT Murphy Reinschreiber checking for leaks in one of Paula's seven ear holes. TOP RIGHT Media magnates Gary Newkirk, Bob Babbitt, and C.J. Olivares eating ice cream at triathlon's mecca. BOTTOM Triathlon's double date, Puntous twins, Dale Basecu, and Marc 'wandering hands' Suprenant.

ABOVE Tony Robertson checking for dirt under his fingernails.

COMRADES

breaking, feeling-hurting outlet for someone's pent-up stress. They don't do it for fame or fortune; they do it because they want to win and winning makes them feel good.

Triathletes are in a unique position. We compete as individuals for the most part. There may be the semblance of a team in the case of international competition, but when the gun is fired, team tactics are never a consideration. (This may change in the future with the advent of draft-legal races.) We are racing for ourselves, for our sponsors and sometimes for our country, but we are completely responsible for our own performance. Yet we travel around the world to many of the same events, sharing plane rides, hotel rooms and most importantly — training sessions. For a triathlete to reach his or her athletic potential, it is almost completely requisite to spend a major portion of time in close proximity to other, like-minded individuals. In other words, the training and preparation necessary to be world class is almost impossible to do alone. And it has always been that way.

Ironman 1979 winner Tom Warren remembers well. "The fondest memories I have of this sport are of the early days, training with Bill Phillips and other members of the San Diego Track Club. There was virtually no pressure to win at triathlon. It wasn't even considered a real sport; it was just a fun way to stay in shape for running and swimming competition. We would head out on these great run/bike/swim training sessions with no plan in mind and just laugh and exercise all day."

Well said. In fact, there are countless stories of individuals who have had their personal records

MIKE PLANT

TOP LEFT *Triathlon* magazine's A-Team: Terry Mulgannon, Daemon Filson, C.J. Olivares, Mark Wendley and Harald Johnson. **TOP RIGHT** Emilio De Soto Sr. and Jr. Hard-working Cuban immigrant and proud, successful son of same. Tenured tri-guys for sure. **BOTTOM** The ties that bind....

RICHARD GRAHAM

DAVID EPPERSON

TOP Howard, Colleen, Erin, Rich and Skid eating barbeque on the porch after a long day of training in New Zealand one spring, a long time ago. BOTTOM LEFT Jim Riley, Jeffrey Essakow, Mr. and Mrs. Tom Thomson and Jack Berghaus. Just another day at the office, eh? BOTTOM RIGHT "If we up our run mileage a bit, maybe include another track session...."

LEFT "Okay, who thinks I have the starting gun in my right hand? How about my left?" **TOP RIGHT** Pre-Spice Girl Power: Liz Bulman, Kirsten Hanssen, Julie Brenning and Gayleen Clews. All of them are still faster than you. **BOTTOM RIGHT** One of the best ways to cool off.

lowered and their social lives raised at the same time. Not that everybody was the best of friends. It's just that when the common goal is to improve one's skills and putting in the long, lonely miles alone is undesirable, the resulting scenario gives a group an arena in which lifelong friendships can easily form. Without a doubt, the guys and gals I've had to hang with have been really good folks. Nearly everybody connected with the sport has been of exceptional character. There have been a few real flakes though, and more recently, power and greed have colored the intentions of otherwise good people.

I can remember watching guys like Scott Molina, Mark Allen and Ray Browning, among others, when they all moved to Boulder, Colorado, in the late 80s. They all raved about the group workouts, the beautiful environment and their rapidly improving race performances. I thought, "Screw that, I'm staying in my beloved North County where there is surf, sunshine and local races." But after a two-week vacation at Molina's house in Sugarloaf above Boulder, I was hooked. The next five summers were spent training and socializing with the growing core group. It was also the best five years of my competitive career. I asked Scott Molina one time if it bothered him that the town was getting so crowded with triathletes. "Not really," he said. "I've always liked to train with other people, even if it meant giving up something. What I got in return was always greater. I couldn't have lasted as long as I did by myself up in these big mountains."

Truth be known, many of the early successful athletes were gradually coming to know that a well-defined, competitive and friendly infrastructure was

TOP LEFT Sean Molina and a buddy out for an easy six on a warm spring afternoon. Is there anything better? TOP RIGHT Long-time race director and athletic entrepreneur Dave McGillivary with his ex-wife, Sue. Dave's contributions to the sport are vast and varied. BOTTOM You go get 'em, neighbor!

COMRADES

paramount to one's success. In the early 1980s, the Big Four had Team JDavid as a lucrative, success-oriented vehicle in which we could train together without the distraction of jealousy or fear. Dave Scott was on his own and in the long run that may have hurt him. Dave once said, "One of the only regrets that I have in this sport is not taking the time to train with the other guys either in Southern California or the early days of Boulder. I think I burned myself out prematurely by always going it alone up on the desolate roads of Davis, California."

But Dave did have the occasional visitor to his Northern California training grounds. He tells the story of the week when a young and very ambitious Mike Pigg joined him. "Mike called me in March of 1989 and decided that we should train together for an entire week. I weighed the benefits and pitfalls of possibly venturing into this torture session with Mad Mike. Without too much prodding, Mike set up temporary headquarters in Davis. After three long, punishing days, Mike, undaunted by my slowing enthusiasm, decided that day four was our long ride day. We ran and swam, then proceeded out on a 137-mile time trial. At 78 miles my entire food and beverage supply was gone along with my pride and ego. My survival skills were heightened to their maximum as I fell in behind Mike, praying that he might want to stop for diner and a nap along the road. My prayers were answered and at 89 miles we stopped. Nearly comatose, I staggered into a convenience store to witness one of the most phenomenal eating performances ever. I was hungry, but Mike was ravenous. He consumed a quart of milk, two berry pies, a

RICHARD GRAHAM

RICHARD GRAHAM

C.J. OLIVARES

TOP Team JDavid hanging out at the Hawi High School pool in October 1983. There are at least ten Ironman championships, eight national titles and two Olympic medals sitting in the bleachers. BOTTOM LEFT Doug and Cyndi Richter (excellent chocolate chip cookies). CENTER RIGHT Andrew McNaughton, Todd Jacobs, Jimmy Riccitello and Tony Richardson discuss the finer points of last night's fight. BOTTOM RIGHT The Seal Beach Boyz: Tom Gallagher and Klaus Barth.

ABOVE Tom Warren (right) during the last few miles of the 1979 Ironman (in which he won). It is a rare photo of a rare individual.

quart of Cytomax, a bag of potato chips, a package of chocolate chip cookies and a half-loaf of bread. Trying to adhere to my published diet, I caved in after witnessing this feat. I indulged with Mike and proudly left with a Twinkie in my pocket. Forty-five miles later my wife Anna drove out to meet us because it was getting dark by then. She snapped a photo that said it all: Pigg, a young puppy bristling with enthusiasm and myself, a 35- year-old weary dog with his tail between his legs."

Listening to Dave tell his tale, remembering what his M.O. used to be, flashing on my own social interactions in the triathlon peloton, I couldn't help but think that we are a subculture that has more than a common interest in three sports, more than a commitment to improving ourselves and our lives. We are somehow committed to each other's interests, each other's successes, because right, wrong or indifferent, our success in this sport is intimately tied to theirs. Sure, you have to be incredibly self-centered for a certain period to win the big races. But those victories are short-lived and hollow unless you can share them with others who have helped you along the way and to whom you will return the gesture. You know, reaping what you sow, blah, blah, blah. "What goes around, comes around." And my favorite: "Be careful who you step on on the way up 'cuz you'll meet them on the way down."

Do me a favor, will you? Take your closest friend out for a 137-mile time trial. Work your ass off to drop him or her. Then take your friend out for a nice meal and a few beers. Send the bill to Mike Pigg with my compliments.

RICH CRUSE

ABOVE Whatever good there is inside you, pass it on.

CHAPTER FIFTEEN

"To err is human, but it feels divine." — *Mae West, 1893-1980*

COASTING

ROBERT OLIVER

By early 1988, the sport of triathlon was going at full speed. Race opportunities seemed to spring up constantly. The standardization of distances had been established and corporate sponsorship was at an all-time high. Other than the ongoing quagmire of politics surrounding the development of an international federation, the sport could do no wrong. Sort of.

As thousands shared the dream, many were realistic in their expectations, spent the time to understand the sport, and more or less, took a long-term view of their involvement. Whether they were elite athletes, race directors, promoters, manufacturers, media types or politicos, the majority of those who became "involved" with the sport on a serious plane, did so with integrity. But there were others, race promoters mostly, who figured they could capitalize on the sport's explosive growth, make a fast buck off of entry fees or sponsorship and move on. It is impossible to note how many unpaid bills were rung up, but as an historical note, I can remember being on a bike ride with Molina and Dave Scott one day, and bored by the regular topics,

COASTING

we added up the amount we had collectively been 'stiffed' by various entities. It was a sad, embarrassing and morbid laugh at the time — all to the tune of a mid-five figure song.

THE RACES

By the mid- to late-'80s, the 'corner race' that existed without permit, aid or glitz, had been replaced by one significantly more organized, more expensive and higher profile. You could still find and enjoy the smallish events, but market demand, like many things in that period of history, called for a bigger, glitzier, fancier and better-made product. The people and events that fueled the demand could be broken down into three categories: 1) The major regional professional races, such as Vancouver International, Patrick O'Riordan's Bermuda, the U.S. Olympians Las Vegas, Michael Braunstein and Kef Kamai's Orange County Performing Arts, Larry King's Kauai Loves You, Renny Roker's America's Paradise Triathlon on St. Croix, and the Voevodin's World Cup in Surfer's Paradise, Australia. They all offered a well-organized race (Okay, almost all of them), good prize money (Mike Pigg's check was for more than $42,000 at St. Croix in 1988), some form of television coverage, and all of them were good fun to go to. The age-groupers showed up en masse and everyone seemed to enjoy the experience.

But some of the promoters either expected more of a return on their investment, lost money, lost interest or ran into unforeseen hurdles at every turn. Of all these events, only St. Croix is still around,

DAVID EPPERSON

PREVIOUS PAGE Sian Welch has had a gradual rise to the top of the sport. Each year she improves, without fail.
ABOVE "Geez, do you think they brought enough stuff? What is this, a Malibu picnic?"

and has been with a different owner for many years, now a well-run and well-respected event.

Other events existed just below the hype and hoopla, races with more of a focus on age-group competition. Races like Wildflower, Panama City, Bakersfield, San Diego International, Columbia, (Maryland), Memphis in May, the Vineman in Northern California, Buffalo Springs Lake, St. Anthony's, Dave MacGillivary's Bay State, Wilkes-Barre, Escape From Alcatraz and the Chicago Sun-Times Tri' offered some decent opportunities for the pros, as well as a chance for age-groupers to race in a well-established and safe event. Nearly every one of these events still exist in the late 1990s.

2) The second category was the 'series' event. Led by the USTS, a number of events would find themselves grouped into a single theme of sorts, in hopes of sharing marketing and production costs. These existed in the form of the Japan Triathlon Series, the French Triathlon Series, the South American Triathlon Circuit, Steve Tebon's South Florida Triathlon Series, Le Coq Sportif International, the New Zealand Race Series, and a handful of small grouped events in Australia. Interestingly, the Triathlon Professional Tour and the Tri-America Series, both in the U.S., only lasted a few years. Danskin has a quite successful women's-only race series and Coors Light sponsored a nationwide biathlon (duathlon) circuit.

3) The last group of events were the ultra-distance championships, Ironman and Nice. By the late 1980s, the feud between the two was all but over and they seemed to co-exist quite peacefully. The Ironman organization was expanding their

ABOVE Klaus Barth, the famous father who finished fourth at the Ironman.

COASTING

race offering to Japan, New Zealand (and soon Europe), and was still considered the "Big One" in most people's book. The interest in Ironman was so high that a complicated form of qualifying was initiated. For a variety of reasons, people still aspired to Kona as the 'ultimate triathlon.' Even if they were just beginning triathletes with a few short courses under their belt, in the back of their minds, lurking like a faint and dull echo, was the idea that someday, maybe, they too could race in the now legendary Hawaiian Ironman.

• • • • •

riathlete magazine ran a graph in their May 1987 issue, depicting the growth rate over the period between 1982 and '87, they told us that the number of races had gone from 600 to 2000, the number of participants from 100,000 to 1,000,000, and the single largest event (Ironman in 1982) at 850 participants to 3471 at USTS Chicago. Nobody seemed to question these numbers because even though there was really no way to get an accurate count at the time, people within the sport wanted to believe that there were a million people just like them. Besides, it helped sell ads, sponsorships and just about anything else that was remotely triathlon-specific and for sale.

What was for sale now was the Ironman itself. Valerie Silk, tired of the politics, the infighting and the constant battle to please everybody, sought a buyer for the event that she had helped nurture and grow from infancy. She at first entered into a loosely structured agreement to sell to a British

TOP Bill and Julie Leach, ready for a cookie and a nap. BOTTOM LEFT "I do solemnly swear...." MIDDLE BOTTOM Hey Kirsten, can you get me a discount on my phone bill? BOTTOM RIGHT "So, ladies and gentleman, these three guys walk into a bar." Val Silk was pretty classy.

firm, but on further inspection she didn't think they would continue the race in the manner in which she had raised it, and bugged out of the deal. The potential buyers cried foul and the first of what was to be nearly a half dozen lawsuits surrounding the sale of the Ironman ensued. Silk had taken on a 49 percent silent partner, reportedly a Honolulu-based construction firm, to raise money a year or two prior. But when the first deal fell through, it became obvious that the event was in play, and several new parties came forth to take a shot at acquiring one of the premier sporting events in the world.

After the dust had settled, it was David Voth, a former director of promotions for the Anheuser Busch-owned Busch Gardens in central Florida, and one Dr. James Gills, a cataract surgeon from Tarpon Springs, Florida, who acquired Ironman. Gills, a devout Christian and one of the wealthier individuals in Florida, was an exceptional endurance athlete and liked everything about the Ironman. Together they formed the World Triathlon Corporation. Voth would run the Ironman as a minority shareholder, and Gill's business people would represent his interest of the reported $3 million sales tag. Unfortunately, it wasn't a good partnership for very long. There had been some slip-ups in the disclosure of what the Ironman name could and could not be used for, and not only did Silk find herself in the midst of another legal fight, but within 18 months, Voth would be gone and replaced with Gills's accountant, David Yates. Yates had his hands full, what with the failure of a startup, short-course series owned by

ABOVE The indefatigable Jimmy Riccitello, climbing the steps on the ill-fated Bahamas Diamond Triathlon run course. There is nothing quite like racing through the small town of a poor country. Nobody quite knows what to think of you.

COASTING

WTC, and the cancellation of a new Ironman franchise event in Cancun, Mexico. But Yates (who resigned from the WTC in March 1998 to spend time with his family) is a fighter and a thinker, and his background is in numbers. He soon figured out that the secret to Ironman's success was in franchise events and licensing. Within two years, under his helm and with the assistance of VP's Ken Murrah and Lew Friedland (who moved into Yates's job), the corporation was profitable.

THE ATHLETES

Once a haven for 'Jack of all trade' athletes and maverick anarchist competitors, triathlon was now creating its own breed of triple-trained people. Harald Johnson, managing editor for *Triathlon* magazine for many years, understood the athletes better than anyone. In a May 1987 article, he stated: "They shared a love of adventure and competition and they didn't want to sacrifice that as they got older and the available sport venues diminished … they were the kind of guys to take a bet on a dare..... But extraordinary prowess in any one sport was no guarantee of success. Balance in training, personal body wisdom … and extreme powers of determination were paramount."

By 1990, especially in the short distances, The Big Four were losing their stranglehold on the podium. Young guys who had grown up with the sport were beginning to come into their own. Men like Kerry Clausen and Andy Carlson, both national-caliber, age-group swimmers, Bill Braun of Boulder, Colorado, Andrew McMartin of Toronto,

RICHARD GRAHAM

ABOVE The best part about kids' triathlons is that they race with their finisher's T-shirts on.

Nate Llerandi, Clark Cambell of Kansas, Wes Hobson, Rob Mackel, Nick Radkewich, a triplet of Aussies with incredible leg speed — Miles Stewart, Brad Beven and Greg Welch — and cycling speedster from Tucson, Arizona, Jimmy Riccitello, who nearly rode away from the pack at his first pro race in 1985 at the Phoenix USTS race. From across the Atlantic, the sport was hearing of two youngsters in their twenties, one from Britain, the other from South Africa, but also living in England, Spencer Smith and Simon Lessing.

For the women, the Puntous twins, Joy Hanssen and Kirsten Hanssen were still the best all-around athletes. Just below the top was Terry Schneider from Santa Cruz, California, Julieanne White from Vista, California, a name that would soon find its way all the way to the top, and Karen Smyers, Katie Webb, Sue Latshaw, France's Isabelle and Beatrice Mouthon and Gail Laurence. But similar to the men, young women who were in their early 20s appeared on the scene and they had already amassed seven or eight years of competitive experience. The two that typify that statement best are the pair of Aussie women, Emma Carney and Michellie Jones. Both women would go on to be considered the best in the world at some time or another.

As far as the mainstream, middle-of-the-packer, again I defer to Harald Johnson. "The average athlete today is less likely to be the maverick of the past, but chances are that he is likely to think of himself as one ... he takes certain pleasure in the fact that certain friends call him 'crazy' for doing triathlons. He's successful in his life and career, but that's not enough anymore; he needs new challenges, wants to find out what he can really do. If he's had to forget fantasies of becoming a professional athlete at least he can be a star in his own age group. And while those broad classifications speak for half the sport's population — men in their mid-20s to mid-40s — their wives, girlfriends, parents and children joined the club. The sport has become a wholesome family affair that can grant a lifetime of fitness."

NOTABLE EVENTS

Not long after the Ironman was acquired by Gills and Voth, they sought to extend the "Ironman Family" of events worldwide. What better way than to group the seven or eight events around the world into an Ironman World Series? On the line was close to $75,000 to the men and women who had the best combined score in up to four events. What this did was put the opportunity out there for a number of long-distance specialists to race four or more Ironman events in one year, hoping to grab the $20,000 first place prize. What it did was shorten a few careers in the process. Pauli Kiuru, Ray Browning, Ken Glah and myself fought it out all year long. Throw in the Nice triathlon and another six-plus hour event in Europe and a few half-Ironman events, and it made for the hardest season of racing in my career.

1990 was also the first year of the ITU Olympic Distance World Championship to be held in America. Florida's Disney World was the spot and the team of race promoters Jim Curl and Carl

COASTING

Thomas, coupled with technical race director Dave MacGillivary, was about the best you could get. Unfortunately, controversy surrounded the race and tainted what could have been a wonderful event. Apparently the Disney folks disallowed much of the sponsorship bannering, claiming conflict with their own corporate supporters. Rumors about the existance of the prize money were reportedly in question. Was the money going to be there? On top of that, a pack formed on the bike and officials were helpless to break it up without disqualifying the entire men's pro field. Greg Welch won for the men and Karen Smyers beat out all the other females. Nevertheless, an "Official ITU World Championship" had been staged and the peripheral benefits, hard as they would be to measure, existed.

. . . . .

1990 saw the first Zofingen Duathlon. There was no prize money at the time, but Kenny Souza went over and helped promote the event for race organizer Urs Linsi. It was the only time he would be able to win what would become the largest run/bike/run event in the world. For the next several years, triathletes, drawn by a large purse, Swiss hospitality and a scenic and challenging course, would win the event. Among the athletes were Mark Allen, Scott Molina and Jürgen Zäck. More importantly, however, Europe was coming into its own with big events, international media and world-class athletes. Every time the results came back to America from a major European event, a new name appeared at the top. From here on,

DAVID EPPERSON

ABOVE The start of the Ironman is one of the most spectacular sights in all of sport. It is something indeed.

triathlon was not simply an American sport. It belonged to everybody and each culture would put their own stamp on it.

. . . . .

The ability for people to learn more about the sport was pervasive. Along with *Triathlete* magazine and *Triathlon Today* (which became *Inside Triathlon* in 1993) there were clinics, camps, coaches, videos, books and a complete infrastructure of 'word-of-mouth' details chronicling the latest race results, vitamin supplement or bike sponsor. This, of course, made it much easier for newcomers to avoid the pitfalls the previous group had fallen into, victims of their own inexperience and naiveté. Guys would show up on one of the group training rides in San Diego, sit in for a couple of weeks until they had the rotation and players wired, and then just start to fly. Some lasted and made it as professionals for awhile, and others fizzled with injuries, burnout and lack of sponsorship. Still, even though certain regions became a variable 'revolving door' of athletic talent, it was an exciting time to be a triathlete.

Soon enough, the fact that all your friends were from different countries didn't matter. Sometimes you felt that you needed a Berlitz language dictionary to carry on a conversation. But there was solace in the fact that you had a floor to sleep on in most of the developed countries. Each country brought its own culture and sense of nationalistic pride. Japan produced some incredible runners who could run through the field, picking up dozens of places in the last 5km. France had more than 500 registered triathlon clubs, modeled after the centuries-old cycling team/village-based system. Germany brought along a sense of committed, science-based training programs that were fueled by a talent pool a mile deep. Australia and New Zealand adapted easily — the triathlon was a simple extension of an aquatic-based lifestyle. Britain, long considered a bastion of reserved, traditional and conservative forms of athletics, was suddenly catapulted into the triathlon limelight when Spencer Smith won the 1993 world championship in Manchester, England, beating South African-turned-Brit Simon Lessing. South America joined the fray with the top-notch triathlons in Santos, Brazil and Pucon, Chile. Athletes such as Cristian Bustos from Chile, Oscar Galindez from Venezuela and Fernanda Keller and Leandro Macedo from Brazil became big names in their respective countries not only from their top results in their region, but on the international circuit as well. Bustos and Keller had both garnered top-three finishes at the Hawaii Ironman, a huge boost to their countries' triathlon programs.

DOWNTURN

The honeymoon had to end at some point though, and as much momentum as the sport had in America, 1991 began a four-year period of diminished growth on the domestic front. In 1992, Anheuser Busch decided against renewing its title sponsorship of the United States Triathlon Series. The series had one year left on its contract and Jim

HARALD JOHNSON

BETTY JENEWIN

Curl, much to his credit, pieced together an abbreviated version of the once mighty series. But, for all intents and purposes, it was merely a better option than to pay back Bud Light the money it had already allocated. CAT Sports president Carl Thomas, the co-producer of the series, resigned his position in December 1992 and shortly thereafter, series administrator Flo Bryan quit and followed Thomas to the Association of Volleyball Professionals. The prize money had all but been eliminated, and there was the nagging issue of the $100,000 Coke Grand Prix Bonus Pool that the athletes still hadn't been paid from the previous year. (They eventually settled for a reported 65 cents on the dollar after CAT Sports sold its interest in The Quarterback Challenge.) In any case, by the end of 1993, USTS was dead and there was a gaping hole on the domestic race scene.

Nineteen ninety-three also brought with it some backlash from years of excessive corporate spending. The Reagan years had given us a glimpse of supply-side economics, and when recession hit, promotional budgets were the first to go. During a recessionary economy, each promotional dollar had to show return on its investment. Even though the demographics of the sport looked good, the numbers were not always big and the spectator appeal was zippo. Triathlon was catching fire around the world but in America, it appeared flat.

Some will argue that the sport never really had a 'bad spot' in the early 1990s, and they are, for the most part, correct. After all, the Ironman, under its new owner, was healthier than ever, and major regional races like Chicago, Panama City,

TOP This poor soul couldn't bring himself to drink his sponsor's stuff. How good could it be with a name like Ultracrud? **BOTTOM** Okay, who slipped me the decaf?

ABOVE Dick and Ricky Hoyt, a heartwarming story, even if you've heard it before.

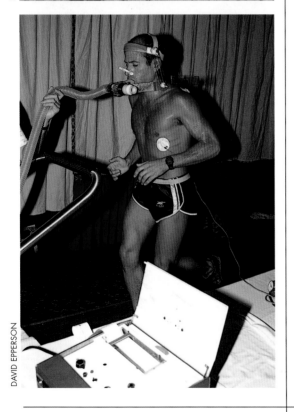

COASTING

Wildflower, and Wilkes-Barre were at all-time highs with entrants. There were still lots of interested sponsors, small start-up companies with triathlon as their key market continued gaining strength, and mainstream interest had never been as good. But insiders who had experienced the meteoric rise of the 1980s had developed an unrealistic notion that growth would continue unabated.

As a testimony to the sport's resiliency, all references to a 'maturation process' aside, triathlon began to gain some of its lost foothold, if only in the minds of the eternal optimists, within 24 months. Interestingly enough, it was the little things. President Clinton wore a Timex Ironman watch. Thomas Magnum, from the Magnum, PI TV show would compete in a triathlon in an episode Paula Newby-Fraser would appear on the Late Night with Conan O'Brien show. Felix Magowan's Inside Communications, publisher of *VeloNews*, would acquire *Triathlon Today*, rename it *Inside Triathlon*, hire *Triathlete* magazine founder Bill Katovsky to run it and force the "other" magazine to keep on its toes. (*Inside Triathlon* was timely, well-edited and backed by a solid professional operation — something that *Triathlete* had let slip.) Dave Scott would come back to do the Ironman at age 40 and darn near win the thing. Simon Lessing would win the inaugural Goodwill Games triathlon in 1994 over Russian Dimitri Gaag in one of the first "draft-legal" races. Mark Allen would beat Frenchman Yves Cordier in a dramatic come-from-behind race at Nice that television was only too happy to milk. Scott Molina would initiate a stellar comeback, where he was the first American

pro finisher at U.S. Pro Championships in Cleveland, Ohio. Steve Locke would take over the helm of Tri-Fed, as a departing Mark Sisson left to explore entrepreneurial interests. Little things that, when grouped together, became bigger things; bigger things with fresh ideas, new blood, enthusiasm.

THE AMERICAN TRIATHLON FEDERATION

Ever since two national federations for the sport emerged simultaneously in 1982, Tri-Fed, which was previously called USTA (United States Triathlon Association) had been mired in conflict. The problem from the beginning was that with only a handful of people willing to volunteer their time to launch something as complicated and ripe for controversy as a national governing body, there were bound to be claims of conflict of interest. In 1982, very few people could make a living off the sport. But a lot wanted to. How many times does a new and charismatic sport come along that is simply a blank page when it comes to the business side? In 1982, there were no pros, very few races, even fewer sponsors, and one paid race director, Jim Curl, from the USTS, who would be able to keep what was left after what he said was "about ten grand to put on five races on the West Coast."

Within a few short years, there were enough people in triathlons to allow an injection of new blood. But the inherent conflict of interest situation spread nationally and resentment toward (what was referred to by some as) the "California Mafia" was high. It was, of course, promulgated at both triathlon-based magazines that showcased

TOP The Big Guy, before he was harpooned by an enemy poison dart. Look for him to rise from the ashes someday at a theater or drive-in near you. BOTTOM Once there was monetary value at stake, the doctors got involved and gradually reduced the guesswork for training.

RICHARD GRAHAM

DAVID EPPERSON

San Diego athletes. USTS and nearly all of the sport's top athletes seemed to be residing in San Diego now.

By 1983, the name was officially changed to The United States Triathlon Federation, and two locals from San Diego ran the organization. Conrad Will was president, and Dennis White, a transplanted East Coaster who had purchased *Running and Triathlon News* from Ed Oleata, the original owner, would serve as executive director. A year later, Verne Scott, Dave's father, took the helm with Carl Thomas (who together with Jim Curl purchased the USTS from Speedo America when it re-organized its U.S. operations), calling the shots from the president's seat. Let's add a few more players so nobody gets their feelings hurt. A steering committee of sorts was formed with people representing many parts of the country. Al James, a race director from Florida, was involved, and John Noll, a bank president and attorney from Illinois, served as president for awhile. Paul Porter, an Indiana insurance specialist, Steve Hegge, a Colorado businessmen/race director, and California's Sally Edwards rounded out the advisory group. Almost all of these people had a real interest in the sport. The fact that some of them enjoyed a simultaneous business-oriented motivation is simply a fact of the small numbers at the time. No one wore more conflicting hats than Carl Thomas, but then again, no one had more to do with the development of Tri-Fed than he. Thomas took a lot of heat for this and maybe he benefited from his ventures, but then maybe he lost money and valuable family time while engrossing himself in the development of a sport that he truly loved.

RUSSELL MOORE

C.J. OLIVARES

TOP Standing with gun swimmers, Tony Robertson, Roch Frey and Rob Mackle. BOTTOM This is the team that the U.S. sent to Avignon for the first ITU world championship in 1989. It included (top left to right) Sue Latshaw, kind of a forgotten hero of sorts, Jan Ripple, mother of two, Laurie Samuelsen, Lisa Lahti, Joy Hanssen, Karen Smyers, and (bottom left to right), Brooks Clark, Ken Glah, Mark Allen, Mike Pigg, Jeff Devlin and Garrett McCarthy.

COASTING

· · · · ·

Mark Sisson took over the executive director's spot of Tri-Fed in 1989 and almost immediately started his quest to add integrity to the organization. Several race directors from around the country took issue with the federation, claiming that the goals were vague and the touted benefits intangible. At the center of this was the insurance and race sanctioning programs. Within a year, Sisson had earned the respect of many by hashing out what had come to be an almost impossible task — making everybody happy. Of course, even Sisson's detente could not last forever. Eventually, a growing sect tired of his "fence sitting" and he left to pursue success in the more black and white arena of private business.

Governing bodies of this sort, whether sports-related or not, are at best a vehicle to promote their ideals and act as clearinghouse for related information, and at worst are a self-serving, bureaucratic, quagmire. Tri-Fed has never fallen into the latter category. It has had its share of troubles — more, in fact, than you would want to know. But for the most part, the people who developed the federation did so because they wanted to see triathlon succeed in a world that tends to shun "new" sports.

THE ITU AND THE OLYMPIC GAMES

To understand the ITU, one needs to have a basic understanding of how and why governing bodies of Olympic sports function. The operative

word in that statement is "Olympic." Governing bodies of sports other than those on the Olympic program have many similarities, but they also have several distinct and noteworthy differences — most having to do with money.

Sports have many humanistic and heroic elements that help make them what they are. The organizations that help to govern them struggle in this department. Don't get me wrong; many organizations are filled with individuals committed to furthering the goals of its constituency, often on a volunteer basis. But for every good, selfless man or woman working for the benefit of the group, there seems to be one who has ulterior

motives, greed for the power associated within and at a minimum, lack of any understanding on how the group can succeed.

Back in 1982, Carl Thomas, who was instrumental in founding the United States Triathlon Association (which became Tri-Fed), began planting the early seeds for an international organization. Thomas understood the long-term importance of a strong world governing body, especially if triathlon was ever to be an Olympic event. Together with Robert Helmick, head of the U.S. Olympic Committee (who would later step down from the post under questionable circumstances), Thomas developed a constitution for an IGB using other Olympic events as examples. At the Ironman in Kona in 1984, 11 countries were represented in what was the first attempt at organization. At approximately the same time, several countries in Europe formed the European Triathlon Union (ETU), electing Con O'Callahan from Ireland as president and Joop van Zanten of Holland as treasurer. The newly formed ETU also believed that a central international body would be good for the sport, but according to a piece at that time in *Triathlete* magazine, were suspect of Thomas, the Americans, and everything else that seemed to stem from Southern California's triathlon community.

Thomas went to the General Assembly of International Sports Federations (GAISF) meeting on several occasions, trying to enlist support for the fledgling Federation Internationale Triathlon (FIT). The Europeans were still slow to support the organization and considered forming their own

ABOVE Pat Griskus, a friend of mine from the East Coast — He only had one leg, and he was a great athlete and a super guy. He was killed by a cement truck five days before the Ironman while training on the Queen K Highway.

ABOVE By the late 1980s, triathlon was considered a serious endurance sport, but still fun to compete in.

ABOVE By 1990, the guys were running fast.

COASTING

IGB on several occasions. Finally, at a 1987 race director's conference in Dallas, with 26 countries represented, the ETU's O'Callahan and van Zanten, along with a Thomas-led American contingency, agreed to a somewhat mutual scenario and decided to try and iron out the differences. The name was changed to Triathlon Federation Internationale (TFI) and it was decided that the group would meet later that year in Amsterdam. Forty-five days before that meeting, the Americans were given an agenda. Sensing that the meeting was stacked against them, the Americans sent only Dave Curnow, a Tri-Fed board member and a San Diego attorney, to the meeting. As suspected, Curnow was outgunned from all sides at the meeting and returned after having been pressured into provisionally joining TFI. Thomas said at the time, "It was a mistake to send anyone because there just wasn't enough time to prepare and too much was at stake." The issues at the time were voting rights, dues, executives and world championships.

The next meeting was to be held around the scheduled 1988 world championship in Canada. The Americans chose not to send anyone (because of the political differences with the European group), but instead sent a memo identifying their four areas of concern before joining the association. Current ITU president Les McDonald is quoted in a June 1988 article on the situation. "I was asked by Jon Noll (president of the old Tri-Fed) to take on the roll of intermediary between the Europeans and the Americans, but I soon found out that the Europeans ... wouldn't play the game. Phil Briars (of New Zealand) and I

RUSSELL MOORE

hammered out a solution to the 14 points (of difference), but they refused to compromise. The obvious gap between their way of thinking and ours soon became insurmountable in Vancouver."

The International Olympic Committee had begun to take an interest in the proceedings and thought that maybe this small group of endurance athletes might be of some use. As an interesting side note, McDonald tells a story of Juan Antonio Samaranch, president of the IOC, sitting in his hotel room at the 1984 Los Angeles Olympics and seeing one of the USTS triathlons on TV.

Samaranch was intrigued and asked one of his aids: "What is that sport there? Go find out more

about it." In any event, McDonald began to take on more of a role in the unfolding story of triathlon's first IGB. He attended a meeting in Stockholm that is connected to the IOC and discovers that the IGB for modern pentathlon (an Olympic event that has been in declining popularity for several years and apparently not one of Samaranch's favorites) has eyes on the sport of triathlon. The motive, it is thought, is that if their organization, the Union Internationale Modern Pentathlon and Biathlon (UIPMB), can latch onto the young, vibrant enthusiasm of triathlon by taking them under their wing, it would help insure their own survival in the Olympics amid talk of cutting events from the program. McDonald, who has worked as a labor union leader for a large part of his life and has experience with the inner workings of sports governing bodies via his involvement with the Canadian Ski Federation, sees the potential for disaster in this scenario. The modern pentathlon group is ripe with conservative, Eastern Bloc bureaucrats who would squash the sport as we know it.

The pivotal meeting would be just before the first, fully sanctioned world championship in Avignon, France in April 1989. What happened next is a story of great interest and note. It seems McDonald knew that TFI was headed right into the hands of the UIPMB, so he changed the time of the Constitution meeting without telling every country, and in the end, had formed a new "alliance" of 15 participating countries, the only one from Eastern Europe being Estonia. (It is interesting to note that the breakup the Soviet Union was helpful in expediting the current International Triathlon Union.)

ABOVE Todd Jacobs, the El Paso Hulkster.

COASTING

program. While he has woven the sport through the intricacies of international sports politics through his cautious and calculating maneuvers, he still lacks the sport-wide support to be truly effective in an incredibly complicated and convoluted arena. Much to McDonald's credit though, not only did he keep the ITU autonomous and out of the quagmire of UIPMB politics, but he single-handedly spearheaded triathlon's quest into the Olympic Games. While there are those who would question whether the ends justify the means, as of this writing, triathlon has not made its Olympic debut and therefore it would be a bit premature to heap criticism until after the verdict is in. Time will tell how this scenario plays out.

The ETU has since become an excellent example of governance, promoting the sport on many fronts. Les McDonald has been the president of the ITU since he was elected at the second ITU Congress in 1989 by a majority of the 15 member countries (there are now 128). McDonald came into this position when he was asked by Samaranch to meet with the UIPMB folks regarding triathlon's potential inclusion into the "Olympic Family." He originally was the chairman of a group of five people who endeavored to produce a working constitution for an international triathlon organization that might be able to piggy-back on the UIPMB as a shortcut to the Olympic

ABOVE The Shell Answer Man, Ray Browning, can't believe anybody would ask him why he left the party early. Lots of training and clinic opportunities popped up.

CHAPTER SIXTEEN

"Man is most nearly himself when he achieves the seriousness of a child at play." — *Heraclitus, c.540-480 B.C.*

OUTTAKES

MIKE PLANT

NATIONAL MEDIA EXPOSURE

I n some ways, the sport of triathlon is full of itself, overly self-absorbed. Blame it on confidence gained through attainment of things considered too difficult for others. I don't know. Justification came in the form of mainstream exposure beyond what the sport-specific magazines published. When triathlon was mentioned in *TV Guide* or the *Wall Street Journal,* it seemed that the duty of its participants was eased. You just got tired of having to say things like, "Well, first you swim...."

As far as I can tell, the first article written about triathlon in "mainstream" journalism was a one-page piece in the April 1979 issue of *Runner's World*. It was entitled "Only the Toughest of the Tough Bother to Apply," and was a race report/history of the 1979 Ironman by a masters runner named Mike Tymn, from Hawaii. It pre-dated McDermott's *Sports Illustrated* article by only six weeks. The first "technically based" piece appeared in the October 1981 issue of *Physician and Sports Medicine* by one Maria Taylor.

Much of the early support for triathlon, in fact, came from the running and scientific communities. Cycling largely ignored the sport for many years, until they discovered the potential new athletes were, as one editor put it, "awkward and inexperienced riders with a credit card and thirst to buy their way onto the winner's podium." Swimming, other than Harald Johnson's *Swim, Swim,* was still largely pool- and age-group oriented. Triathletes were interesting 'sidebars' that filled a small editorial and reader interest. But the running community threw caution to the wind and covered the sport like it was here to stay. Writer Al Gross wrote an excellent 10-page spread for the May 1982 issue of *Running Times,* in which he explored almost every angle of the sport, including "talk of an Olympic Triathlon soon."

The television side wasn't as clear cut. *Time* and *Newsweek* may have only included triathlon in their "lifestyle" sections; unable to put a label or pigeonhole the new sport, they simply reported it as an interesting sporting sidenote without passing judgment on the mindset or motivation of the athlete. But television, in some ways, struggled badly to find a way to bring the sport to living rooms around the world. At best the sport is difficult to cover from a logistic point of view. You just can't place one camera in the transition area and cover the event.

Viewers have become spoiled by multiple camera angles, instant replay, competitor background interviews, the whole shabang. ABC Wide World of Sports at first tried to cover the sport as a race, but found that watching one guy ride his bike along the side of the road for five hours was interesting for about two minutes. They then went to the "freak show" approach, portraying

RICHARD GRAHAM

PREVIOUS PAGE This bike course is surrounded by yuppie condos now. **ABOVE** The start of some biathlon, excuse me duathlon, somewhere. Kenny Souza, #1, protecting his boys.

the athletes as masochists. Finally, with the advent of motorcycle cameras, human interest stories, a budget to reflect the size and stature of the event and 10 years of trial and error, the network coverage of not only the Ironman, but events such as Escape From Alcatraz and Nice, have developed a sellable balance that incorporates just enough of each group that is attracted to the sport (if not the television show) to keep most people happy.

As an interesting side note, the legalization of drafting at ITU World Cup events was, at one point, put off to "television's request" for a more exciting and "visual" format. Now I don't doubt that when a winner is DQd for drafting after they cross the finish line, it looks pathetic on the box, nor do I doubt that there are high-ranking individuals at the networks and in cable access production companies that favor a pro-drafting format. But in my research, I could not find *one* person in a decision-making capacity at a major television network that cared one way or another about drafting. As long as they had "access" to the race and it all unfolded during the event, they seemed satisfied.

Without a doubt, drafting-legal events can be exciting. But if the very nature of the sport is altered for the sake of promotion or publicity ... well, you have to ask yourself if we've gone too far.

PRETENDERS TO THE THRONE

The true history of triathlon may continue to take the track that I have laid out in this book; the road that began with Don Shanahan and Jack Johnstone and Dave Pain of San Diego. I believe it the best history, though not the *only* one. Hopefully the evidence presented, corroborated by many, will establish a "family tree" of sorts for future generations to feel a part of, should they feel so motivated. I am sure, however, that some will take exception to this line of thinking, this lineage dating back to a swim/bike/run triathlon in 1974, a triathlon that *directly* links Commander John Collins of Ironman fame to the second installation of said event in San Diego's Mission Bay. I stand behind this chain of events though. The dates and distances may be off by a day or a week or a mile, but if it is starting point of the sport that you are looking for, I believe this is it.

That said, I will attempt to place similar multisport events into some historical context as they relate to Fiesta Island in the early 1970s:

Eppie's Great Race: In Northern California, in and around the capital city of Sacramento, exists the small chain of 24 hour, Denny's-ish diners called Eppies. It is owned by 69-year-old Eppie Johnson, a tall, muscular, bear of a man some would call crusty. Back in 1974, Eppie and friends had discussed the idea of staging an event consisting of a kayak/bike/cross-country ski. Eppie would end up steering the proposed event away from the proposed Lake Tahoe region back to Sacramento, and include the simplicity of running. His chain of restaurants had grown to five by then and he offered to sponsor the race in return for the title.

The first event was staged in and around the American River and the adjacent bike path in July 1974, a full two months prior to San Diego Track Club's inaugural Mission Bay Triathlon. The event,

RICHARD GRAHAM

RICHARD GRAHAM

TOP Joel Thomson at the Desert Princess Duathlon. He was a very good athlete and one day just decided to be a doctor. We said "Yeah, right." Seven-and-a-half years later he has an M.D. behind his name and we are still riding that little groove up and down PCH. BOTTOM Rare is the race when you can look all around and not see another competitor.

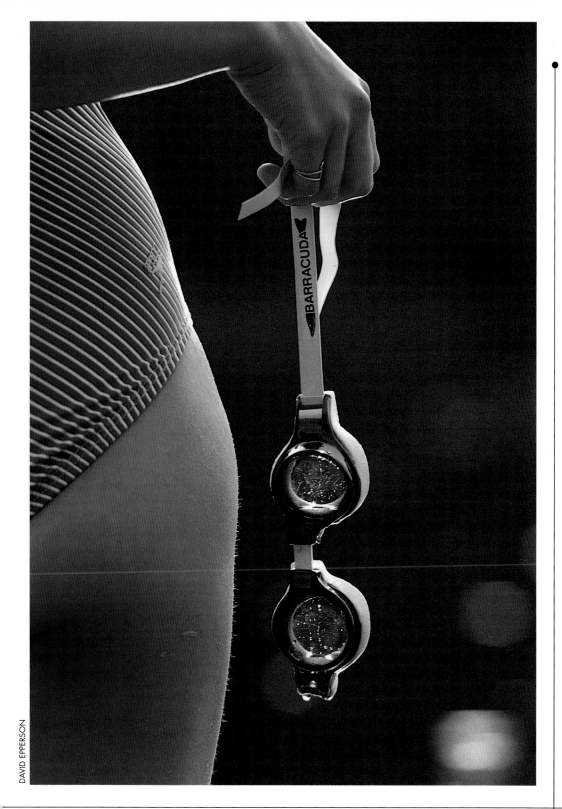

ABOVE Who says athleticism cannot be artistic?

which would come to be called The Great Race, began with a flat, 6-mile run, followed by a 12-mile bike ride and a downstream, 6.3-mile paddle. In 1974, there were 52 teams and no individuals. The following year, one person, a guy named Pax Beale, competed in the event all by himself when his teammates failed to show up. Interestingly enough, Beale warned Johnson after the race that in the future, more and more people would want to compete as individuals and he should give serious thought to how he wanted to see the race grow. In the beginning, people paddled anything that floated. But it became apparent that certain boats were faster than others and the race favored a strong paddler. Local athlete Mike Gammon, from the nearby town of Carmichael, said this: "Eppie's is sort of like a triathlon, but not really. If you can't paddle well, you get beat bad. If you want to do well here, you have to learn to paddle a downriver boat at a high rate of speed."

As the Great Race grew from 50-some teams to 800 overall competitors in 1980, the number of individuals grew to 25 percent of the field. Eppie had turned over the helm to race director Shirley Wiltwaganer. "We had to create 22 different categories of boats to keep it fair," Shirley remembers, "but the number of individuals continued to grow. I think they get about 2000 people now, almost half of them individuals." At that time, it was obvious that The Great Race (which in 1984 registered the title "oldest running triathlon in the country") was being propelled by the growing interest in triathlon. Eppie Johnson realized this and knew he would have to put a lid on the event. When I asked him to recall the growth in the early years, he simply replied, "It was my race, I'll let as many damn people as I want in." I admire that. Johnson went out on a limb, spending his own money putting on a race that is 25 years old in

1998. Is it the first triathlon ever staged? Well, is a triathlon only swimming, cycling and running? The dictionary says so now; it didn't back in 1974. What Eppie and his Great Race did was provide an opportuni ty for multisport athletes to experience all that any event has to offer. So what if you go downstream in a boat instead of on your tummy?

• • • • •

In 1986, John Du Pont, of the Du Pont chemical dynasty, and the great-great-grandson of Eleuthere Irenee Du Pont, who established the gunpowder mills in Delaware that eventually developed into the globally powerful corporation, entered the triathlon scene. He lived on the family estate, an 800-acre place outside Newtown Square, Pennsylvania, called Foxcatcher Farms. Du Pont had tried out for the 1968 Olympic modern pentathlon (a para-militaryish event consisting of horseback riding, fencing, shooting, swimming and running that receives little attention outside the Olympic Games) team. And while he failed to make the team, he went on to support it in other ways, including the facilitation of their training at his farm. Since modern pentathlon included two of triathlon's three events, Du Pont and other pentathletes were naturally attracted to it.

In a March 1986 article in *Triathlete* magazine, Du Pont was quoted as the winner of the first 'triathlon' held in the United States. "We held our first triathlon in 1966," says Du Pont in the article. "At one time there were six of us....We first swam 3000 meters, then we ran 4000 meters

and that was followed by 20 rounds of pistol shooting. I won the competition."

The article continues: "The triathlon event grew more popular during the next few years. There would be up to 200 people competing … the thinking back then was: As long as John wants to do it on his estate, its fine — let him do it."

The question continues. Does a non-swim/bike/run event constitute a "true" triathlon, at least, as we know it now? Does it matter? (As a matter of note, John Du Pont was convicted of murder in 1997 for the death of Olympic wrestler Dave Schultz on Foxcatcher Farms in January of 1996.)

• • • • •

On other fronts, Ironman winner Tom Warren remembers competing in what was billed as the Clear Lake Challenge back in 1974, as does Andy O'Leary, who actually predates Warren's involvement by one year, when he placed third in 1973. The Clear Lake Challenge was a 7-mile run, a 3-mile swim, a scramble to the top of 2000 foot Mt. Konocti, and a 3- mile return swim. The 'official' results from the 1973 event show Peter Toennies of Coronado winning in a time of 4 hours and 27 minutes. What ties this early run/swim/run/swim event to San Diego's Mission Bay is Toennies, O'Leary and Warren. They had all driven hundreds of miles to compete in a multisport event. They also came back and told all their San Diego Track Club friends about it.

We also have an interesting story by writer Len Wallach, from the June 1984 issue of *Triathlete* mag-

DAVID EPPERSON

ABOVE Dave, Dave ... first it was the lead vehicle situation and now this. Crossing the yellow line to cut the tangents. Ironman 1986.

azine, in which Wallach claims to have participated in triathlons while growing up in Honolulu. Wallach writes, "Local park and recreation directors were always putting together "Saturday Specials" for the playground regulars, and it was natural that someone would come up with a swim/bike/run combination as part of a single package." He continues the story: "It wasn't a sophisticated event, nor was it bound by a traditional sequence. The usual order proceeded thus: The contestants bicycled down the boulevard, got off their bikes and ran along the sand back to the starting point. Then they swam to complete the event." Wallach doesn't include places, dates or distances. It may be a bit too low key, even by triathlon's early standards, to warrant any substantial mark in the history of the sport. It does warrant further investigation though, if only for interest's sake.

In some ways you could say that other multi-sport events, spearheaded by the sport of duathlon, were in competition with triathlon. Believe it or not, there was a time when people weren't sure of the sport's future, not sure that there would be a race to compete in next year, let alone next month. "Maybe it's just a fad," they'd say. "Maybe it'll go the way of frisbee golf or lawn darts."

Finally, there is always France's Charles Secter and his September 1921 event in Marseilles. Remember?

FORGOTTEN HEROES

Triathlon, in its short history, has had any number of people who have logged heroic efforts. And though the competitors have garnered the

TOP "There it is again. A big black fin." Pre-race psyche-job. BOTTOM Kim Bushong: Pound for pound, the world's greatest eater.

ROGER LEE

ABOVE Anne Dandoy and Sally Edwards. Two different styles, two classy and talented athletes.

lion's share of the known stories, there remain many untold tales of average racers, supportive families, physically challenged competitors, and men and women in the associated business whose efforts shall long be forgotten. In a sort of tribute to all those, and in no particular order, here are a few forgotten heroes of triathlon's first 20 years:

Tom Price

A little known competitor from Canada who stopped while leading one of the early Canadian Ironman events to help a fallen comrade.

Dr. Bob Laird

The only medical director the Ironman in Kona has ever known. He has invested countless hours into supporting those competitors whose grasp has exceeded their reach — and that is a big number. Laird is a pediatrician by trade, but knows more about sports medicine that most who specialize in the field. The Ironman would not be the same without people like Dr. Bob.

Other health practitioners would also become a big part of an inner working circle of support that the athletes depended on. Dr. P.Z. Pearce from Liberty Lake, Washington; Dr. Paul Copesky, D.C., from San Diego; and even massage therapists like Dave Richardson and Michael Rubano, had names within the sport.

Brad Kearns

Kearnsy was the first multisport athlete to use the new aerodynamic handlebars from Boone Lennon. It was at the 1987 Desert Princess Duathlon and Brad

OUTTAKES

was all too happy to share the outstanding results with his fellow competitors. Some guys would have hidden them from the others.

Linda Sweeney Hunt

As an overall female winner of the Ironman Triathlon, you'd think that Linda Sweeney Hunt's name would carry some distance. Not true, though. If any person has come on to the triathlon scene, made a statement, and moved on without fanfare, it is Hunt. Okay, so there were only 320-something people entered back in 1981; it is still the Ironman and the course has changed oh-so-slightly. If anything, her performance is even more awe-inspiring due to the lack of precedence. Up until 1981, only *three women* had finished Ironman, and that was on a much easier Oahu course. It must have been a bit unnerving, pedaling away from the field with a huge lead, thinking that she had to get off the bike and run a marathon. Sweeney had done a few shorter triathlons back home in San Diego and only went to Kona at the urging of friends. She had grown up as an age-group swimmer, had done a bit of running and cycling for fun and fitness, but the Ironman — that was a different story. After beating pre-race favorite Sally Edwards by well over a half hour, Sweeney was unclear as to her triathlon future. A foot injury kept her out of the rest of the 1981 season — not that there were many races to attend anyway. In 1982 she married national 10,000 meter record holder Thom Hunt and moved to Eugene, Oregon, to facilitate his run training. And that was about it. College, a career, other interests — triathlon was put on the shelf, not to be taken off

DAVID EPPERSON

ABOVE The darkest hour is just before the dawn.

except for the occasional dusting. It did have an effect, though. Sweeney Hunt has continued to be attracted to freelance-type jobs that allow her the flexibility to train, if for no other reason than to stay fit. When people ask her about her athletic past, she is almost hesitant to mention her Ironman victory, afraid that, like times before, they won't believe her. "It was almost like another life," she recalls. " I was right there, and then I moved on to a different life."

William R. Katovsky

William Katovsky, or Bill, is an odd sort. He doesn't look like he 'belongs' to the sport of triathlon. Admittedly, he finds it implausible that a self-confessed, cause-oriented, political science student would end up as a founder of a sports magazine. His story is addressed to some extent at other junctions of this book, but I feel it necessary to note that it was Bill's creative flair and quest for unique looks at the sport that added panache to a sometimes mundane and overly technical sport. He was able to chronicle the subtle nuances that other journalists failed to have an eye for, let alone create the interest in, in a quirky sidebar to triathlon. He sold his majority interest to French publisher Jean Claude Garot nearly a year after starting *Triathlete,* and came back for a short stint with *Inside Triathlon* when his long-time peer, Felix Magowan, launched the publication in 1992. He is still involved in some ways with multisport publications, and enjoys competing in the odd triathlon or adventure race.

George Isom

A race director from Texas, he volunteered to be on several Tri-Fed committees and basically worked his ass off for several years for free. There are lots of George Isoms out there. I don't recall all their names. There was a guy named Fletcher Hanks form Maryland who used to put on what he called

TOP The winningest woman in Ironman history, Paula Newby-Fraser. BOTTOM Mike Pigg and I had to spend a whole day out in the desert doing a photo shoot for Tinley Performance Wear, so we decided to bring along a couple of my dirt bikes. Between shots, we would jump on the bikes and disappear over the sand dunes. Not very professional, but a lot of fun.

the "Equilateral Triathlon," because the swim was almost five miles long. It used to piss him off that the swimmers always got short-changed in the event distance category, so he held his own race with his own distances.

Jim Bates, from Kelowna, B.C., Canada

Just a guy who owned a small running and bike shop who decided to help out with a local triathlon. The next thing he knows, he is knee-deep in several aspects of the sport. He loves it, but it doesn't really justify the time he spends on it. I could go on and on. These men and women are everywhere. Without their efforts, the sport would never have survived, let alone reach a point where it is healthy and prosperous. They are truly forgotten heroes.

Sean and Phil Molina

The "other" Molina brothers who competed and did quite well. Sean actually won the Baltimore USTS one year. He was coached by Marc Evans of Tri-Athletics West, and in some ways, had more talent that his famous older brother. The historical note here is that there are many siblings, friends, training partners and a host of other individuals who may have done something significant. Their contributions, however obscure some 10, 15 or 20 years later, are dually noted and Sean Molina will accept thanks on your behalf.

The CAT Sports crew

The team that worked at CAT Sports in the late 80s was very good. Confident to a fault at times, not only did they manage the nationwide United States

CAROL HOGAN

COURTESY USTS

TOP LEFT John Duke heading out onto the run of the Ironman, wondering if the ABC cameras are pointed at someone else because he has a whole PowerBar stuffed into his mouth. **TOP RIGHT** Ouch, that looks painful. **BOTTOM** It's a dog's life. The new K-9 Oakleys.

HARALD JOHNSON

ABOVE Much to his chagrin, the new race director thought that the competitors could do the three sports in any order they'd like.

OUTTAKES

Triathlon Series, in many ways they artificially "propped up" the sport. It wasn't just Carl Thomas, Jim Curl and Flo Bryan; there was an entire office and field crew doing the work, carrying out the edict and dreams of those "upstairs" to little fanfare of their own. Marsha Smilkensen, Ellen Hawthorne Duvall, Karen Cosgrave, Tim Downs, Mary Jane Shoevers, Perry Levy, Mindy Metzger, Susan Sullivan, William De Belles and Kai Palchakoff were all part of a hard-working team that was instrumental in putting the sport on the map. The series was a huge undertaking, bigger than most people realize, including those who were at the heart of it. In the end, the size and underlying overheads were just too difficult to maintain without sacrificing the quality of the events. The organizers went on to other areas of sports promotion and marketing, successfully applying the skills they had gleaned as part of the CAT Sports crew.

The "small business" of triathlon

If there has always been one area of the sport that is overlooked when historical credits are handed out, it is the "little guy" (or gal) who makes a go at a type of business associated with triathlon. Take Mike Reilly, for instance, who as a sales rep for various manufacturers of sports-related products, has to keep his finger on the pulse of what is hot and what is not. Moonlighting as a race announcer and publisher of a local event guide, his involvement is varied and complex. He is also a "friend" of the sport.

Or consider Steve and Annie Hed

Manufacturers of aerodynamic wheels and miscel-

DAVID EPPERSON

RICHARD GRAHAM

RUSSELL MOORE

TOP San Francisco is arguably the best running city in the country. Joanne Ernst. BOTTOM LEFT This is Jimmy Riccitello when he was 16. BOTTOM RIGHT Trish the Dish, Mission Viejo Triathlon, 1993.

laneous after-market items intended to give us a speed advantage, they built the business out of a spare bedroom and a few hundred bucks that Annie (formerly McDonald) won as a pro triathlete in the late 1980s. Ten years later, they continue to focus primarily on research and development rather than profit. Most of Steve's ideas eventually show up as a competitive product, slightly altered by the copycat manufacturer, but one born out of the Hed's R&D lab in the basement nonetheless.

I could go on and on:

Race directors Rick Kozlowski, a San Diego native; Jeff Sheard of Columbus, Ohio; Jan Caillé, big chief of the Mrs. T's Chicago Triathlon; Dave Horning; Leon Wolek; Michael Epstein of Los Angeles; sports promoters/marketers Dave McGillivary, Scott Zagarino, Graham and Karen Fraser, Steve Tebon, Mike Greer, Robert Vigorito and John Duke; small manufacturers Emilio De Soto of De Soto Sports, Danny Abshire of Active Imprints, Jim Rice of Sole Performance, Dan Mayer of Cycle Technology, Tim Twardzik of Mrs. T's Perogoies ... all have created a variable "cottage industry" closely aligned with the sport, providing goods and services for those of us who are attracted to the lifestyle.

The educators: The coaches, exercise physiologists, camp counselors, keynote speakers, all the people who do the research and spread the word. Folks like Marc Evans from Truckee, Nevada; Roch Frey, coach and husband of 1997 Hawaii Ironman winner Heather Fuhr, from Edmonton, Canada; Dr. Herman Falsetti of Irvine, California; Dr. Jim Stray Gunderson of Dallas, Texas; Jaci VanHeest from the

ABOVE Winter triathlons: A chance to wear those funny stretchpants year-round.

OUTTAKES

Olympic Training Center in Colorado Springs.

May they rest … Kay Rhead, Nick Rott, Kef Kamai, Pat Griskus.

FAMOUS DQS

USTS National Championships at Hilton Head, 1989: Jimmy Riccitello, a veteran pro from Tucson, Arizona and a regular on the USTS circuit, finishes second overall to give him the number two slot in the season-long Coke Grand Prix. His pay-day equals a well-deserved $24,000. Drafting is rampant, however, and many of the top finishers are given a time penalty. Jimmy, one of the few who stayed clear of the cheating (due to his strong anti-draft stance and cycling abilities), is actually given a penalty for going outside the yellow line while trying to avoid another rider. His payday goes from $24,000 to $1000. Eventual winner Louis Murphy, an obscure runner who drops from the sport soon thereafter, says little about the situation during his awards speech. Riccitello is supported by many of the other competitors, who admit to riding outside the line in an attempt to avoid the huge pack, which is witnessed by two draft marshals for a large portion of the race. The situation is made worse when several athletes hear one of the officials say to Jimmy, "Hey Jim, it's only $23,000." It is a low point for all involved.

World's Toughest Triathlon, Lake Tahoe, California, 1987: Jaqueline Shaw is leading the race and fails to stop and put her foot down at one of the only stop signs on the mostly rural 120 mile bike course. She goes on to win but is DQd and loses

ABOVE See your future, be your future. Sooner or later, we all come over to the dirty side. **OPPOSITE PAGE, TOP** Tom Warren had competed in something like 15 Ironmans in a row when, one year, he didn't go. When I asked him why, he just said, "Well, I'm not really sure. The day I was supposed to go, I just felt like doing something else."

the $10,000 first place award.

Ironman Hawaii, 1986: Patricia Puntous wins and crosses the finish line to much emotion and tears. An hour later she is told that she is disqualified by officials for drafting. Paula Newby-Fraser is moved up from second to first. It is a bad situation for everybody involved.

Mission Viejo Triathlon, Orange County, 1993: Jimmy Riccitello again. He's got a 1:10 lead over second-place Greg Welch as he dismounts the bike and begins the run. He is in the best shape of his life and needs the Mazda Miata that goes to the winner. At the two-mile mark he still has 45 seconds over a hard-charging Welch. An official on a motorcycle pulls up to him and disqualifies him on the spot for a helmet chin strap penalty. At the time, there was no three-minute penalty.

Bermuda Triathlon, 1987: A tightly bunched group of pros (at least 20) turn the bike ride into a peloton as the narrow, winding road offers little room to spread out in the one lane provided. Nevertheless, it is mass cheating and DQs are fast and furious at the finish. My off-the-back finish takes me from 27th to 9th (I think) in one fell swoop.

Nice triathlon: Late 1980s, Erin Baker is handed a cup of water from her sister when she has trouble getting fluids on the run course. Many of the other athletes have turned to outside aid to prevent dehydration. Baker is singled out, disqualified and loses the $10,000 first prize.

OTHER MONUMENTAL SCREW-UPS

Wildflower Triathlon, 1994: Someone forgets to put a course marshal at the run turnaround and the top six runners go a half mile

past before realizing their mistake. Race director Terry Davis dips into his own pocket, takes complete responsibility for the snafu and pretty much pays everyone who was at the race.

Horny Toad Triathlon, 1983, San Diego: The lifeguard staff is seriously undermanned, so they have no time to set up a whole swim course for the 1.5-mile swim. One buoy is placed approximately three-quarters of a mile out. I get to the that buoy, look back to shore, and realize we are a long way from land.

Springtime 1988, the Long Beach Convention Center: A press conference for the just-announced World Port International Triathlon in Long Beach, California. The proposed date is October 2, the Mayor of L.A. is there, everybody is psyched. Six weeks later, the whole thing is called off, without explanation.

Chicago Sun Times Triathlon, late 1980s: One of the competitors is set to enter the water of his first triathlon and is dressed in his best cut-off jeans. Trouble is, he hasn't swam since he was a kid. He jumps off the seawall into Lake Michigan and goes right to the bottom. Race organizers pull him out and institute a "swim competency" certificate program for the next year.

Atlanta USTS, 1984: The lake is fogged in until 15 minutes before the scheduled start. When it lifts, Jim Curl looks out over the course and fails to spot the far buoys. He asks the race director how long the course is and she replies, "1500 meters, just like you asked." Jim then asks her if she knows how long a meter is. "Of course," she says, holding her hands approximately 12 inches apart, "just a bit longer than a foot."

BOTTOM In 1978, race promoter Dave McGillivary decided to run across the United States to raise money for charity. He met this guy at a hunting camp outside of Sandpoint, Idaho. He rode next to him for 800 miles, then made a left turn near the Missouri border.

CHAPTER SEVENTEEN

"Man is most nearly himself when he achieves the seriousness of a child at play." — *Heraclitus, c.540-480 B.C.*

CURRENTS

ROBERT OLIVER

The sport of triathlon is different now than it was five, 10 or 25 years ago. It has matured for sure, some will say for the better, others for the worse. In any case, it is different, as it must be. Growth assured of us of that. How could you even conceive of putting 2000 competitors, let alone 200, on a Fiesta Island multirun/multiswim course? Early races may have been unorganized, but for the most part, they were safe enough. The competitors themselves defined the early days; their eccentricities, their courage, their maverick personalities and yes, their odd quirks. The sport is too big now to be defined simply by its clientele. It is a tree that has grown roots and sprouted branches in many directions, each of which has taken on its own personality. Some exist for the unadulterated love of the athletic lifestyle that it portrends. And other arms have sprung out of a profit-motivated greed. Mostly they balance each other out. But even those who seem to have their fingers on the pulse of the sport cannot always tell the good guys from the bad guys. People slip and justify their questionable actions in all sorts of ways. "Hey, I vol-

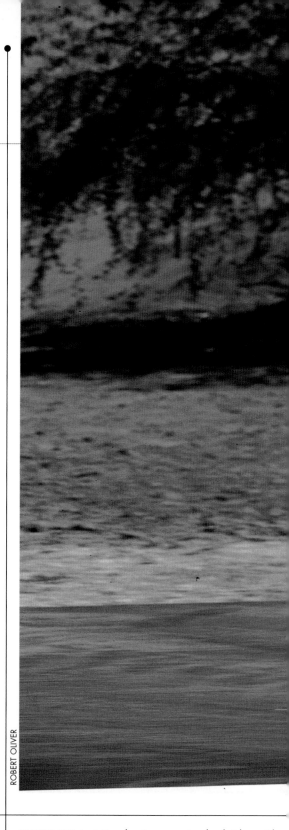

unteered my ass for 10 fucking years," they claim, "this sport owes me!" But does it? Do we not reap what we sow? Are we not lucky that we even had the *opportunity* to be involved in what we love?

The late 1990s is a somewhat tumultuous time in the sport of triathlon. There is conflict at the highest level. The World Triathlon Corporation, keeper of the Ironman flame, filed legal action against the International Triathlon Union over matters pursuant to ITU's claim to the name "world" in conjunction with anything triathlon-related. Something as innocuous as drafting on the bike has become a hotly debated issue. Gaining an advantage over a competitor by riding in their slipstream, has become our sport's Vietnam, abortion and capitol punishment all wrapped up into one. Come on folks, get a life! You know when you're cheating. We used to be able to police ourselves, go up to someone after the race and have words with them.

Right, wrong or indifferent, we are a fragmented group. If Juan Antonio Samaranch and the International Olympic Committee think that the Olympic triathlon that opens the Sydney 2000 Games is truly representative of our sport's rank and file, well then, they have been sold a bill of goods. The Olympic Games allow drafting. Ninety-five percent of the sport's participants worldwide will argue against this because it goes against the nature of our sport, the very conceptual creativity upon which our short history lies. The ITU's treasurer, Mark Sisson, who was instrumental in the pro-drafting format, has been quoted as saying that triathlon allowed drafting in the early days. Except

for a few isolated cases, this is unequivocally false. I competed in dozens of races throughout the 1970s and except for Verne Scott's Davis Triathlon, none of them allowed drafting.

The point is not to belabor an issue that has been argued ad nauseum; if there is one thing that we have failed at while parenting this child sport, it's that we have, in many cases, failed to reach a consensus, to compromise. I am not sure if this is because the sport simply attracts headstrong, iron-willed individuals, or because the turnover rate among those who lay claim to a professional position inside the sport is almost nil. In some ways it's almost a big circle jerk. You go to a meeting, look around, see the same 25 or 30 people that have been involved for 10 or 15 years and think, "Geez, maybe we should try to make the pie bigger instead of continuing to steal each others pieces."

The lack of cohesion and commonality, however ironic, do not necessarily detract from the sport. If anything, it gives the athlete choices that may not have existed without the current of dissension. A competitor can vote for a particular style of race with his or her attendance. A corporate sponsor can, with a bit of research, determine which athlete will represent the product with integrity and which one is a fabrication of a creative sports agent's hype. The weekend warriors who are the heart and soul of our sport are not dumb. They know which events are safe, well-run and fairly priced. They watch the other athletes, read the magazines, read between the lines — they may not like all the political jockeying that goes on, but if it ultimately means a better product

ROBERT OLIVER

PREVIOUS PAGE Lori Bowden in a spectacular bridesmaid performance at Ironman 1997, completing a one-two sweep for the Canucks.

ABOVE Cristian Bustos, one of the gutsiest people you will ever meet, reborn from the ashes of a near fatal crash. A core guy.

CURRENTS

from which to choose, then they will tolerate it.

Indeed, amid the confusion, there still exists a solid vein of core opportunities for athletes of all sizes and shapes to seek out and grab hold of.

THE RACES

A triathlete, depending on where he or she lives, may have as many as 100 or as few as two chances to compete in seasonal races within a few hours' drive of his/her home. The distances will vary greatly, with the majority still falling into the 1.5kmS/40kmB/10kmR category. (At various times this has been referred to as the USTS distance, the short course, the Olympic and the Classic distance.) The trend, though, is away from this and toward the shorter sprint distance — a course that the average person can train for and complete in an hour or so a day.

At the same time, the Ironman events continue to grow in popularity, albeit at a much slower rate. These seem to be fueled by triathletes looking to validate their careers with the penultimate challenge. One often fails to consider one's self a "real" athlete unless he or she has done an Ironman, much like the 5km runner who has aspirations of a marathon. This is, of course, ridiculous. The Ironman, any Ironman, is beyond the capability of many casual participants if for no other reason than they lack the confidence and training time needed to finish. Yet they are still triathletes, enjoying the intrinsic benefits of all the sport has to offer.

Other areas showing strong signs of growth are in the off-road triathlon (lake swim, mountain

ROBERT OLIVER

ROBERT OLIVER

ROBERT OLIVER

TOP Thomas Hellreigel, the new Ironman champion and part of the new breed of European speed demons. **BOTTOM LEFT** Brazil's Fernanda Keller, always a strong contender at "The Show," collects her third bronze finish in 1997. **BOTTOM RIGHT** Switzerland's Natascha Badmann rides a bike like she was shot out of a cannon. A virus thwarted her '97 Ironman race. Like Arnold, she'll be back.

ABOVE Lucky because no Luc? Nah. Basic tools plus hard work plus opportunity equal success.

bike, trail run), stage race (multiday events, usually pro only), and loop course categories (criterium-style, draft-legal, mostly pro). There also seems to be a renewed interest in the half-Ironman distance, although the selection is still quite limited. The strong events that have been around for a number of years (Wildflower, Columbia, Buffalo Springs Lake, St. Croix, Panama City, San Diego International, Chicago Mrs. T's) all seem to be healthy, supported by the thousands who have participated one year or another.

THE ATHLETES

The athletes of today are different from the ones of yesterday, yet they retain commonalities. We still are attracted by the unique challenge of testing oneself against a distance, against a three-disciplined course, against oneself. At the professional level though, much more is at stake. A win at the Hawaiian Ironman is worth a minimum of $100,000 in prize money, bonuses and sponsorship. When I won in 1982 and '85, it was worth a koa wood trophy, minus the expenses we had to pay. And that is okay. The level of competition then was a fraction of what it is now.

The amateurs still face the same hurdles, like stray dogs on a training ride, or a course marshall who inadvertently sends you the wrong way on a course. In some ways, the sport is safer because of improved training methods, closed courses and lifeguarded swims. But some folks just lay it on the line more, too. Go to the finish line at Ironman and watch as every seventh or eighth competitor struggles almost violently to reach the carpeted gates of triathlon heaven. Maybe I didn't notice, but I just don't remember people putting themselves that close to the edge as they do now.

Former *Sports Illustrated* writer Barry McDermott agrees: "The event is so different now, it is almost life-threatening," he says. "The attraction to finish Ironman is so strong, it's like climbing Everest — people are just going to suffer and get hurt. It is a major sports spectacle, not just a test of one's character."

As a group, triathletes are still a wonderfully interesting lot. There exist many characters, as in the early days, but they seem to be swallowed up by the seething mass of competitive humanity. The pros are much more serious though, friendly enough, but intense nonetheless. I suppose that's what happens when you put a whole bunch of money on the line instead of coupons for dinners at the local steak house. And they deserve what they make. I can remember going to a meeting of several pro athletes in 1983, and having sports promoter Larry King (ex-husband of Billie Jean King) tell us that if we played our cards right, within three or four years most of us could expect to be able to earn a pretty good living from the sport — upward of $50,000 to $100,000 per year. That seemed like a lot of money back then, as it still is today. It took 10 years longer than Larry's prediction to come true, but at least for the top 15 or 20 in the world, that vision has come true.

Not that it matters, but since some people keep score by one's earning power, the best of the best, athletes like Britons Simon Lessing and Spencer Smith, Australia's Emma Carney, Greg Welch and Brad Beven, Germany's Jürgen Zäck, Lothar Leder and Thomas Hellriegel, Canada's Peter Reid, Carol Montgomery and Heather Fuhr, America's Jimmy Riccitello and Kenny Glah, and

ROBERT OLIVER

TOP Japan's Hideya Miyazuka has been one of the best triathletes from the land of the rising sun for some time now. He was a landscape guy before starting a career track that has taken him around the world representing his country.

TOP LEFT Ironman winner Heather Fuhr chatting with fellow Canadian Graham Fraser. "So Heather, what do you think of the current political climate in Somalia?" "Well Graham, I'm glad you asked." **BOTTOM LEFT** Actress Alexandra Paul on her way to a strong, critic-silencing performance at Ironman 1997. A staunch environmentalist and a really nice lady, Paul put her career on hold to finish the race with integrity. She finished with more than that — like a few thousand new believers. **RIGHT** Tim DeBoom of Boulder, Colorado, and Peter Reid from north of the border out for a little Saturday afternoon jog when a race broke out around them.

CURRENTS

Belgium's Luc Van Lierde ... all of them should expect to earn substantially more than that in the latter years of the 1990s. Marketability is sometimes as valuable as competitive success, but in the end, the promotional dollars that find their way into the pockets of men and women who write on their tax return under profession, "Athlete," are derived by their ability to drive sales of a product, their very association with "widget X" should somehow motivate the customer's buying decision.

How this dovetails into the big picture of triathletes is a somewhat more complicated equation. We have become somewhat jaded by the behavior of some professional athletes in America. Stories of NBA stars holding out for $22 million instead of $20 million per year, positive drug tests or worse, governing bodies *covering up* positive drug tests — all have given the average Joe a justifiably cynical attitude toward guys and gals who get paid to race when they have to cut back on the monthly budget to justify another $65 entry fee. Rightfully so. Some of these guys are jerks. But a lot of them are solid, honest people, the best in the world at what they do, amazing in their athletic talent.

In triathlon, the separation between pro and amateur has always been minimal. In what other sport can you find yourself on the starting line of the biggest event in the world, lined up next to the defending champion, trading best wishes if not tension-easing smiles? I'm a decent tennis player. Do you have any idea what it would take for me to get to play Wimbledon? If this is a bit too Walter Mitty-ish for the purist among you, tough luck. Triathlon was born on the fringe and if it is to

TOP LEFT Jürgen Zäck has nearly completed his Southern California apprenticeship. Two more seasons in North County and he will earn a new 6-feet 10-inches Thruster from Encinitas Surfboards. TOP RIGHT Sian Welch, lookin' sweet, riding smooth. BOTTOM John Maclean, physically challenged? Maybe. Physically able? Absolutely.

ROBERT OLIVER

succeed in a realm of homogenized, pre-fab sports, we must push it off to the left from time to time, give Joe-bag-of-donuts a chance to be a paper lion for a few hours. The trickle down theory is alive and well in this sport. If a race lands the big sponsor, that windfall should show up in reduced entry fees. If it doesn't, don't race. Ever hear of supply and demand?

THE MEDIA

The media has finally figured out what the sport is all about and how to cover it. Oh, you will still get the fresh, young reporter right out of a college journalism class who will ask something like "How long do you get to rest between events?" or "don't your legs get sore after all that exercise?" But as a group, especially in the vast black hole of television, we are more understood than ever before — or at least we are not portrayed as masochistic crazies. Mainstream media play in the *Washington Post*, the *Wall Street Journal* and the *New York Times* have given cause to thousands of intrigued individuals looking for a challenge. Captains of industry, political aspirants, uptown socialites and factory line workers alike will see a little piece in the back of the sports section. It will ignite a small ember that either grows into a fiery inferno or goes out when they move on to the next story about an NBA player fined for punching a referee. It has to start somewhere.

ABOVE Wingnut and Feather, side by side, in sync, a moment in time not to be repeated, but cherished forever.

CURRENTS

THE FEDERATIONS

The vast majority of triathlon participants do not know, nor do they care, what goes on in the boardroom of their national federation. Maybe they read the platform of a potential board member in some publication and decide they like the dude. So they vote for him or her. But mostly they ignore stuff like that. After all, they have lives outside of triathlon; they have a career, a family, other interests. They simply can't justify the time needed to decide if candidate A is better than candidate B.

I'm interested in other sports, but I don't care too much about the politics of any of them. Maybe, though, I will go and sign up for a moto-cross race and some official will tell me I can't race because the particular tread pattern on my tires has been disallowed by the National Off-Road Motorcycle Association … or some such group. I won't have any different tires in my truck so I will climb in and drive the three hours back home, seething at the rule that prevented me from reaching my goal, if not having a hell of a lot of fun. All the while I will be thinking of the letter I will write or the local representative I will contact. Would it have helped if I was just a tiny bit more involved? Probably not, but you must never forget that if you choose not to be involved, you must accept the decisions of those who take the time to do so. Jimmy Riccitello is one of the most apolitical people I know, yet he sat on the Tri-Fed board as an athlete's rep for four years. I asked him once how he was able to handle all the legalese. "It's just a game really," he said. "You either

TOP LEFT The Great White Rasta and one of America's hopes: Cameron Widoff. BOTTOM LEFT The other DeBoom, Tim's brother Tony, working…. TOP RIGHT Les McDonald, architect of the International Triathlon Union (ITU). CENTER RIGHT Race director Sharron Ackles BOTTOM RIGHT Former president of the World Triathlon Corporation and tireless anti-draft proponent, David Yates takes the microphone at another gala awards ceremony.

play it or you are at the mercy of the person playing on your behalf." True enough.

Tri- Fed, which became USA Triathlon in 1996, has had several recent years of stability. There are still rumors and accusations of favoritism, and conflict of interest, but for the most part, the leadership of executive director Steve Locke has been relatively smooth, at least compared to earlier years. On the world front, the ITU, under the tightly controlled helm of Canadian Les McDonald, continues to find itself under constant scrutiny from professional athletes, competing race promoters and dissatisfied national governing bodies. At the same time though, its World Cup circuit continues to attract dozens of the fastest short course triathletes in the world in search of the lucrative prize money.

The ITU has been a hotbed of controversy since its tumultuous beginnings in the late 80s. McDonald, a clever politician, has almost single-handedly achieved the seemingly insurmountable task of gaining a spot on the Olympic program for triathlon. Other sports try for decades to gain a coveted slot. Les, shrewd and experienced in the inner workings of international sports politics, wove the sport through the quagmire of glad-handing, deal-making and backroom negotiations. But McDonald's critics, who are many, argue that his uncompromising, single-minded ways that put the sport in the Olympics, has also stifled creativity, entrepreneurial endeavors, and the devil-may-care rebelliousness upon which the sport was founded.

It poses the basic question: Does an organization that is supposed to serve its constituents have the right to push the very nature of the sport in a

TOP The venerable Kenny Glah, probably has as many top 10 finishes at Ironman as anyone. Always laying it all out there, daring someone to knock it off. Sometimes they do, sometimes they don't. On his report card next to effort there is always an A. BOTTOM LEFT Imagine a race without volunteers? Mike Swan from Goleta, California can't. BOTTOM RIGHT Lothar Leder, part of the ultra-strong German contingent. Like many of the Germans, he at first seems a bit aloof. But on further inspection, he is a hard-working, down to earth, fun-loving guy.

CURRENTS

direction that may either insure a healthy longevity and/or squelch the inner soul that so many find so attractive? The biggest single issue is, of course, drafting. And even though it exists primarily in the pro-only ITU World Cup circuit, you can see it beginning to permeate other smaller, amateur-influenced events.

McDonald, for his part, believes that the ends will justify the means. Maybe it will. Nobody knows. But very few are comfortable with the methods used by the ITU to achieve its goals. For the time being, the organization and its stated objectives are firmly ensconced on the road to the 2000 Sydney Olympics. If its detractors are unhappy, they will have to take well-planned and executed action to force the hand of ITU.

All of this political maneuvering is commonplace in the sport's governing bodies. One has only to look at the inner workings of the NGBs that govern triathlon's three disciplines. It is an ongoing dichotomy with few altruistic undertakings on one side, and multiple, unnoticed acts of personal heroism on the other. Somehow they exist on the same plane, a sometimes mutually beneficial relationship unfolding. And other times they threaten to terminate each other, negating or compromising the very sport for which they exist.

An amateur athlete need not find him or herself wrapped up in these, sitting on committees, helping to dictate rules and regulations. Some may be drawn to that, finding the process intriguing, which it certainly can be. But most are not, choosing instead to spend what little time they have training, racing and sharing the fitness experience. At a mini-

TOP Give it up for the top five women overall at Ironman 1997: Heather Fuhr, Lori Bowden, Fernanda Keller, Wingnut Ingraham and Sian Welch. Women, you can take off those goofy green wrist bands now. BOTTOM The next Big Four? Thomas Hellriegel, Jürgen Zäck, Lothar Leder and Peter Reid. Toss in an absent Luc Van Lierde and things are heating up quickly.

mum though, they should understand that things are rarely what they appear to be and behind each tear-jerking Olympic moment, there is an equally emotional action of a different sort. Besides everything we know sport to be, it is also a business, a form of entertainment and a profitable career for those who claw their way into a paying position. As long as we are aware of those facts, we can endeavor to play whatever game needs playing on a level field.

THE INDUSTRY OF TRIATHLON

Back when the sport had its humble beginnings, few people were able to glean an income off it. Prize money was nonexistent until 1982, and slow-growing for the next five years. Ironman did not even offer a purse until 1986. Corporate sponsorships of athletes and events were equally slim until approximately the same time. But gradually a cottage industry was formed, branching off into several directions.

The key players who fanned this flame were Carl Thomas of Speedo, Mike Gilmore of *Triathlon* magazine and Sally Edwards of Fleet Feet stores. Ironically, Thomas and Gilmore attended college across town from each other, at archrival schools UCLA and USC. Both men knew all too well that if the sport was to grow, someone would need to guide it into, and hopefully through, all the various entities necessary for it to grow and prosper. Sponsors needed to be convinced that this was a proper vehicle to align their products with, race entrants were needed to fill up the events, a magazine or two could tell the story and a governing body might

facilitate a lot of the above, or at least offer some credibility to those that feel that any sport lacking a central clearing house has not reached its potential.

So Gilmore became publisher of *Triathlon* magazine, and along with his editorial partners Harald Johnson and Penny Little produced a slick little mag. Thomas would go on with his own partner Jim Curl and produce the Unites States Triathlon Series, and Sally Edwards would not only start the Fleet Feet chain of running stores, but write numerous books on the sport. Thomas has moved into the

entertainment field, Gilmore remains involved as marketing director for the ITU, and Edwards gives clinics on the Danskin triathlon circuit, does corporate training and continues to write about the sport.

Many of the top athletes can earn up to six figures in prize money and sponsorship, event sponsorship is on the rebound after the recesionary slowdown of the early 1990s, and small manufacturers continue to use triathlon as a key market in their start-up strategies. Several companies that aligned themselves with the sport in the

early days have gone on to great success — Oakley, PowerBar, Giro helmets — while others have their niche in triathlon and continue to branch off into new areas (Hed wheels, Litespeed bikes, Champion Nutrition). And some of the larger, more established corporations continue to support the sport on many fronts (Reebok, Timex and Shimano). The triathlon media enjoys two healthy publications: Felix Magowan's *Inside Triathlon,* currently edited by Chris Newbound, and Jean Claude Garot's *Triathlete,* run by John Duke and the La Jolla Holding Group. Both appear poised for steady growth in the coming years.

With the Sydney Olympic games just a couple short years away, NGBs in dozens of the participating countries around the world have begun to direct money into triathlon development programs, hoping to place one of their countrymen or women atop the winner's podium. Only a few short years ago, opportunities such as this did not exist for any athlete, regardless of their athletic ability or won/loss record. Now, five to 10 of the best athletes in more than a dozen countries can expect some support from their NGB. This seems to be one of the first tangible benefits of Olympic inclusion.

"THE FEELING"

While all of this business and politicking goes on around us, thereis still the simple act of competing; the act of preparing one's body for a great challenge and going out to meet that challenge. At times, we who are deeply involved in the sport tend to lose sight of that. Caught up in

ABOVE In the battle of the comeback stars, Kirsten Hanssen beats Julie Moss at Ironman 1997. Third place in the women 35-39 has got to be thinking, "Didn't you two already have your 15 minutes of fame?"

the current deal or ruling or race or rumor, we tend to lose touch with what originally attracted us to the sport. All the peripheral goings-on tend to be distracting; they create animosity, greed and cynicism. The opportunity for us to pull back on the stick, to reverse the spin that skews our thinking, is always there. The best events are not always the biggest, the richest or most publicized. Sometimes they are not even the most organized. Same goes for athletes, companies and friends. It is up to each athlete to seek out and find who and what he feels most comfortable with.

The best example of this is former pro triathlete Joy Hansen. Hansen was quite good, a former national class runner and winner of numerous USTS events in the late 1980s and early '90s. She had problems, though; the psychological pressure that she placed on herself to succeed at everything she did was overwhelming. One day she just broke, suffered a nervous breakdown of sorts and was unable to compete for a long time.

Gradually, she realized that what was important was the simple joy of participating, of preparing herself for an athletic task and then just going out and doing it, consequences be damned. It is with this renewed outlook on competition that Hansen rebuilt her life. She is not an isolated example of this either. Holding onto that feeling is sometimes as important as the training itself.

ROBERT OLIVER

ABOVE A golden moment for Peter Reid (fourth) and Lori Bowden (second) in 1997.

CHAPTER EIGHTEEN

"Excuse me while I kiss the sky." — *from "Purple Haze", Jimi Hendrix, 1943-1971*

RANDOM THOUGHTS

TRIATHLON TWINS

COURTESY USTS

The sport of triathlon has had no less than a half dozen sets of twins who have reached some level of competitive success. I find that to be one of the more unique nuances that seem to be woven into the culture of this sport. I don't know if it is just the simple mathematics of chance, or if athletic talent is carried over from the binary aspects of prenatal development. Maybe it's just really worthwhile to have a dependable training partner. Wherever the case, here is a partial list of triathlon twins:

1. Wally and Wayne Buckingham: Two of the best triathletes in the world back in 1975, when only two or three races existed anywhere.
2. Joan and Joy Hanssen: Great runners. Joy especially was one of the fastest women on the USTS circuit in the late 1980s.
3. Sylviane and Patricia Puntous: Canadian duo with a one-two punch.
4. Jan and Diane Girard: Texas gals, depend-

able and consistent.

5. Michellie and Gabrielle Jones: Michellie, of course, is one of the best women in the world in the late 1990s. Her sister only races for fun and fitness but is still quite good.

6. Isabelle and Beatrice Mouthon: France's answer to all of the above.

THINGS THAT CHANGED THE SPORT

1. Wave starts: This was Jim Curl's idea. He needed to allow more people into his races, but couldn't imagine sending 2000 athletes running into the water at once. He actually got the idea from the Bolder Boulder 10km.

2. Aero' handlebars: There is some discussion on who came up with the idea first. Bike equipment manufacturer Richard Bryne designed a pair for one of his friends competing in the Race Across America at least a year or two before Boone Lennon took the idea to Scott USA and licensed the concept. Lennon says he came up with the idea while noting the position of downhill ski racers. Whatever the situation, Scott brought them to market and changed the way triathletes and cyclists rode forever. It also put the rider in a position to help employ certain muscles that were more developed in runners, thereby helping that group.

3. Wetsuits: O'Neill Wetsuits of Santa Cruz, California is the oldest wetsuit company in the world. In 1982, they gave me several prototype "swimming" wetsuits targeted at the emerging

LOIS SCHWARTZ

DAVID EPPERSON

PREVIOUS PAGE "Men, this is a very dangerous mission you have volunteered for." TOP Puntous twins from the Great North of Montreal, Canada. BOTTOM The Loch Ness Monsterette. Nice suit. Bet it floats you well, Julie.

ABOVE A lean Molina passes Charlie Graves over a bridge of troubled waters.

THOUGHTS

triathlon market. Basically they were 2mm vests with a hood attached and didn't help much at all. The idea of providing flotation at the same time just didn't click yet. In late 1983, Australian triathlete Marc Dragan and a few of his friends had some 2mm "farmer john" style suits with 3mm leg panels and high cut legs that really seemed to help. Dragan noticed that his swim times were substantially better and had a custom suit built that was a bit thicker but was made of more flexible neoprene. He wore that all year in 1984 even if the water was hot. He also told very few people of his find.

Just about a year later, Dan Empfield redesigned the suits available to the point where they really helped a poor swimmer feel more comfortable in the water. His Quintana Roo (a state in Mexico where Empfield used to vacation) wetsuit has been the most widely used suit for nearly a decade.

What the swimming wetsuit did was allow competitors to race in less than ideal conditions. Before the advent of wetsuits, hypothermia was a real concern. Triathlons were scary enough for a lot of people without freezing your ass off.

4. Television coverage of triathlon: Starting with ABC's Wide World of Sports coverage in 1980, TV brought the sport into the homes of millions who wouldn't otherwise know it unless they happened to take a walk down to the beach on a Sunday morning.

5. Triathlon in the Olympics: As of this writing, the first Olympic triathlon is still two years

DAVID EPPERSON

ABOVE Ah, the dreaded 'Kona Shuffle.' None are immune. Sooner or later, the road will reach up and grab the ankles of even the best of them. How one handles that is more a measure of courage and heart than fitness and age.

TOP Down this path is the way to athletic salvation. Do not stray from its course. **BOTTOM LEFT** Manny, Moe and Jack. **BOTTOM RIGHT** "At the YMCA," Marc Suprenant, as Cali as a dude from the Cape can get.

away, but it has already had a big effect on the sport. National Olympic Committees around the world have poured hundreds of thousands of dollars into the coffers of their sports' governing bodies to try and develop talent that will eventually bring home medals.

There has been a price, though. Drafting on the bike, a concept born out of the need to avoid controversy at the Olympics, is now fully legal at the International Triathlon Union's World Cup events. There are more rules, more standardization and more bureaucracy. In truth, the jury is still out on whether an Olympic triathlon has been worth the price.

MULTISPORT OPTIONS

Before triathlon became enamored and then committed to swimming, cycling and running, there was talk that maybe the sport shouldn't commit itself to just these three and only in such an order. Of course, lifeguard-based run/swim biathlons were quite popular at the time, and the occasional canoe event would filter into the mix, but for the most part, "triathlon" was simply a near-generic term used to describe an event that consisted of three events. But even as the sport gradually accepted swim/bike/run as the norm, a few other formats would emerge and, for a period, thrive in the new arena of multisport fascination.

Duathlon was born of the run/bike and then run/bike/run as a viable alternative to not only those who didn't like to swim, but to those events

COURTESY JOHN HOWARD

TOP This was the shot for an ad we did at Tinley Performance Wear. I really like it, but wasn't sure if people 'got it.' **BOTTOM LEFT** Portrait of a gnarled, ageless warrior: Sir John Howard. **BOTTOM RIGHT** This expression is usually followed by the most infectious laugh around. C2, Colleen Kashansky.

LEFT Best shot of Dave ever taken. October 1982, he had the fastest splits in all three sports. **RIGHT** "I really enjoyed my time as a triathlete, but it was time to move on." Kathleen McCartney.

contested in colder, waterless climates. It was and is an excellent starting point for any athlete who has hesitations about open water swimming or who finds the whole idea of competing in three sports just a bit overwhelming. Duathlon reached its peak in popularity in 1990, when Kenny Souza was king and the Desert Princess Run/Bike/Run was the big event. Coors Light also sponsored a successful series of shorter events, consisting of a 5km run, 30km bike and a 5km run. The big names, besides Souza, were George Pierce, Michael Tobin, Liz Downing, Greg Stewart, Jay Larsen and the odd triathlete who opted for a swimless event. Running specialists were attracted to the sport, as evidenced by Olympic gold medalist Frank Shorter's run at the master's division record in Palm Springs's Desert Princess. Miler Steve Scott had a go at a race or two and was surprised how much snap a 20 mile bike ride can take out of one's legs.

But for one reason or another, duathlon never really made it over the "hump" into the same arena as triathlon — until the Powerman came along. A product of Urs Linsi and Bruno Imfeld, bankers from the small Swiss town of Zofingen, the Powerman and its incredibly difficult course, its highly competitive field and its large prize purse, all contributed to its immediate success. Urs and his Swiss-efficient staff would follow up the ultradistance duathlon with a worldwide series of shorter events. Without the Powerman programs, duathlon would find it hard to maintain stature in the world of international sporting politics. In any case, it is still a big part of the family of multisport events and a viable addition to that genre of competitive opportunities.

ROBERT OLIVER

FUNNIEST TRIATHLON STORIES

Souza the jetsetter

At the peak of the Coors Light Biathlon Series, Kenny Souza was nearly unbeatable. At one point he had the opportunity to meet Brewing Mogul Peter Coors, who invited Souza to join him in his private jet on a trip to San Diego for the Coors Light event. After takeoff, Peter tried to discuss various business matters with the young Souza, who feigned interest but had little to add to the conversation. After several periods of long silence, Souza excused himself and went to the back of the plane to talk with Peter's 14-year-old daughter. They spoke of MTV, Nintendo tactics and favorite ice cream flavors, hitting it off like a couple of long-lost pals.

Live by the sword…

The first Avia Scramble was a long, gnarly off-road running race that was to award money and prizes

for first, second and fourth place … that's right, nothing for third. With a half mile to go, I was in third place, just over a minute behind Kenny Souza in second and some hotshot runner in first. I had this brainstorm that I would hide behind a tree until the third-place guy crossed the finish line and then come out, finish fourth and collect the award (I think it was a mountain bike) for fourth place. It worked perfectly until I found out, after crossing the line in third, that the first-place guy had gotten lost and Souza had won. So instead of collecting the $1500 for second, I outfoxed my way into third and took home nothing but the mud on my face.

Bar-Wars

When a few of us showed up at the Ironman in Kona with new Scott DH aero' bars in the fall of 1987, many of the other competitors were incredulous. The Euro' dudes in particular were pissed they didn't have the goods. By Friday before the race, though, the more creative ones had paid a visit to the local plumbing supply store and had tried to build their own. When two of them tried to check in their bikes with plastic PVC pipe extending out the front, the mechanics on the pier said, "So, what type of irrigation are you running out here on your bars?"

My kingdom for a shoe

Back in 1980-something, Dave McGillivary was the race director for one of the Boston USTS events. Now if you know Dave, you'll understand that he wanted to put on the best event of the year. So Dave comes up with this elaborate course with the start, the bike finish and the run finish all miles apart.

ABOVE Duathlete Michael Tobin, great all-around athlete and nice guy.

TOP LEFT Pre-PowerBar race food: black licorice and masking tape bananas.   **BOTTOM LEFT** One of the few times you are glad to see a cop in the rearview mirror.   **RIGHT** When Dirk Aschmoneit came to San Diego from Germany to train, all he wanted to do was marry a California "beach bunny." He got his wish.

THOUGHTS

You had to put your running shoes in a bag so that they would get trucked to the spot where the bike leg ended. Well, as it turns out, one of the trucks carrying 500 pairs of shoes breaks down and when all of those competitors get to the transition to start the run ... you guessed it, no running shoes. Some people ran barefoot, some people borrowed shoes from spectators, some ran in their cycling cleats and some just turned their bikes around and rode back to the start in disgust. It wasn't funny then, but it is now.

BK's bum

In 1986, a young pro named Brad Kearns won the now defunct Penrod's Triathlon in Fort Lauderdale, Florida. He had to sprint the last quarter mile to beat local favorite Rob Roller. When the volunteer went to pull the tag off the bottom of his number, she gave a mighty tug, just like she had been shown, and off came the number ... with Brad's running shorts attached. The local news station caught the whole thing and used the footage for its local play of the day. Kearns can recite the dialogue verbatim. The newscaster says: "Here he wins the whole triathlon and what does he get for a prize? He gets his pants pulled down in front of hundreds of onlookers! Those triathletes are nuts! Now, on to the weather...."

RICHARD GRAHAM

DAVID EPPERSON

TOP LEFT Duathlete Liz Downing was one of the only women to be consistent in this run/bike sport. **TOP RIGHT** Greg Welch can make you laugh. The guy runs pretty quick, too. **BELOW** This guy used to be a 90-pound weakling. Ah, the metamorphosis of the species.

ABOVE Sean Molina, tailgating.

"Come my friends. 'Tis not too late seek a newer world." — *Alfred Lord Tennyson, 1809-1892*

WINDOWS TO THE FUTURE

DAVID EPPERSON

Triathlon appears to be at a crossroads now, but then again, it seems to face directional changes on a near-constant basis. At the risk of dating myself (which I have done since the first chapter), and more importantly, this book, I will endeavor to make several predictions of things to come in the sport. As we all know, unforeseen events will inevitably play havoc with those who look for slow and predictable change. I would not have predicted 10 years ago that the sport would be in the 2000 Olympics; 15 years ago I would not have predicted that the Ironman winner would take home a check for $30,000; and I would not have predicted in my early 20s that I would still be competing seriously in my early 40s.

We are faced with constant change requiring decisions at every turn of the pedal. How we choose will dictate in which direction the sport grows. Do you think drafting should not be allowed? Stay away from events that allow it. Do you find a particular sponsor deceptive or over-priced? Don't buy their product. Vote with your attendance and your wallet. The sport is still

WINDOWS

small enough that the "everyman" has his or her say.

But where will triathlon go? Will the numbers of entrants continue to grow? Will it become more and more of an international sport, finally severing its Southern California roots completely? Will off-road triathlons become the next rage? Will kids' triathlons reach into each and every neighborhood like basketball or soccer? Will short, loop-style courses with drafting create a format for spectator appeal? Will the Ironman distance also become an Olympic event? Will the political infighting that continues to exist within our sport ever give way to a model of compromising synergy?

Sometimes we get so wrapped up in our own world of triathlon, we fail to see the "big picture" in which it exists. It takes an individual who has stepped away, retired from their involvement, to give us a shot of reality. Erin Baker left the sport at the top and never looked back. When I asked her to explain, she said, "I think it showed just how sane I really was that my life never entirely revolved around the sport." *Triathlon* magazine cofounder and editorial director Harald Johnson, in a farewell message, wrote, "Don't take anything, even the triathlon, too seriously. Instead, have fun and stay healthy." Mike Plant, journalist, said in his final issue of *The Plant Report*, "I'm sure there was a time when the hearts of most of the sport's movers and shakers were in the right place, when the excitement of watching a new sport grow, and of being a part of that growth, was also their inspiration. But too many years on the financial tightrope and too many hours at the bargaining table have left many of our best jaded and cynical,

DAVID EPPERSON

RUSSELL MOORE

PREVIOUS PAGE We will continue to be attracted to "The Hub," whatever it is. TOP Even with increased organization, standardization and a half a dozen other "izations," athletes will still be able to find the odd neighborhood event where the trophies are in laughter and the victories are in smiles. BOTTOM LEFT People of all sizes and shapes will continue to be attracted to the sport for deeply personal reasons. BOTTOM RIGHT Triathletes around the world will learn bike-handling skills.

ABOVE We will still find beauty in all aspects of a fitness lifestyle.

WINDOWS

de-sensitized to the moral impact of political incest and commercialization. The end has come to justify the means, I'm afraid, and that's a shame, because it used to be that in this sport the finish line didn't matter so much as long as you had fun along the way." True enough.

Carl Thomas, cofounder of the USTS Series, had this to say about the future direction of triathlon: "It is something to see an "idea" go from just a notion to an event in the Olympic Games. It is not every day that the opportunity to be involved in that process comes along ... at any level. Yes, the sport is different, but people can still go to the fringe of civilization and do the "corner race" if they want." In a *Triathlete* magazine article 11 years ago, well before he moved into a different arena, he said: "Our future? Well, I can tell you that we're in this thing for the long haul, and without a doubt our best years are still in front of us."

William Katovsky, founder of *Triathlete* magazine and a true bohemian among us, has this to say about the future of our sport: "We need more interesting aspects of sport, more personalities and maybe even more controversy that the public can understand. Triathlon can be a boring sport, very dull. But when it becomes a metaphor for life, reflecting the subtle nuances of our society, it becomes attractive to everyone."

Baker and Johnson and Plant and Thomas and Katovsky. They are no different than any of us. They have changed, moved on, grown ... maybe learned a few things along the way. All of them were intimately involve with the development of triathlon at a young age, each in his or her own

DAVID EPPERSON

ABOVE A major national kids triathlon series will emerge.

ABOVE Wave starts will grow.

DAVID EPPERSON

ABOVE "Family style" events will become popular, in which kids can compete with their parents.

way. And now they live outside the microcosm of this sport (although Plant is involved in a new version of the USTS Series and is serving as vice president of marketing for Quintana Roo). The vision they shared is common to many of us and still specific to their own version and their own personal needs. It is a reflection of how far we've come, yet how far we still have to go, that we can still remember those who made a difference, yet not dwell on a quirky and sometimes incestuous past.

Barry McDermott, the *Sports Illustrated* writer who penned the Tom Warren piece on the 1979 Ironman, no longer writes for a living. He sells real estate in New York. When queried about the future of triathlon, he says: "The event is so different now. It is no longer life-threatening. Roads are closed to traffic. People know how to train. It is a legitimate sporting event. But back then it was truly a test of one's character, like climbing Everest without oxygen."

Another writer who has covered the sport since its early days is Ken McAlpine. McAlpine began writing about triathlon as a budding journalist for small, California regional publications like *Competitor* and *City Sports*. He is now a regular with *Sports Illustrated*, *Outside* and *Men's Journal*. "Back then," he recalls, "we were missing the point. Most of the journalists didn't realize what they were looking at."

He explains: "We certainly didn't recognize the athleticism. Yeah, some of the guys were fruitcakes, but they were talented fruitcakes. Nowadays we understand what's going on out there. The athleticism is incredible, maybe too much so. There is a

TOP As the world's population ages, the 50-54 age group will post times as fast as the pros. BOTTOM America will rebound as a powerhouse of athletic talent.

perception that some of the best in the world are part of one giant lab experiment. It may have been a strange chemistry before, but more along the lines of a Timothy Leary class."

When pressed to predict the potential changes in coming years, he is hesitant. "The Olympics will lend a certain legitimacy to the sport. I am curious to see how it will unfold. The Games don't make or break a sport, but they sure can help if run in a proper fashion."

If there is one issue that parallels the questions of growth in the sport, it is the Olympic Games. Triathlon will open the 2000 Olympics in Sydney, Australia. Will it help grow the sport? Has it already caused irreparable damage to the very pretense upon which the sport was founded? Or has the sport outgrown it innocence, lost forever the casual camaraderie that permeated those laid back events of the early 1980s? There is no question that triathlon has more rules and regulations than ever. But it is also safer, better-publicized and more fair as a competitive outlet. In many ways, it is reflective of the Olympic Games themselves. The public, coerced by the IOC party line, hold the Games up on a pedestal, revering them like possibly no other social institution of the past 50 years. To many of us, they are the penultimate icon of the human condition, at once peppered with hope, struggle, triumph, tragedy and victory of every shape and color. Beneath that, behind the five rings, lies the largest unregulated financial entity since the Roman Church. It is pure naïveté if one thinks that sports and politics don't mix. In the case of the Olympic Games, they are as intertwined

ROBERT OLIVER

ROBERT OLIVER

TOP Madam Pelé will continue to play havoc with a few on the Queen K Highway. BOTTOM Physically challenged athletes continue to break down old barriers.

as a plant that climbs an old fence as it grows. Money reigns supreme over athletic performance. Quid pro quo is standard operating procedure at the highest levels. And that is Okay. While the purist may cringe at the backroom negotiating that goes on, in the end it works. The Olympic Games have survived wars, depressions, droughts, deaths and crass commercialism. They remain a stable yet political entity that answers to no one in particular but is beholden to the two billion viewers that witness the world's best do their thing every four years. As long as we don't hold any illusions as to their supposed integrity and altruism, let the Games go on. As Les McDonald, president of the ITU said, "Sport is a precious legacy we inherit from those who went before us. In spite of wars, revolutions and boycotts, the Modern Olympics have survived and are almost 100 years old. Dull would be of heart who has not nurtured the Olympic Dream, however modestly. We have an obligation to add to the dream. There are other reasons to strive for the Olympics. To help achieve the goal, to be above all races, above all political systems and beliefs ... and "to unite the youth of the world in friendship, youth and peace." Lofty words indeed, though difficult to embrace when one finds him or herself struggling to make ends meet; maybe a business entity has spent years building up its own equity in a similar arena; then one can easily pass off such high flown declarations as shallow and unrealistic.

All we can really hope and strive for in this unfolding tale of sport is a level playing field, where people play straight up, without hidden agendas and ulterior motives. I really don't care if a particular city is awarded the Olympic Games because they courted the IOC members better than another city. I really don't care if drafting is allowed in a particular race, I don't even care if

TOP Duathlons will make a comeback and Kenny Souza will again lead the charge. BOTTOM Competitors will still revel in the celebration of their own success, regardless of the time and place.

WINDOWS

another competitor is using illegal drugs ... I just want to know the truths, the real reasons behind it all, so that I can make my decisions based upon reality, not half-truths and propaganda; so that my course of action, whether proactive or dismissive, can be made with an educated mind.

Maybe the Olympics will be the best thing to happen to triathlon in a long time. And maybe they won't make much difference at all. Some sports, as it is, don't really fit into the sometimes stifling mold of Olympic competition. Take snowboarding, for instance. At first, all the top riders thought it would be such a cool thing. But as the resulting politics and finally the Winter Olympic Games in Nagano, Japan unfolded, it was painfully obvious that the devil-may-care spirit and semi-anarchistic nature of the sport's constituents would not fit well with the IOC's conservative cloak and dagger activities.

In any case, the sport continues to unfold, bringing with it a continuous opportunity to put oneself out on the fringe. Many of the same faces are still involved with the sport, directing the races, writing the stories, courting the sponsors, doing well in the pro, then age-group competition. Sometimes it looks like people are hoping to get a bigger piece of the pie instead of making the pie bigger. But at other times, one is witness to a newcomer, completely stoked with the rapture of finishing their first race. The smile on their face goes from one ear to the other. And it is easy to forget the problems that the sport faces. After all, it is only that, a sport. Maybe even a silly one at that. Three different sports rolled into one; who would have thought that it would have any appeal? And where does that appeal come from?

TOP LEFT International athletes around the world will remain competitive, but will also forge friendships that transcend borders, languages and cultures. **TOP RIGHT** Kenny Glah will win the Ironman on his eighteenth try, at age 37. **BOTTOM** Bikes will continue to get more exotic, with increased sponsor billboard space being a major factor. Steve Ferrario of Bassi Ranch riding "the toaster."

ABOVE Ironman will cease to hold its "diaper dash" for adults due to lack of interest.

WINDOWS

Is it the challenge of it all? Is it a metaphor for our times of relative comfort and standard of living, the fact that there are no wars and few real causes that this generation has embraced? Is it that swimming is a unique opportunity for a human to propel his or herself through a completely different environment? Is it that cycling is a unique statement of man's approach to use technology to improve his efficiency? Or is it that running is the most basic and oldest form of human powered locomotion, steeped in fits of raw and uncompromising survival? Or is it something more, something unexplainable at the very core, when patronized by shallow attempts at relevance, only to fall farther from explanation?

Get up before the sun one day, have a steaming cup of good coffee, put on your favorite running shoes and head out very, very slowly. Force yourself to stay well within your feelings, holding back the pace until the sun peaks over a distant hill. Now pick it up a bit, just a little, feel the earth moving beneath your feet like a familiar carpet set in motion. Smell the fresh cut grass in your sleepy neighborhood, listen to a dog bark, an old pick-up truck cough to life. Wonder why the rest of the world isn't right along side you, and be glad that they are not. Turn the dial another notch now, feeling the blood vessels open up and let the warm blood carry the oxygen to the muscles that are beginning to work in syncopated time. Look up into the sky and accept whatever climate and conditions that the Great Spirit, or whatever you call Him, has dealt upon the Earth for the day. Laugh out loud that you can do whatever it is that you do and cherish it, no matter how small it is. All of this is still free. And it is yours for the taking.

RICHARD GRAHAM

ROBERT OLIVER

TOP Scenic courses like this, on Catalina Island, will become increasingly desirable, but harder to secure. BOTTOM People will finally realize the invaluable contribution of medical personnel like Drs. P. Z. Pearce and Bob Laird, of the Ironman medical staff.

ABOVE We will each strive for peace and beauty that exists in the nature of sport, try to find some meaning through it all, and apply it to our daily lives with the same depth of feeling that first put us in motion.

ABOUT THE AUTHOR

Scott Tinley has been competing in triathlons since 1976. He is known as an outspoken spokesperson for the sport. He founded Tinley Performance Wear and sold the company to Reebok. He has successfully turned his triathlete lifestyle into a comfortable living situation. He won the 1982 and '85 Ironman competition in Hawaii, and remains a world-class triathlete by qualifying, competing and placing in many international triathlon events. He lives in Del Mar, California, with his wife and two children.

OTHER BOOKS FROM VELOPRESS

VELO *press*

Perfect Circles *by Greg Moody*
Team Haven rides again! The long-anticipated sequel to *Two Wheels* begins with the mysterious death of a professional cyclist in the Netherlands, and takes the Haven peloton through the grueling Tour de France. Will Ross is back in great form as the aging team lieutenant determined to place his team in Le Tour, cycling's most prestigious international event.
400 pp • Paperback.
1-884737-44-7 • P-CIR $12.95

The Athlete's Guide to Sponsorship *by Jennifer Drury and Cheri Elliott*
How to find an individual, team or event sponsor
This concise yet comprehensive step-by-step guide is for any athlete, team, or sport event planner who is considering sponsorship.
1-884737-45-5 • P GUI $14.95

John Wilcockson's World of Cycling *by John Wilcockson*
John Wilcockson, editor of *VeloNews*, has reported on every major bicycle race, including the Tour de France, for thirty years. His writing brings to life all the various facets of the fascinating sport of professional cycling and its leading racers and personalities. This book features sixteen pages of color photos by Graham Watson, as well as stories on Greg LeMond, Lance Armstrong and many other top stars. Essential reading for the cycling fan!
336 pages • hardcover • 16 pages of color photos
1-884737-50-1 • P-WOC $24.95

The Triathlete's Training Bible *by Joe Friel*
This volume is the most extensive training guide available for triathletes. Joe Friel, a nationally recognized authority on endurance training, integrates the latest research on training, nutrition, and techniques with everything needed for planning your workouts. The result is a "must" book for every triathlete wanting to train smarter, not harder, and achieve their best results!
400 pages • paperback
1-884737-48-x • P-TRIB $19.95

The Cyclist's Training Bible *by Joe Friel*
Hailed as a major breakthrough in training for competitive cycling, this book helps take cyclists from where they are to where they want to be — the podium.
288 pp. • Photos, charts, diagrams • Paperback.
1-884737-21-8 • P-BIB $19.95

***Inside Triathlon* Training Diary** *by Joe Friel*
Combines the best in quantitative and qualitative training notation. Designed to help you attain your best fitness ever. Non-dated, so you can start at any time of the year.
240 pp. • Spiral-bound.
1-884737-41-2 • P-IDI $12.95

***VeloNews* Training Diary** *by Joe Friel*
The world's most popular training diary for cyclists. Allows you to record every facet of training with plenty of room for notes. Non-dated, so you can start any time of the year.
240 pp. • Spiral-bound.
1-884737-42-0 • P-DIN $12.95

The Giro d'Italia *by Dino Buzzati*
Coppi vs. Bartali at the 1949 Tour of Italy
The 1949 Tour of Italy was perhaps the most famous Giro of them all, pitting bitter arch-rivals Fausto Coppi and Gino Bartali as they battled it out on roads still marked by World War II. Buzzati's account is a true classic of cycling journalism that pulls the reader right inside this famous race. This edition comes complete with maps and illustrations of the race, as well as an introduction by *VeloNews* editor, John Wilcockson.
paperback • maps and illustrations of the tour
1-884737-51-x • P-GRO $16.95

Mountain Bike Owner's Manual
by Lennard Zinn and the Technical Editors of VeloNews
This illustrated guide is small enough to pack on trips yet filled with enough comprehensive information to help out with any situation one can encounter on the trail including information on bike and trail safety, tools, proper clothing, emergencies, and repair tips on all major components.
96 pages • illustrations, charts • paperback
1-884737-52-8 • P MBO $9.95

Zinn & the Art of Mountain Bike Maintenance, 2nd Edition
by Lennard Zinn
Guides you through every aspect of mountain-bike maintenance, repair and troubleshooting in a succinct, idiot-proof format.
288 pp • Illustrations • Paperback
1-884737-47-1 • P-ZYN $17.95

Off-Season Training for Cyclists *by Edmund R. Burke, Ph.D.*
Burke takes you through everything you need to know about winter training—indoor workouts, weight training, cross-training, periodization and more.
168 pp. • photos • Paperback.
1-994737-40-4 • P-OFF $14.95

Bicycle Racing in the Modern Era *from the editors of* VeloNews
These 63 articles represent the best in cycling journalism over the past quarter century.
218 pp. • Paperback.
1-884737-32-3 • P-MOD $19.95

Tales from the Toolbox *by Scott Parr with Rupert Guinness*
In his years as a Motorola team mechanic, Scott Parr saw it all. Get the inside dirt on the pro peloton and the guys who really make it happen ... the mechanics.
168 pp. • Paperback.
1-884737-39-0 • P-TFT $14.95

Single-Track Mind *by Paul Skilbeck*
The right combination of scientific training information, bike-handling skills, nutrition, mental training, and a proven year-round training plan.
128 pp. • Photos, charts, diagrams • Paperback.
1-884737-10-2 • P-STM $19.95

Weight Training for Cyclists *by Eric Schmitz and Ken Doyle*
Written from the premise that optimum cycling performance demands total body strength, this book informs the serious cyclist on how to increase strength with weight training, as cycling alone cannot completely develop the muscle groups used while riding.
160 pp. • 40 b/w photos • Paperback.
1-884737-43-9 • P-WTC $14.95

Cyclo-cross *by Simon Burney*
A must read for anyone brave enough to ride their road bike downhill through the mud.
200 pp. • Photos, charts, diagrams • Paperback.
1-884737-20-X • P-CRS $14.95

The Mountain Biker's Cookbook *by Jill Smith*
Healthy and delicious recipes from the world's best mountain-bike racers. The ideal marriage between calories and the perfect way to burn them off.
• 152 pp. • Paperback.
1-884737-23-4 • P-EAT $14.95

Barnett's Manual *by John Barnett*
Regarded by professionals worldwide as the final word in bicycle maintenance.
950 pp. • Illustrations, diagrams, charts • Five-ring loose-leaf binder.
1-884737-16-1 • P-BNT $149.95

Half-Wheel Hell, and Other Stories *by Maynard Hershon*
Hershon explores our perception of ourselves and our sport with humor and sensitivity.
134 pp. • Paperback.
1-884737-05-6 • P-HWH $13.95

Tour de France THE 75TH ANNIVERSARY BICYCLE RACE
by Robin Magowan
Magowan's fluid prose style brings to life the most contested Tour de France as if it were yesterday.
208 pp. • Photos and stage profiles • Hardbound.
1-884737-13-7 • P-MAG $24.95

Eddy Merckx *by Rik Vanwalleghem*
Discover the passion and fear that motivated the world's greatest cyclist. The man they called "the cannibal" is captured like never before in this lavish coffee-table book.
216 pp. • 24 color & 165 B/W photos • Hardback.
1-884737-22-6 • P-EDY $49.95

Bobke *by Bob Roll*
If Hunter S. Thompson and Dennis Rodman had a boy, he would write like Bob Roll: rough-hewn, poetic gonzo. Roll's been there and has the T-shirts to prove it.
124 pp. • Photos • Paperback.
1-884737-12-9 • P-BOB $16.95

A Season in Turmoil *by Samuel Abt*
Abt traces the differing fortunes of American road racers Lance Armstrong and Greg LeMond through the 1994 season. Revealing, in-depth interviews show the raw exuberance of Armstrong as he becomes the top U.S. road cycling star, while LeMond sinks toward an unwanted retirement.
178 pp. • B/W photos • Paperback.
1-884737-09-9 • P-SIT $14.95

**FOR ORDERING OR MORE INFORMATION, PLEASE CALL VELOPRESS, TOLL FREE: 800/234-8356
OR VISIT OUR WEBSITE AT WWW.VELOCATALOGUE.COM**